C000142814

ATHENIAN TRAGEDY IN PERFORMANCE

STUDIES IN THEATRE HISTORY AND CULTURE

Edited by Heather Nathans

ATHENIAN TRAGEDY IN PERFORMANCE

A GUIDE TO
CONTEMPORARY
STUDIES AND
HISTORICAL
DEBATES

Melinda Powers

University of Iowa Press
Iowa City

University of Iowa Press, Iowa City 52242
Copyright © 2014 by the University of Iowa Press
Printed in the United States of America
Design by April Leidig
www.uiowapress.org

No part of this book may be reproduced or used in
any form or by any means without permission in
writing from the publisher. All reasonable steps have
been taken to contact copyright holders of material
used in this book. The publisher would be pleased to
make suitable arrangements with any whom it has
not been possible to reach.

The University of Iowa Press is a member of Green
Press Initiative and is committed to preserving
natural resources.

Printed on acid-free paper

ISBN: 978-1-60938-231-5, 1-60938-231-5 (pbk)
ISBN: 978-1-60938-257-5, 1-60938-257-9 (ebk)
LCCN: 2013953636

For Mom and Dad

CONTENTS

ACKNOWLEDGMENTS

This book began with a performance, when I first crowned my head with ivy and sang *Bacchae*'s odes in the Barnard/Columbia Ancient Drama Group's production of Euripides's masterpiece, in Ancient Greek. Many years have passed since my first year at Columbia, and many friends, colleagues, students, and teachers too numerous to name have helped me along the way to produce this book. Nevertheless, some special thanks are needed.

I would first like to thank Helene Foley, who has loyally guided me over the years, from instructing me during my first semester at college to offering her comments on the penultimate draft of this manuscript. Sue-Ellen Case, who supervised my PhD work, is another dedicated teacher and mentor. A great source of inspiration, she has helped me to develop into a scholar of theatre and performance. This book also could not have been written without the help of Thomas Postlewait, who edited this book—one of his last for Iowa before retiring as series editor after two decades. I am profoundly grateful for his tireless editorial guidance. He has been as much a determined teacher and mentor as an editor. I hope this final version rewards his interest.

Oliver Taplin, Nancy Rabinowitz, Peter Meineck, Glenn Most, and Peter Pormann have graciously offered their time to read early drafts of chapters. Amy Richlin, Carla Melo, Hana Thalova Salussolia, and especially Mary Louise Hart have been a continued source of encouragement. My CUNY colleagues, particularly Pat Licklider, Marny Tabb, Allison Pease, and Jean Graham-Jones have created a supportive environment, and my students, graduate and undergraduate, have motivated me with their curiosity, enthusiasm, and hard work.

CUNY's union, the Professional Staff Congress, has assisted my research by funding me with course releases, payment for the images, and an assistant, Benjamin Gillespie, who helped with preparing the works cited pages. Grateful thanks are also due to Holly Carver, Catherine Cocks, Karen Copp, and Charlotte Wright at the University of Iowa Press; to Gary Jay Williams, who provided me with a detailed and most helpful reader's report; and to Carla Bertini at IKONA, Robbi Siegal at Art Resource, and Thomas Volpe for their kind help with image permissions.

My warmest heartfelt thanks go to Joe Smudin, a kind and generous presence who has sustained me through this process. And finally, I would like to thank two of my dearest teachers, critics, and supporters: Frank and Winifred Powers, to whom I dedicate this book.

ATHENIAN TRAGEDY IN PERFORMANCE

INTRODUCTION

This book presents an introduction to the analytical and creative ways that scholars of fifth-century Athenian theatre use the historical sources—and the lack of them—in descriptions and interpretations of the ancient plays and their performances. How does analytical skill combine with imaginative muscle to address the known and the unknown, the historical record and the holes within it? I have chosen to explore this question not by attempting the formidable task of offering a comprehensive study on the topic but rather by discussing a few recurring and familiar methodological issues that arise in select scholarship on fifth-century Athenian theatrical space, audience, chorus, performance style, costuming, properties, gesture, and the mask.

In order to focus my discussion further, at the end of each chapter, I use Euripides's tragedy *Bacchae*,[1] staged in 405 BCE at the annual Dionysian festival, as a case study. Investigating the information that this text does—and does not—provide about the operation of these performance practices in its historical staging, I explore critical historiographical questions related to the tension between the study of a drama as literature versus its role as a record of a historical performance. I of course recognize the difficulty of addressing in a single book the many complexities of my diverse subjects of Athenian performance practices, Euripides's play, and historical methodologies. However, by combining these three subjects and narrowing my discussion to a selection of scholarship related to *Bacchae*'s late fifth-century performance, I am able to explore with greater specificity the limitations in the sources and the problems related to their interpretation, both of which are an essential part of understanding the historical subject itself.

For instance, because the sources do not make clear whether women attended the performances, disagreement exists over the presence of women spectators in the theatre. Many scholars argue that women were present, others insist on their absence, and yet others hedge their bets. The coauthored textbook *Theatre Histories: An Introduction* (second edition, 2010) remains noncommittal. It avoids the hot topic of women's attendance. Instead, the authors focus on a paradox. The plays present strong female characters, but Athenian society confined women's role to the domestic sphere. The authors attribute this practice to the expectations of the Athenians for their "theatre to stage contemporary cultural issues in its dialogic process, stirring debate."[2] By contrast, Oscar G. Brockett directly addresses the presence of women in the audience. In his third edition of *History of the Theatre* (1977), he explains that women were indeed present: "It has been suggested that each tribe had its own section and that within these areas one part was set aside for women. . . . Seats were also reserved for other priests and priestesses. . . . The audience was composed of women, men, boys, and slaves" (36). However, in the coauthored tenth edition of *History of the Theatre* (2008), Brockett and Franklin J. Hildy add a disclaimer to this statement: "The audience certainly included men and boys, but there is considerable scholarly debate as to whether it included women or slaves. Seats were reserved for certain state officials, visiting ambassadors, and persons the state wished to honor along with the priests of Dionysus, other priests, and perhaps for priestesses" (29). Brockett and Hildy's revision is a reminder that our knowledge of Athenian theatre often rests on shifting sands. What was once a solid assumption can easily become an uncertainty.

The limited historical record is partly responsible for such modifications. Scholars must rely on primary sources such as archaeological remains, vasepainting, sculpture, lexicons, epigraphic records, such as the Fasti,[3] ancient commentaries or *scholia*, and the manuscripts and papyri that have preserved the dramatic texts, their fragments, and other literary, historical, and philosophical texts. These problematic and often partial historical sources have presented difficulties not only to authors of general histories but also to specialists, for even the most specialized studies cannot avoid conjectures, speculations, and the all too redundant disclaimer, "although there is little evidence, I will argue." For example, in his general history for *The Oxford*

Illustrated History of Theatre (2001), Oliver Taplin, a specialist in the study of the performance of ancient Greek drama, hedges his position on women with a "probably." According to Taplin, "the vast majority of the audience consisted of Athenian citizens; there were definitely boys there also, but probably not slaves. . . . It is much disputed whether women were admitted to the *theatron* at Athens, but probably they were not. Their presence, if they were there, leaves no trace in the contemporary evidence."[4] Taplin's expert opinion on this issue has not gone unchallenged. One recent work on the audience, David Roselli's *Theater of the People* (2011), makes a strong case for women's attendance, and other classicists concur.[5] These varied points of view are unavoidable, for the task of classicists and theatre historians is no simple matter of making right or wrong arguments or deciding between correct or incorrect interpretations. What scholars know is always framed by what they do not know. This relationship, or rather this gap, between the uncertain evidence and interpretive assumptions is the topic of this book.

As an introductory study in historiography, or the methods and approaches to historical study,[6] this work presents an atypical investigation of classical theatre and drama. In the usual model of investigation, scholars aim to construct a persuasive argument and thereby engage in the familiar two-part process of reviewing previous scholarship before positing their new interpretations. They conduct research on the available sources, analyze them, and attempt to present them as credible evidence, but in the process, whenever they confront the many holes in the historical record, they often argue around the missing pieces, close up these empty spaces, and try to leap across the gaps. In this historiographical study, I reverse this usual process by contemplating the inexact nature of the study of Athenian tragedy and its performance. Instead of trying to bridge the gaps, I delve into them. Instead of following the traditional formula and presenting a new argument on the nature of Athenian performance, I aim to understand the subject better by investigating the shared historical issues, problems, and perplexities that all scholars confront as they interpret and explain fifth-century Athenian theatre. That is, I confront the historiographical issues directly.

To address these topics, I have divided the study into six chapters: Theatrical Space; Audience; the Chorus, Music, Movement, and Dance; Performance Style; Costuming and Properties; and Gesture and Mask. I begin by discussing the elements that shape and inform and are informed by the performers, and I ultimately move to the performers themselves. I have focused on these six basic attributes because the topics have generated several debates that illustrate the methodological problems confronting anyone who is interested in Athenian theatre, from an undergraduate student to a leading specialist.

Each of the chapters has two parts. Before turning to my case study of *Bacchae* in the final section of each chapter, in the first part, I examine some of the interpretive methods at work in a few contending perspectives and arguments that several recent scholars have made on a specific historical issue. For example, I consider the ways in which scholars identify, analyze, interpret, describe, explain, and present the limited historical sources as evidence for their arguments. How do scholars manage the contradictory nature of some of the sources? How do they confront, ignore, speculate, or make conjectures about the gaps or absences in the historical record? What methods do they apply in developing interpretive arguments, and what are the advantages and disadvantages of these various methods?

Some difficulties that arise in these scholars' arguments are ones that all historians face, such as problems with periodization, synchronic approaches, and biased sources. Other concerns are specific to classicists, for example, the limited source material that creates the need to mix and match sources from disparate genres (e.g., comedy, tragedy, philosophy), locations (Greece/Italy), and periods (fifth century/fourth century). Still other problems are specific to performance historians, such as the conflation of characters with actors, the ephemeral nature of performance, and the risk of anachronism in using practical theatre experience to interpret historical performance practices. Some topics, such as problems with interpreting the visual record, recur in several chapters, but I explore specific aspects of each topic in relation to the performance practice at hand. For example, in chapter 3, I discuss problems with the visual record by examining the difficulty of reconstructing dance moves from static images, but in chapter 5, I consider the challenge of interpreting the so-called Pronomos Vase (figures 1, 2, and 3) through reproductions instead of a firsthand viewing. In some cases, I highlight the historiographical problems. In others, I discuss the ways that scholars attempt to overcome these obstacles with interpretive strategies, such as identifying interpretive patterns in the historical sources, reading literary sources in relation to visual material, applying the kinesthetic understanding of theatre practitioners, and making arguments *ex silentio*, i.e., from a silence in the sources. The choices of topics and debates that I have made are in the service of my overall aim: to examine the methods of scholarship, the unavoidable challenges inherent in the task, the debates that ensue as a result, and the underlying reasons for the abundance of diverse interpretations of Athenian tragedy and its performance.

Thus, I have not attempted to present a comprehensive study of each performance topic or of every scholarly argument on a topic, nor have I offered an interpretive catalogue of the wide range of methods and theories in historiography. Instead, I have chosen a few representative case studies that reveal a cross section of the complications that appear in current scholarship on Athenian tragedy in performance. For example, in my chapter on the theatrical space, I focus on the evidence and debates over a circular versus rectangular *orchēstra* (playing space), but I do not consider, for instance, the evidence and debates on the *skēnē* (stage building). My analysis of these historiographical issues in current scholarship can serve as a reflection on the state of the craft for specialists, an overview of the subject for non-specialists, an introduction to historical writing for students, a reference for further reading, and a clarification of several general misconceptions about, for example, the shape and size of the fifth-century performance space, the identities of the spectators, the nature of the costumes, and the functions of the mask and the chorus.

Without question, my study of this subject has profited from the valuable scholarship of performance scholars and historians, such as Clifford Ashby, Charlotte M. Canning, Marvin Carlson, Sue-Ellen Case, Tracy C. Davis, Susan Leigh Foster, Bruce McConachie, Joseph Roach, Wilmar Sauter, and especially Thomas Postlewait, who has served as my editor on this project. My study of the source material has greatly benefitted from the solid foundational studies of Sir Arthur Pickard-Cambridge's *The Dramatic Festivals of Athens*[7] and Eric Csapo and William J. Slater's *The Context of Ancient Drama*,[8] and I have also learned from the studies of many other classicists whose work in part serves as the focus of this study: Eric Csapo, E. R. Dodds, Pat Easterling, Helene P. Foley, John Gould, J. Richard Green, Simon Goldhill, Edith Hall, Lloyd Llewellyn-Jones, Peter Meineck, David Roselli, Richard Seaford, Oliver Taplin, David Wiles, and Froma Zeitlin. Their contemporary scholarship in English appeals to an interdisciplinary audience and demonstrates in its great variety and sophistication the challenges inherent in a study of fifth-century plays, their theatrical elements, potential performances, and setting within the context of the religious festivals central to Athenian society, its culture and values. Because ancient history is a subfield of classics, most of these classicists would probably not regard themselves as historians of the ancient world, but I usually refer to them as such, for the complications that arise in their studies often relate to the historical task.

Their current research on which I focus is part of a long tradition of scholarship in classics. In this tradition, philology has been paramount, but very few recent scholars have restricted their research to textual criticism alone. In the study of the ancient plays and their performances, the borders between the subdivisions of the field of classics (e.g., textual criticism, epigraphy, papyrology, literary criticism, cultural studies, ancient history, art history) are porous. The skills and approaches required by the subject are many and often overlap. Each individual study has its own justification. Each deserves an examination in terms of a scholar's specific agenda for the specific work at hand. Scholarship rarely fits easily into one single area of study, and scholars often vary in their choice of source material, techniques, methods, aims, and agenda from work to work. Accordingly, my intention is not to distribute scholars and their works into separate, distinct, or opposing camps, such as ritualist, feminist, poststructuralist, and so forth. Nor do I wish to rank scholars, or judge whose methods and arguments are right and whose are wrong. Instead, I introduce and examine a cross section of the representative research methods, arguments, and debates in current research on fifth-century performance.

I have selected *Bacchae* as a case study because the tragedy provides more evidence on fifth-century Athenian performance than any other extant play. While fourth-century sources that comment on performance, such as Aristotle's *Poetics*, Demosthenes's speeches, and various iconographic sources, are relatively ample, only a handful of fifth-century sources directly related to Athenian theatre have survived. Two of these key works date to approximately the same year as *Bacchae* and thus help to contextualize its performance practices: Aristophanes's *Frogs*,[9] performed the same year as *Bacchae* in 405 BCE, and the Attic vase attributed to the Pronomos Painter, painted circa 400 BCE (figures 1, 2, and 3).[10] Both sources provide critical information on costume, mask, gesture, performance style, and other aspects of performance. In addition, two extant tragedies (produced posthumously), Sophocles's *Oedipus at Colonus*, 401 BCE, and Euripides's *Iphigenia at Aulis*, 405 BCE, help to contextualize *Bacchae*'s dramaturgy.[11] In my interpretations of the play, I have relied as much as possible on these late fifth-century treasures as well as on some early fourth-century ones, such as the so-called

Chorēgos Vase (figure 9), in an attempt to reconstruct, as far as is possible, the historical performance context in which *Bacchae* participated.[12]

Bacchae was said to have been produced posthumously at the Dionysian festival in 405 BCE, perhaps directed by Euripides's son,[13] but Euripides apparently composed the play at the court of Archelaus in Macedonia. The process of this composition is uncertain,[14] but whatever Euripides's method, this "text" or some version of it was delivered to Athens, probably as a written document but perhaps orally. The first extant written copies of this "text," on which editions and translations of *Bacchae* are based, appear in fragmentary form on papyri, dating from the second century BCE to the fifth century CE. The first complete, or near complete, accounts of the play are two fourteenth-century manuscripts commonly known as P and L, Palatinus 287 and Laurentianus xxxii, the latter of which preserves only lines 1–755.[15] These manuscripts may derive from versions of the play taught in schools, and perhaps for this reason, the manuscripts offer little information about performance. There are no speaker headings, stage directions, or actors' notations. Thus, the manuscripts, which date to approximately seventeen hundred years after *Bacchae*'s performance at the Dionysia, are problematic, if not anachronistic, sources for a study of the 405 BCE production, yet while the relationship between the extant manuscripts and *Bacchae*'s ancient performance is uncertain, most scholars take a correspondence for granted.

Assuming the manuscript is similar to the fifth-century version, the play is an excellent resource for the study of Athenian performance, partly because it features Dionysus, the god of theatre and the mask, as a central character. Moreover, the tragedy stages a dressing-up scene in which Dionysus directs his nemesis Pentheus in how best to perform the role of a maenad. This critical scene, with its self-reflective commentary on theatrical presentation, offers clues about theatrical space, audience response, and the conventions of performance style, costuming, mask, and gesture. *Bacchae* is also one of the few, if not the only, extant plays that does not present a methodological problem in studying the depiction of everyday dress and gesture on theatre vases in relation to the descriptions of costume in the text. The direct correlation between the many images of maenads on late fifth-century vase-painting (e.g., figures 3, 7, 8) and *Bacchae*'s description of the maenad chorus's movement, gesture, and costume prevents this dilemma. For the convenience of specialists and nonspecialists, parenthetically in the *Bacchae* section of each chapter, I have cited lines from Richard

Seaford's edition of the text, which includes an English translation next to the ancient Greek.[16] Unless otherwise indicated, all translations are my own.

Although *Bacchae* is not the only play to which I refer in this study, by narrowing my interpretive focus to a case study of a single play and its historical context, I am able to explore in greater depth both the rich detail that a text provides about its performance and critical historiographical questions related to this information. How can scholars interpret the historical and cultural significance of a tragedy from a complex text with limited information about the performance practices in which it participated? How can scholars understand performance practices in general with only partial knowledge of their operation in a play's fifth-century performance? How do scholars, trained in a tradition influenced by Aristotle's marginalization of spectacle (*Poetics* vi. 1450b 15–20), address or ignore the double identity of the extant texts, which are crucial sources on fifth-century performance, religion, and culture, but are also only a part of the historical 405 BCE performance witnessed by the ancient audience? In other words, how do current scholars, whose fields have long privileged the study of drama as literature, negotiate the study of a text with its absent historical performance?

Inevitably influenced by my observations of many contemporary productions of *Bacchae*[17] and my experiences with performing in the play, I explore such questions by presenting both a theatre history and historiography. In chapter 1, for example, I present a theatre history of *Bacchae*'s spatial operations. In this interpretation, I, like most scholars, depend on the play-text as evidence in order to present what I deem to be a probable argument. At the same time, when I present my argument, I apply my historiographical lens to acknowledge and confront the ways in which the historical performance could have differed from my interpretations. In this way, I attempt to maintain my historiographical focus by raising the specter of the unknown performance to illustrate the complications with my own interpretations and methodologies as well as those of the other scholars whose work I discuss. Through this two-part process of presenting both theatre history and historiography, I attempt to achieve my overall objective, which is not necessarily to present a convincing argument about *Bacchae*, to identify any right or wrong interpretations, or to solve or try to solve the common methodological problems that arise in scholarly investigations. Rather I want to explore in each chapter the shared problem of deciphering the complex nature of a play-text, which gives historians glimpses of the past while denying a full view.

In my chapter on audience, I first consider the homogenization of the audience in studies of *Bacchae*, and I then suggest that this tendency contributes to an oversight of the contribution of women's possible presence in creating the "theatrical event," Wilmar Sauter's term for the joint creation of meaning from the actions and reactions of both performers and spectators.[18] In chapter 3, I use textual clues to posit a model for excavating choral performance while simultaneously recognizing the gaps in my interpretation. In chapter 4, I focus on the problems with the information that the dressing-up scene provides about performance style in order to argue that a limited understanding of performance style impedes interpretations that speculate on *Bacchae*'s commentary on democracy. In chapter 5, I discuss the uncertainties over the play's costuming and properties in order to question the common claim about the feminine or effeminate appearance of Dionysus in the play. In my final chapter on gesture and mask, I present methods for reconstructing the gestures of Pentheus in the dressing-up scene, and I illustrate the issues that surface in arguments about the ritual or comic connotations of those gestures as well as Dionysus's so-called "smiling" mask.

Through this discussion, I want to suggest that while a close study of the texts is necessary for literary, cultural, and performance studies, play-texts can also be misleading evidence for the study of plays, their performances, and the historical context in which they were situated. The absence of knowledge about the performance practices with which a play-text cooperated corrupts the ability to appreciate, understand, and explain the historical theatrical event, as it was experienced and created by the fifth-century audience in the Theatre of Dionysus. To explore these points, I investigate the issues, questions, and problems that arise in the study of fifth-century, especially late fifth-century, Athenian tragedy in performance in order to highlight the challenges of studying a play-text and using it as evidence. My method is to present both a history and a sort of negative history. I present my own and other scholars' interpretations of historical sources, but I also identify the knowledge gaps within such arguments and foreground the questions that scholars often need to explain away in the effort to make credible arguments about Euripides's *Bacchae*, the performance elements with which it cooperated, and the historical context in which it was situated. At the same time, I do not attempt to propose what, in my opinion, is the best method of passage through these knowledge gaps. I do not pose any solutions or answers to the shared historiographical problems and issues that I identify. Instead, I focus on the inherent difficulties of the historical task, but in the process, I by no means intend to imply that these difficulties and their resulting debates make scholarship futile. Rather I aim to demonstrate that the historical process is a continual, collective effort. The recurrent, cooperative mediation of the many sophisticated studies, disagreements, and unresolved debates moves knowledge forward and produces a deeper understanding and appreciation of the known—and the unknown—aspects of the performance of Athenian tragedy in the late fifth century BCE.

1 THEATRICAL SPACE

The study of Athenian theatrical space is a complex endeavor. Complicated and sometimes conflicting terminology abounds: diegetic space or the narrated space of the dramatic text, offstage space or indexical space, which is indicated by the onstage narrative, mimetic space or the scenic space of the acting area also known as iconic space or onstage space, spatial patterning or blocking, the physical space of the building, audience space, rehearsal space, and front and back of the theatre space.[1] In addition, much uncertainty exists about the elements that comprise the fifth-century performance space, for example, the location of the theatre, its structure, its material, the *skēnē* (stage building),[2] *paraskēnia* (side-scenes) and *proskēnion* (what is in front of the stage building),[3] the *skēnē*'s roof,[4] the doorway(s) to the *skēnē*, scene painting,[5] the *ekkyklēma* (wheeled device for rolling out bodies),[6] the *mēchanē* (crane),[7] the possibility of a low raised stage,[8] the altar and tomb,[9] the shape of the *orchēstra*,[10] the use of the side entrances,[11] and the audience's bleacher seats.[12] Many debates have been waged over questions related to these components, such as where the *skēnē* was located, when it was introduced, and if it had a roof and doors. However, most current scholarship agrees that the fifth-century Theatre of Dionysus was not the 30,000-seat stone structure of popular imagination but instead had wooden bleachers that seated an audience of no more than 4,000 to 6,000.[13]

Recently scholars, such as David Wiles, Lowell Edmunds, and Rush Rehm, have produced a variety of studies on the fifth-century performance space. For example, Wiles in his *Tragedy in Athens: Performance Space and Theatrical Meaning*, which I will later discuss in detail, refers to his approach as structuralist but also draws upon Henri Lefebvre's *The Production of Space* in order to discuss Athenian tragedy in terms of a performance set in social space. Lowell Edmunds's *Theatrical Space and Historical Place in Sophocles' "Oedipus at Colonus"* examines the use of space in Sophocles's play through Michael Issacharoff's and Anne Ubersfeld's semiotic theories, but, employing the work of cognitive psychologist James J. Gibson's *The Ecological Approach to Visual Perception*, Rush Rehm, in his *The Play of Space*, has criticized Edmunds's study as aiming at "taxonomic completeness rather than at an understanding of dramatic action and spatial interaction" (2). In the process, Rehm aims to avoid the problems of the reduction of space into a text to be read (8) and the construction of space in terms of structuralist binaries (1).[14] These studies are some of the many that disagree over the theatre building, the stage space, the uses of it in stagecraft, the relationship of theatre to fifth-century cultural perceptions of space, and sometimes all of these topics at once.

Instead of addressing these many topics and their related studies, in this chapter I limit my investigation to a critical debate over the shape of the playing space (*orchēstra*) in two recent works: Clifford Ashby's *Classical Greek Theatre: New Views of an Old Subject* (1999), and David Wiles's *Tragedy in Athens* (1997). Ashby and Wiles are both theatre historians and practitioners who present distinct approaches to the material that yield divergent conclusions.[15] Their debate thus serves as an excellent case study through which I can discuss the questions and problems that arise from historiographical issues, such as the influence of cultural and individual perspectives on historical assumptions, arguing by analogy, assuming the ideal case, and using theatre practitioners' instincts to interpret historical performance conditions.

After examining Wiles and Ashby's debate over the Theatre of Dionysus's *orchēstra*, I then turn to a study of another type of space: the fictional or imaginary space within a play-text. Using Wiles's theory of spatial practices as a model, I attempt to uncover the spatial operation of Euripides's *Bacchae* within the physical space of the fifth-century theatre in order to emphasize that the unresolved debates over the Theatre of Dionysus are not futile. Rather such critical debates, which are endemic to the historical process, have provided valuable interpretive tools for a variety of studies including my own.

Nevertheless, as the historian Michael Stanford has explained in *A Companion to the Study of History*, any historical account "is best understood as a model; that is, helpful, but not to be confused with reality" (131). If this statement is true of historical accounts in general, it may be especially true of historical accounts of performance, for a fifth-century play-text is no simple synecdochic substitute for the unknown and absent historical performance of *Bacchae*. Instead, as classicist Richard P. Martin has well stated, "timing, gesture, voice inflection, tempo, proximity to the audience . . . the setting . . . are factors that determine the meaning of the actual words spoken by a performer as much if not more so than the literal meaning of the words themselves."[16] Mindful of this notion, I explore the gaps in the historical sources, methods, issues, and debates related to a study of the physical space of the fifth-century theatre and the fictive space of a late fifth-century text.

Debates over the Shape of the *Orchēstra*

Athenian performance space, however defined, begins within the parameters of the Theatre of Dionysus, but even this most basic starting point presents serious difficulties to historians. The material remains of the fifth-century theatre include a small arc of less than a dozen stones—only a few dozen stones from which a multitude of stories have developed.

These stones lie among many others, because the theatre was continually rebuilt. The first reconstruction occurred probably in the second half of the fifth century BCE, most likely in conjunction with the construction of the Odeon of Pericles built around 440 BCE.[17] This renovation was one of many to follow in subsequent generations, and these various reconstructions have contributed to the present image of the Theatre of Dionysus (figure 4) and the ambiguity surrounding the dimensions of the fifth-century theatre's *orchēstra*.

Ever since Wilhelm Dörpfeld conducted his 1880s excavation of the Theatre of Dionysus, the scholarly community has been in disagreement over the nature and significance of this space. According to David Wiles, whose survey I here summarize,[18] Dörpfeld linked a rough arc of stones with a smaller line of stones "in order to project a circular boundary for a primitive acting/dancing area with a diameter somewhere between 24 and 27 metres."[19] From this configuration, one could infer that the rough arc of stones "should belong to a wall which supported a circular dancing area half cut into the hill-side and half extending from it."[20] Dörpfeld's successor, Ernst Fiechter, disagreed with this view. Proposing a more symmetrical and orderly shape, he dismissed as coincidence that the "other smaller group of stones on Dörpfeld's circumference formed a tangent with the new circle . . . since these stones could have had no structural function buried deep in the midst of the presumed terrace."[21] Fiechter instead "introduced a new smaller circle centred on the axes of the later auditorium and *eisodoi*, and at a tangent to a later stage wall."[22] This model was favored by scholars such as Pickard-Cambridge, but views of the orchestral shape as a quadrilateral began to surface with Carlo Anti's work in 1947.[23] According to Wiles, "Margarete Bieber helped to popularize his [Anti's] work, favouring a polygonal auditorium in the second edition of her *History of the Greek and Roman Theater*," and later, Elizabeth Gebhard[24] and Anti's pupil Luigi Polacco[25] continued to promote this view of a quadrilateral shape.

Instead of resolving these previous debates over the *orchēstra*'s shape, recent scholarship has instead replicated them. Donald Mastronarde has stated that "our uncertainty is well illustrated by the recent advocacy of the view that we have been wrong to imagine a circular orchestra for this period."[26] Since Mastronarde, Wiles has argued again for a circle. He asserts: "The facts are extremely clear. On the one hand, there is no evidence that the auditorium in the Athenian Theatre of Dionysus was ever rectilinear, and on the other, Dörpfeld offers the only acceptable explanation for the ancient arc of stones and for the sudden emergence of circular theatres across the Greek world."[27] Moreover, Wiles contends that a rectangular shape would have been too small to have accommodated the fifty-member dithyrambic choruses which performed in the space, although in making this claim he does not consider the clear difference in size between ancient Greek adult males and their 1900 CE European counterparts.[28] Despite Wiles's assertions, the current consensus of classicists is again moving toward a rectilinear view of a theatre. Hans R. Goette has most recently presented a reconstruction of a quadrilateral *theatron* and *orchēstra* based on archaeological research at the site.[29] But his discussion still does not directly respond to Wiles's points regarding how a rectangular orchestra could have accommodated a fifty-member chorus, or what, besides the Theatre of Dionysus, would have inspired the building of circular theatres in the fourth century BCE. After decades of studies, the scant remains of the fifth-century Theatre of Dionysus continue to leave little certainty or agreement over its structure. Despite the impressive rigor and erudition of the scholarship, on all sides of the debate, Rehm's words seem to have well summarized the problem: "We begin by reconstructing (with unavoidable speculation and simplification), the fifth-century theatre per se."[30]

Wiles and Ashby: Generational Cross Talk

In order to illustrate further the contending views of the shape of the *orchēstra* and to clarify some of the related historiographical issues, I will now consider the specific positions of Wiles, who argues for a circular shape, and Ashby, who argues for a rectangular one.[31] While both theatre historians are also practitioners who share an interest in applying performance-based hypotheses, Wiles's *Tragedy in Athens* and Ashby's *Classical Greek Theatre* represent two distinct eras of theatre history methodology. Ashby's work represents an empirical approach to stagecraft characteristic of previous generations, while Wiles's work bears the imprint of the academy's revolution in studies of language and culture. The distinct training, perspectives, and methodologies of these scholars in part influence their descriptions and analyses, for in the words of historian E. H. Carr, "the historian is just another dim figure trudging along in another part of the procession. . . . The point in the procession at which he finds himself [or herself] determines his [or her] angle of vision over the past."[32] In other words, as my bracketed comments indicate, historians themselves can be historicized. The individual positioning of Wiles and Ashby in part contributes to their opposing conclusions about the *orchēstra*'s shape.

Ashby draws on his extensive fieldwork, conducted at over one hundred ancient theatre sites, and applies it as evidence to revise previous assumptions about the Athenian theatre, including its architecture, use of space, time of performance, and the three-actor rule. In his concluding chapters, he then posits three methods of validation: by authority, by repetition, and by experiment. He explains that validation by authority and repetition has led to many misuses of evidence, and he further suggests that validation by experiment in modern theatres can offer an effective means to test canonical, historical suppositions. Privileging practitioners' instincts in the interpretation of the sources, he constructs a narrative using the sources related to the theatre itself and ignores the additional sources, beyond the immediate space of performance, which construct the religious, social, and political contexts of the dramatic festival.

Wiles, however, views this additional evidence as crucial for the study of theatre. While he refers to his methodology as structuralist,[33] his overall approach is complex. He engages with structuralism, but influenced by

Henri Lefebvre's *The Production of Space*, he also aims to provide a materiality to his study.[34] For example, he does not take a Euclidean view of space but, like Lefebvre, insists: *"(Social) space is a (social) product."*[35] In so doing, Wiles discusses the Theatre of Dionysus in terms of Lefebvre's "absolute space," i.e., space that is "religious and political in character,"[36] not like "abstract space," which, produced by capitalism, divides the civil and religious spheres.[37] Drawing on these insights, Wiles thus aims to reconstruct Athenian "spatial practices," Lefebvre's term for "what members of a society actually do, how they have learned to live and work in space, following practices that ensure social cohesion."[38] Accordingly, Wiles's interest rests not only in the theatrical space but also in the ways in which the Athenian audience, whom he assumes are male,[39] thought about space and in terms of space. How was the theatre's spatial arrangement socially conditioned?[40] How was the male audience conditioned to see? In this way, *Tragedy in Athens* helped to pioneer the study of Athenian drama in terms of its religious, social, political, and especially performance context.

Therefore, despite the contemporaneous publication of their works, Wiles and Ashby engage in a type of generational cross talk. Ashby examines the sites of ancient theatres to "seek explanations for some of the puzzling contradictions found in the standard histories of Greek theatre" and to formulate answers to questions posed by his students.[41] He aims to present "new views of an old subject," but Wiles seeks to shift the mode of viewing entirely. He insists that the sites of the ancient theatres and the performances within them cannot be divorced from the cultural, political, and religious forces inscribed in their construction. At the same time, both scholars share an interest in validation by experimentation, studying many theatres as opposed to just one, debunking conventional views of the theatre's space, and drawing on a variety of evidence (archaeological, literary, visual, and practitioner experience). These distinctions and commonalities between them represent the communal and communicative process that advances scholarly methods as well as the understanding of a given subject.

The Debate over the Theatre at Thorikos: Cultural Blinders

In making their cases for the shape of the Theatre of Dionysus, Wiles and Ashby make a comparison to the Theatre at Thorikos (figure 5). However, they disagree about the shape and function of this sixth-century BCE deme[42] theatre, which is the only theatre from this time to have survived intact and which does not have a clearly defined shape. On the one hand, if the theatre has a rectangular playing space, as Ashby posits, then no precedent would exist for a circular playing space in the Theatre of Dionysus, so from where would the idea of the circle have come? On the other hand, if Thorikos was a squashed circle, as Wiles suggests in "Seeing Is Believing," could its playing space have been a proto-circular shape? Thus, each scholar's view of the theatre's shape, i.e., each scholar's way of seeing, influences his distinct conclusion.

In making his case, Wiles argues that "the deme theatres provide misleading evidence for the Theatre of Dionysus in Athens insofar as they are both small and multi-functional."[43] He suggests that the social function of Thorikos overrides the theatre's function for performance, which is why the *orchēstra*'s shape is not a classic circle. "The Thorikians," he argues, "were plainly not concerned in the first instance to create a harmonious architectural composition, but were adapting a sacred space that lay above the bodies of their ancestors" (31). Ashby does not consider the social functions for the space. He focuses only on the theatre's dramatic function and disagrees with previous scholarship, such as that of Pickard-Cambridge and Walter Miller, which argues that a circular shape was necessary for Thorikos to function as a theatre.[44] "Imbued with the concept of theatrical circularity," he suggests (39), Pickard-Cambridge and Miller simply saw what they wanted to see.

However, according to Wiles, in his essay "Seeing Is Believing," Ashby's argument suffers from the same methodological problem that Ashby identifies in Pickard-Cambridge's and Walter Miller's works: seeing what one wants to see. Wiles explains that Ashby saw Thorikos as having a straight line of curved seating because he "aligned his camera to take a shot along the front rows of seats to emphasize the long straight line and minimize the impact of the curves."[45] According to Wiles, this technique "manipulates language to suggest that the curved sides were a later addition."[46] Wiles further explains that there is no archaeological evidence to suggest that the curved sides were a later addition or "for the 'rectangular' performance area somehow existing independently of the shape defined by the auditorium" (219). Illustrating these problems with Ashby's argument, Wiles states: "The question is, how do we see this shape [figure 5]? Is it a failed rectangle or a squashed circle or does it have a completely different formal logic?" (218).

Addressing this question, he discusses the geometry of Thorikos to offer "a vivid case study of how historians project onto the past an idea of performance space that legitimates theatre practices in the present" (217). For his specific questions about Thorikos relate to a larger historiographical question: "Do we see what is there, or do we see what our culture has taught us to see?" (216). He states, for example, that "after 1917 people *saw* differently. For us today, soaked in Pablo Picasso's modernist mode of seeing the world and his particular abstraction of the visual process, it is hard to recover an older way of seeing and appreciate the lost pleasures of pictorial theatre" (217). Wiles implies that Ashby's culturally determined modes of seeing caused him to misinterpret the shape of Thorikos, whereas Greek archaeologist Clairy Palyvou, exposed to performances at Epidauros, viewed the space as circular. In this way, "Seeing Is Believing" emphasizes the importance of learning to see in ways that lead to a better assessment of the shape and function of a historical space.

This key point raises yet another historiographical issue: to what extent is it possible for historians not to see as culturally and historically constituted modern individuals? It has become almost a truism that individuals and their modes of seeing are culturally constructed, for according to Michel de Certeau, "discourse can be dissociated today neither from the origins of its production nor from the political, economic, or religious praxis that can change societies and, at a given moment, make various kinds of scientific comprehension possible."[47] Thus, as James Clifford has noted of ethnographers, historians too "seem to be condemned to strive for . . . true encounter while simultaneously recognizing the political, ethical, and personal cross-purposes that undermine any transmission of intercultural knowledge."[48] In other words, historians, like ethnographers, constantly need to adjust their cultural blinders. How Ashby and Wiles negotiate their cultural positioning to represent a past culture in its own terms is part of the historical problem that leads to their disagreement.

Arguments by Analogy

Making another argument by analogy, Wiles and Ashby speculate about versions of ancient dance performed in the Dionysian theatre. Even though rectangular choreography could be performed in a circular space and circular choreography in a rectangular one, they both lean toward an either/or argument. If the dance was a certain shape, then so would be the *orchēstra*. Either the *orchēstra* would have been built to accommodate the dance, or the dance would have developed according to the shape of the space. According to this logic, Ashby argues that the choral dances tended toward a rectangular pattern in the rectangular-shaped theatre, and Wiles instead suggests the circular shape of, not the dramatic dances, but the dithyrambic ones for which, he argues, the Theatre of Dionysus was solely built.[49] The scholars' use of yet another analogy in their debate raises the question of the extent to which arguments by analogy can be helpful or misleading.

Because in chapter 3 I address the controversy over the shape of dramatic dances, I here focus on the complications related to determining the dithyramb dance's shape. The point is important to Wiles's argument for a circular *orchēstra* and is a complex issue on which scholars disagree. Noting as his source only the late second-century author Athenaeus, who "contrasts four-square and circular choruses [*kuklioi khoroi*],"[50] Sir Arthur Pickard-Cambridge in his *Dithyramb, Tragedy and Comedy* has suggested that "at Athens the dithyramb was danced and sung by a chorus of fifty men or boys. The name 'circular chorus,' which always means dithyramb, was *probably* [italics mine] derived from the dancers being arranged in a circle, instead of in rectangular formation as dramatic choruses were."[51] Pickard-Cambridge tentatively suggests a circular shape, but recently, theatre historian Graham Ley has been firm: "These *choroi* were called circular and we have no reason to doubt that description."[52] While Pickard-Cambridge hedges his position and Wiles and Ley are assertive, classicist David Fearn has questioned the relationship of dithyrambs to the term *kyklioi choroi* (circular dances). In his 2007 work on the subject of Bacchylides's dithyrambs,[53] Fearn suggests that *kyklioi choroi*[54] referred to a wide variety of choral performances, such as those described in Homer and Archaic poetry.[55] He states that because dithyrambs were a subcategory of *kyklioi choroi*, Pickard-Cambridge's "straight-forward elision of *kuklios khoros* with 'dithyramb'" has been misleading (166), for not all *kyklioi choroi* are necessarily dithyrambs nor were *kyklioi choroi* exclusive to the Dionysia.[56]

Fearn's study raises questions about the nature of the dithyramb and especially its relationship to circular dancing. Were all *kyklioi choroi* circular dances or only the dithyramb? Or were none of the dances circular? While Pickard-Cambridge has suggested that "a dance especially associated with the dithyramb was the *tyrbasia*,"[57] Fearn is clear that "we have no information about how exactly an individual *kuklios khoros* was arranged in performance,"[58] yet he also speculates that "although we do not know exactly how *kuklioi choroi* were arranged in performance, *it seems likely* [italics mine] that they would have been highly suited to fit the performance of the *geranos*, a dance with 'twisty' connotations" (248). These scholars have attempted to associate a certain dance style with *kyklioi choroi* such as the dithyramb, but because of the lack of specificity in the evidence, their suggestions rest more in the realm of possibility than probability.

Although the term is the primary evidence suggesting a circular dance, *kyklios choros* does not necessarily imply anything about the dance's arrangement. *Kyklios* could have referred to the entire dance, a part of a dance, or even none of the dance. Or *kyklios* could have referred to an earlier form of the dance in the performance of Dark Age Homeric or Archaic poetry, but the dance could have changed its form by the classical era. In any case, what *kyklios choros* meant to the Greeks may surely be different from what scholars assume today. Was it a circle? Or did it refer to a serpentine style of weaving in and out and creating a series of half circles? Or did it refer to the nature of the accompanying music?

Despite these uncertainties, scholars continue to reinforce the view of the dance as circular. Some, such as Ley, Wiles, and Peter Wilson, suggest the connection between Athens's democratic political system and the Athenian theatre's building design, but the association of the circle with democracy may be nothing more than a wishful metaphor. Karen Bassi has made this point in her review of Wiles's *Tragedy in Athens*: "When generals and tyrants stand in the center of the orchestra, as they do in the examples Wiles cites from Plutarch, are they playing the democrat or usurping the role of the collective?"[59] There is nothing intrinsically democratic about the shape.

Nevertheless, Wiles's 1997 work simply states that "the principal dance at the festival of Dionysus was the dithyramb, and this was consistently known in antiquity as the 'circular chorus'" (49). As the source for this claim, he cites not Pickard-Cambridge's *Dithyramb, Tragedy and Comedy*, which as previously mentioned cites Athenaeus as a source, but rather *The Dramatic Festivals of Athens*, which references as evidence Aristophanes's *Frogs* (fragment 156.10 K.–A.) and Aeschines III 232.[60] However, these ancient sources merely refer to *kyklioi choroi* with no explanation about the dance's shape, yet Wiles nevertheless assumes from the term *kyklios* that the dithyramb must have been a circular dance in honor of Dionysus, even though the evidence for this assertion is uncertain.

Ignoring the point that the dithyramb had top billing at the festival, Ashby focuses instead on the dance of the dramatic choruses, which he argues tends toward a rectangular, not circular, pattern. Later sources do suggest that the dramatic choruses tended toward a rectangular shape, but these sources, as I discuss in chapter 3, are not only ambiguous but also contradict evidence in the dramas that at least some of the choral dances were circular, such as that of the Erinyes in the so-called binding song in Aeschylus's *Eumenides*. In any case, Ashby bases his assumptions about choral dancing primarily on contemporary forms of Greek folk dancing and not any ancient source. He contends that folk dancing, when the dancers are not being observed, gravitates toward a circular shape; but theatrical dance, which is meant to be observed, abandons its center focus for its presentation to others.[61] Although Ashby recognizes that "theatrical practices of one era can[not] be automatically transferred to another" (xviii), he here judges his generalization about folk dancing to be a valid point of comparison. Nevertheless, his assessment risks projecting the present onto the past[62] and raises the problem of anachronism built upon a shaky argument by analogy.

The dance may have adjusted to the gathering of the spectators who could have circled around the performers. At the same time, the performers may have danced in horizontal lines in order for spectators to see the performers better, or perhaps the shape accommodated both circular and rectangular dances. Despite the uncertainty, Wiles and Ashby both assume that, in some way, the shape of the theatre followed or somehow accommodated the shape of the dance. In a perfect theatre, that might be the case, but assuming the constitution of an ideal theatre presents another historiographical topic.

Assuming the Ideal Case

Both scholars rely on their experience as practitioners to persuade readers of their views of the theatre's shape, yet they disagree on which shape would have best served the demands of hearing and seeing a performance. Wiles assumes that a circular space would have presented the best-case scenario for sight lines and acoustics. He suggests that "there is an applied common sense behind Vitruvius' statement that sound travels in circles like the ripples set up by a pebble thrown into a pond, and that interruptions to the circle disturb the flow of sound."[63] He further argues that Polacco's model of a trapezoidal auditorium, on which Ashby relies, has "sightlines and more importantly acoustics [that] would be inferior to those offered by a more-or-less circular auditorium, considerations which become more pressing in proportion to the scale[64] of the theatre."[65] In contrast to Wiles, another theatre practitioner, classicist Peter Meineck has argued in "The Embodied Space" that a rectilinear *orchēstra* would instead be a superior shape. Meineck contends that "although not impossible to surmount, the evidence from modern theatre practice is that round stages require specific blocking and staging and acoustical attention that may not have been best suited to the ancient conditions of masked frontal drama" (34). While Wiles suggests that the circular *orchēstra* has aesthetic and functional superiority, Ashby and Meineck assert, on the contrary, that a rectilinear shape was functionally superior. Despite their distinct views, all of these scholars assume that the shape of the *orchēstra*, whatever it was, functioned well and best accommodated the cultural, aesthetic, and practical needs of its audience.

Practitioner Instinct

Although Wiles and Ashby take opposing positions on the shape of the *orchēstra*, they both agree that the altar within it was not a permanent fixture. A portable altar may have been used, or perhaps there was never a major altar at all in the Theatre of Dionysus. Aware of these possibilities, they again rely on their instincts as theatre practitioners. They reject the idea, proposed by Dörpfeld and Reisch, that a permanent altar was positioned in the center of the Theatre of Dionysus. Ashby does not find the ancient evidence for a permanent fixture to be convincing because of its impracticality for staging.[66] He instead suggests that the altars mentioned in the text were temporary. He argues that any permanent altar would have "sat on the periphery of the orchestra; from this position, they could maintain a prominence without constituting a major obstacle to dramatic performance" (59). Wiles also rejects the idea of a permanent altar in the center of the theatre, and he posits the *orchēstra*'s midpoint as a powerful focus.[67] Instead of imagining a permanent altar fixed upon this point,[68] he argues for a movable stone, the *thymelē*, which could serve as a focal point like a hearth. This *thymelē* would have served as the focus for ritual activity, such as "the pouring of libations, and the purification of the theatre by *periestiarchoi*—'the men who go around the hearth.'"[69] Wiles argues his case by citing examples of marking stones in the theatres at Epidauros, Aigai, Dodona, and Eretria. However, like Ashby, his instincts as a practitioner seem most to convince him. "Focus," he argues, is the "*sine qua non* of a satisfactory performance space. . . . For the analysis of 'focus,' we have to turn to theatre practitioners, for the problem lies outside the normal discourses of classical scholarship."[70] This "focus on the centre point" is a central tenet of Wiles's theory of the Dionysian theatre's spatial practices, which I will discuss further in the *Bacchae* section of this chapter. Like Ashby, Wiles has little concrete evidence for his theory of this center-point, but he relies primarily on a kinesthetic understanding of the space to make his claims. This kinesthetic sense, while difficult to quantify in objective terms, can serve as crucial evidence, a point which I discuss further in chapter 6, when I consider the degree to which the instincts of modern practitioners can serve as reliable evidence for theories of ancient masking practice.

While not yielding the answers hoped for, the debate between Wiles and Ashby does raise important questions. If the Theatre of Dionysus's *orchēstra* was not circular, why would later fourth-century theatres have emerged with a circular *orchēstra*? From where would this idea have come? Wiles's theory that the Dionysian theatre was built to accommodate the god's dance of the dithyramb provides a good reason for the development of a circular shaped *orchēstra* that was copied in the fourth century because it proved to be aesthetically and acoustically superior. At the same time, Meineck, who argues for a rectangular *orchēstra* in the Theatre of Dionysus, has provided another convincing response to the question. He argues instead that a circular *orchēstra* developed in the fourth century to accommodate various factors of the Hellenistic theatre, such as its institutionalization, growing audiences, acoustic properties, and focus on star actors.[71] Clearly many contending ideas, assumptions, and questions emerge as scholars attempt to work with ideas of dance, masked acting, and theatrical space and relate them to the potential political, religious, and performance functions of the theatre. The arguments on both sides are strong and complex, but perhaps only future excavation will help to clarify the issue.[72]

Bacchic Space

Having discussed the architectural space where actors presented the plays, I will now turn to my case study of *Bacchae*, where I will demonstrate the dynamic interaction[73] of the physical space of the Dionysian theatre with *Bacchae*'s fictive or imaginary space.[74] Both seen and unseen space operate in the fictive world of the play, and the bodies of actors both produce and inhabit the play's imaginary space by moving through the physical space[75] and producing spatial patterns, which in western theatre is known as blocking. According to Wiles, the geographical coordinates of the Theatre of Dionysus (north, south, east, west) help to articulate binary oppositions expressed in the tragic plays, such as human/divine, male/female, Greek/

barbarian. The actors' movements, their entrances and exits on the *eisodoi* for example, create meaning on this spatial grid. Following this theory of Athenian spatial practices,[76] which illustrates the visual presentation of a play's binary oppositions,[77] I will attempt a reconstruction of the space of *Bacchae*'s 405 BCE performance, for as Wiles states, his argument for the theatre's spatial practices stands independently of the argument that the *orchēstra* was circular.[78] Then, after presenting what I deem to be a probable function of *Bacchae*'s spatial operation as well as the complications with that interpretation, I will ultimately suggest that the play defies Wiles's model of spatial operations by undermining the dichotomies upon which his theory partially depends.

In the Theatre of Dionysus, the audience faces south. This one piece of certain evidence is crucial, because scholars can use it to determine the audience's orientation to the directions of east and west. In *Bacchae*, the god and his foreign chorus of Asian[79] women would have most likely entered from the geographical direction of the east, the direction from which Dionysus in his prologue indicates they traveled. Alternatively, they could have entered from the west, and the east could have represented the direction of Mt. Cithaeron and the town. However, if this were the case, the words of the text, which state that the chorus has arrived from the East would contradict with the spatial positioning of the theatre building. The geographical spatial coordinates of the theatre would not have corresponded with the fictive space of the play. Another possibility is that one *eisodos* (entryway) could lead to the town and the other to the mountain. In this case, Dionysus and the chorus could have arrived from either direction, but if, as Wiles argues, the *didaskalos* (director)[80] arranged the movement with an awareness of the theatre's coordinates, then the words of the text should correspond with those coordinates. At the same time, it is possible that the audience would not have expected the geographical coordinates within the fictive world of the play to adhere literally to those of the performance space and surrounding landscape. In this case, none of these possible entrances can be determined with any certainty, but *if* the *didaskalos* wanted to establish visually the conflict between Dionysus and Pentheus, the chorus and Dionysus would have entered through the opposite *eisodos* from that which Pentheus enters. Therefore, an entrance from the east, i.e., the audience's left, while not certain, does seem probable.

This interpretation results in a coordination of the fictive space and physical space according to the following scheme:

SOUTH

Orchestra

EAST   Dionysus and chorus   Mt. Cithaeron, Town   WEST

Audience

NORTH

The coordinates of the outdoor theatre have the audience facing south in the direction of the *orchēstra*. Therefore, stage right is to the east and stage left is to the west. In this arrangement, Pentheus should enter from the west *eisodos* (stage left), because although he initially heard the news about Dionysus when he was out of town (215), he has also heard news, likely while in town, that the Theban maenads have been caught and put in prison. Because Mt. Cithaeron is beyond the town walls (1222–26), the same *eisodos* should lead to both places, and the chorus and possibly Dionysus would have arrived by the opposite *eisodos*, which leads to the East. In this case, Dionysus (east/left) and Pentheus (west/right) would have arrived from two opposite directions. In order to maintain continuity, the chorus in the Parados (the opening choral ode) would have arrived via the east *eisodos* and Agaue, who comes from Cithaeron, would have arrived via the west *eisodos*.

Alternatively, if the two opposing *eisodoi* were instead to represent Cithaeron (east) and the town (west) and if Dionysus and the chorus were to arrive from Cithaeron and Pentheus from the town, then the opposition between the sweet chorus and the terrible Theban maenads would be lost, because Agaue would arrive through the same *eisodos* as the chorus did earlier. For this reason, the Dionysus/chorus/east/left and Pentheus/Agaue/west/right design seems more probable. Such a use of space would set up visually the *agōn* (contest) between Pentheus and Dionysus as well as the tension between the true followers of Dionysus and the crazed Theban maenads.

Several examples support the interpretation that one *eisodos* (west/right) leads to Cithaeron and the town and the opposite *eisodos* (east/left) leads to the East, from where Dionysus and the chorus arrive. For one, in the Prologue (62–63), Dionysus states that he is going to join the women on Cithaeron. Later, a servant brings the disguised god back on stage (434ff.) together with news from the public prison that some of the Theban maenads, whom Pentheus had earlier announced were imprisoned (226–27), have escaped (443–46). Thus, the servant appears to have brought the god, who was earlier on Cithaeron, from the direction of the prison, which, like the Athenians' own public prison near the Acropolis, may have been in town. Second, Dionysus plans to lead Pentheus through the town on the way to Cithaeron to make the king the laughingstock of Thebes (854–56), and third, Pentheus fears being seen by the Cadmeians on the way to the mountain (840). Furthermore, the first messenger states that the Theban maenads ransacked Hysiai and Erythrai, which are settlements at the foot of Mt. Cithaeron (751–54), and Cadmus states that he heard, after he was back inside the walls of the town, of Agaue's exploits on the mountain and so turned back to Cithaeron in order to recover Pentheus's remains, with which he arrives onstage (1222–26). This operation of fictive space could best be articulated by having one *eisodos* (west) lead both to the town and Cithaeron. Dionysus and the chorus would then have used the other *eisodos* for their entrance from the east. In this way, the use of space would visually establish the *agōn* (contest) between the characters as well as that between the true worshippers of Dionysus and the raving lunatics on the mountain.

Even so, other possibilities cannot be ignored. The east and west *eisodoi* could have led to the opposite locations of Cithaeron and the town. If this arrangement were the case, the characters could have exited through the *eisodos* associated with the town and traveled through offstage space to Cithaeron, which is associated with the opposite side of the stage. However, this option would be problematic for the eventual exit of Agaue, who would either have had to exit in the direction of the town or in the direction of Mt. Cithaeron. As an exile, she would not likely exit the stage in the direction of the town, and she clearly asks her escorts to lead her to where she may never again set eyes on Cithaeron (1381–87). However, if Agaue did indeed exit the stage (she may not have), then a configuration of the west *eisodos* leading to the town and Cithaeron and the east *eisodos* leading to the East would make sense. Then, her exit along the *eisodos* through which Dionysus and his chorus arrived would help to establish her status as an outsider, an exile.

Despite the various possibilities that were available to the *didaskalos*, I would argue that the text clearly suggests that one *eisodos* leads to both Cithaeron and the town, and the performance thus set up a strong structuralist opposition that designated the chorus as outsiders and emphasized them as "other." My interpretation is structured according to the following scheme:

SOUTH

(the playing space)

UPPER

Dionysus *ex machina*

Son of Zeus

God

EAST		WEST
Dionysus		Pentheus
Asian maenads		Theban women
Asian cities		Thebes
Nature		City
Dancing	Orchestra	Killing
Ecstasy		Madness
Vengeful		Violent
God		Human
Appropriate worship		Frenzy
Asia		Cithaeron
LEFT		RIGHT

LOWER

Dionysus disguised

Pentheus, Son of Echion

Mortal

(where audience sits)

NORTH

In this diagram, the contest in terms of upper/lower, left/right, and east/ west plays out according to a scheme somewhat different from that which Wiles has posited for Aeschylus's *Oresteia* and Sophocles's *Antigone*.[81] In Wiles's interpretation of spatial practices, the left side of the spectrum refers to the wild female and the right to the civilized male, and the movement in *Oresteia* and *Antigone* is from left to right, with the left typically more threatening than the right and the right appearing to subsume, incorporate, or overcome the left. In *Bacchae*, the reverse occurs. The left, while threatening too, should in theory be more benign than the right, for the god and his chorus cannot and should not be more threatening than the violence on Cithaeron, especially since the violence is the result not of accepting but of hubristically rejecting the god. In the end, from the audience's perspective, which always faces south, left/east finally overcomes the right/west, so the movement in *Bacchae* is not from left to right but rather from left to right to left, i.e., left and right trade places.[82]

This proposed use of space presents a problem for the traditional structuralist schema[83] of the play, which associates Cithaeron with the wild as opposed to the civilized city, but this mix-up could be the very way in which Euripides's dramaturgy used the traditional modes of the theatre to make meaning through breaking the expectations associated with those conventions. Whereas Rehm argues that this confusion demonstrates that "there is something too neat about its [the structuralist interpretive scheme's] application to the different spaces of *Bacchae*,"[84] I would suggest that this confusion might be the play's very point, since it illustrates spatially the god's challenge to traditional boundaries. Accordingly, through the operation of the fictive or dramatic space within the physical space of the theatre, *Bacchae* raises the question of the extent to which Euripides may have innovated and challenged typical uses of theatrical space, for the play poses a challenge to any singular definition of the spatial operations of the Athenian theatre.

In the process of making this argument about *Bacchae*'s fictive space, I have illustrated the close connection between textual analysis and performance analysis, but at the same time, I must acknowledge that the texts are only one part of the larger equation. The ephemeral nature of performance may have undermined what the text suggests, for the *didaskalos*'s choices, the reasons for them, and the audience's expectations for the use of space are clear gaps in the historical record. The study of the communication codes of a static text, even when that study considers the performance aspects of that text, is not the same as a study of the semiotic and phenomenological codes in a multidimensional, live, historical, fifth-century performance.[85] In other words, the extant text is no simple blueprint or plan for the historical performance, nor is it a basic directive or diagram for controlling the performance event. Nevertheless, inspired and informed by the many debates about the architecture of the Theatre of Dionysus, I have here attempted to present a possible if not probable hypothesis about *Bacchae*'s spatial practices in its 405 BCE performance by reading the play's fictive space in relation to the physical space of the theatre. For making judgments and assertions, however flawed or incomplete, is essential to the advancement of knowledge in any historical subject.

2 │ AUDIENCE

The ancient evidence testifies to an Athenian audience characterized by
its demonstrative communication. Whistling, hissing, and heel-drumming
in the theatre were apparently as common as shouting, interrupting, and
scowling in the law courts,[1] yet this lively crowd has left no surviving personal recollections, diaries, reviews, registers, or recordings to complement
accounts of them by Aristophanes, Demosthenes, Plato, and Plutarch.[2] Left
with many questions as a result of these absences, scholars have contended
over subjects from the size of the audience[3] to the exclusion of women from
the event. Debates continue over how to read the sources, what to do when
they are in disagreement, and how to judge which are reliable.

In some studies, specific topics, such as judging the contests,[4] or specific
authors, such as Plato and his characterization of the audience,[5] have served
as a subject. Other studies focus on the decoding of the expectations set
up by the performance.[6] Some scholars study the emotional impact of the
dramas on the audience[7] and the influence of audience response[8] on a play's
meaning.[9] Others study the role of the audience in Aristophanes[10] or the
ways in which the social fabric of Athens affected the dramas.[11] Still others
focus on the audience's identity. The plays may not have been directed at a
homogenized male citizen audience, but instead at a heterogeneous audience which included women and foreigners, who may have influenced both
the composition and reception of the plays.[12]

Despite the diversity of these approaches, two key questions have continued to emerge in the scholarship over the years: who was in the audience and how did the spectators respond? But as studies in performance have demonstrated,[13] these who and how questions present a pervasive problem even for studies of contemporary audiences. Who "they" are in an audience is not always easy to determine. Nor can scholars objectively assess how "they," whoever they may be, may have responded and so created the performance.

In order to explore further these critical problems of defining the audience and its responses, I have chosen to feature the topic of women's presence in the fifth-century theatre, because from Böttinger's 1796 refutation of Casaubon's 1592 claim that women were present, the question of women's attendance has continued to spark debate.[14] I here feature one recent debate on the subject, in Simon Goldhill's "Representing Democracy: Women at the Great Dionysia" (1994) and Jeffrey Henderson's "Women and the Athenian Dramatic Festivals" (1991), in order to explore historiographical topics such as arguments *ex silentio*, synchronic approaches, and periodization. I then discuss the problem of assessing individual audience response through a consideration of David Kawalko Roselli's *Theater of the People: Spectators and Society in Ancient Athens* (2011), a study that questions the common practice of constructing a singular view of a homogenized audience comprised of citizen males. In the final section of this chapter, I use my historiographical lens to explore the issue of homogenizing the audience that emerges in three distinct interpretations of *Bacchae*'s dressing-up scene, by Helene P. Foley, Richard Seaford, and Kirk Ormand, before I bring into focus questions about the potential impact that women's possible presence could have had on the theatrical event. In the process, I argue that ignoring the possibility of women's presence in the 405 BCE audience limits interpretations of *Bacchae*, for the play's historical and cultural significance depended not on its role as a work of literature to be read but on its function as a theatrical event in which the audience shapes the performance's meaning.[15]

The Science of Instincts and Opinions

Many classicists have commented on the difficulty of addressing the question of women's presence. David Roselli, for example, has called the topic "something of an academic battlefield."[16] Simon Goldhill too contends that "the presence of women at the Great Dionysia is a hotly contested subject."[17] Because no direct evidence can provide a clear solution to the problem, Goldhill has explained that "the debate has tended to rely on analogies with other Athenian festivals, general suppositions about the role of women in Athenian culture, oversimplified interpretation of difficult and ambiguous sources, and, all too often, mere hypothesis—'gut feeling'" (62). As a result, classicists often approach the subject armed with a series of disclaimers.[18]

Helene P. Foley, for example, opens her 2001 *Female Acts* by explaining, "Greek tragedy was written and performed by men and aimed—perhaps not exclusively if women were present in the theater—at a large, public male audience."[19] She notes, "I am of the *opinion* [italics mine] that a limited number of (perhaps predominately older or noncitizen) women were present along with metics, foreigners, and slaves, but that the performances were primarily aimed at citizen men."[20] Peter Arnott surmises: "There are many things we do not know about the Athenian audience. It is still not certain, for example, whether or not women were admitted (though it is a reasonable surmise that they were)."[21] Csapo and Slater assert that the "testimony . . . shows *clearly* [italics mine] that women (and boys) were present," but in a classicist's version of legalese, they remind readers that this claim is "in our opinion."[22] Performance theorist Sue-Ellen Case in her "Classic Drag," a seminal feminist critique of Greek drama, suggests both possibilities, stating that based on the evidence "it would seem appropriate that women were not in the audience. Or, in the context of chapter four [of *Poetics*], that they would be inferior members."[23] However, David Kawalko Roselli's most recent study *Theater of the People*, which I will discuss later, emphasizes the opposite case and argues for the importance of women to the ritual function of the event.

Given the paucity of evidence, instinct and intuition, cultivated by years of careful training, are often a scholar's best resource. Many solid arguments have developed from instinct and enlarged an understanding of historical topics. Trusting a scholar's subjective sense is often prudent. The problem here is that so many expert opinions remain in disagreement.

Henderson's "Women and the Athenian Dramatic Festivals": Arguments *Ex Silentio*

One such disagreement emerges in Jeffrey Henderson's "Women and the Athenian Dramatic Festivals" (1991) and Simon Goldhill's "Representing Democracy: Women at the Great Dionysia" (1994). While the question of women in the audience is a centuries-old debate, the works of these classicists represent intellectual developments that are characteristic of recent decades. Goldhill has helped to pioneer the application of poststructuralist theory to classical literature, and Henderson too has been on the vanguard of opening the field to twentieth-century–inspired questions and approaches instead of relying on a traditional philological approach that "can have (or can be made to seem to have) right and wrong answers (textual 'authority')."[24] Despite this similarity, the opinions, methods, and approaches of these classicists are distinct. Through stylish, well-crafted arguments, each presents opposing positions on the question of women's attendance, and in the absence of definitive answers, rhetorical techniques become crucial in the process of delivering persuasive arguments based on subjective sense.

Henderson's argument draws primarily on the works of Aristophanes and Plato, which are the key literary sources on the audience, yet his argument begins by addressing not the information in these sources but rather the lack of information in them. A silence in the sources serves as evidence for his argument. Because no extant source directly mentions women's exclusion from the event, he uses this silence as evidence for women's presence. In other words, he posits that if women were excluded from the audience, then the sources would have made that fact clear. To support his claim, Henderson poses various questions: why would women have excluded themselves, how could women have passed on myths to their children (if we are to believe Plato's suggestion of this custom[25]) without attending, and why would drama have addressed topics of interest to women if they were not present? Finding no clear answers, he further explains that the exclusion of women from the political sphere of the democracy would not have transferred to their exclusion from the theatre, for women participated in religion and cult, and the procession at the Dionysiac festival (*pompē*) included women. At this point, he then shifts the question to the types of women who would have attended the dramatic performances. Attentive to class differences among fifth-century women, he contends that "it is conceivable, for example, that poor women, women with small children to care for, women from distant demes, or women for some reason shy of public visibility would have been less likely to attend than others."[26] Because no source testifies to the absence of women, and some sources, such as Aristophanes and Plato, suggest women's presence, then women, at least some women, must have been there. Therefore, Henderson's argument is primarily *ex silentio*. Many of his claims rest on a silence in the sources about the absence of women from the event. If women were excluded, then the sources would have clearly indicated their absence.

One complication with such an approach is that the same silence could be interpreted to support the opposing view. In a presentation delivered at Columbia University on October 15, 2011, Oliver Taplin used an argument *ex silentio* to suggest that women were not present in the fifth-century theatre. His paper attempted to establish the absence of women in the fifth-century theatre and their possible presence in the fourth-century theatre, and he based his argument in part on the lack of any direct reference in Aristophanes to women in the theatre. He suggested that if women were present in the fifth-century audience, then surely at least one reference to a woman would have appeared in the Aristophanic corpus, for the comedies are full of direct address references to male audience members. Henderson and Taplin both recognize a silence and use it as evidence, but they disagree on its meaning. Does no mention of exclusion mean presence, or does no mention of presence mean exclusion?

These questions yield others as well. What does silence mean, and in what ways does its meaning depend upon historical and cultural customs? Silence is often ambiguous, and particularly on the subject of fifth-century women, it may relate to custom, not exclusion. For example, an acknowledgment of a woman's presence in the theatre audience could have been undignified. Women could have been present, but to paraphrase Pericles in his Funeral Oration, the best women should not be spoken of either for good or bad. In the law courts as well, women were not normally mentioned by name unless they were dead, dishonorable, or associated with the opposing speaker.[27] Thus, in the case of women's presence in the fifth-century theatre, arguments *ex silentio* are problematic. Because of fifth-century social taboos related to the naming of women, a silence in the sources may have more to do with social propriety than actual practice.

Goldhill's "Representing Democracy": Synchronic Approaches

Whereas Henderson focuses primarily on a close study of the event in the theatre and its related evidence, Goldhill takes a synchronic approach to the question and considers the framing institutions of politics and society that contribute to the identity of the Dionysian festival. Insisting that his interest is "in historiography as much as in the Realien,"[28] he shifts the focus in his investigation from an analysis of familiar sources and issues to one of underlying concerns, such as the questions asked, the sources used, and the methods for examining them. However, while Goldhill is interested in historiography, he also presents a history by situating the festival within Athenian social topography in order to suggest his "strong view" on women's exclusion. His point is to move the question "away from the re-reading of a few well-known so-called testimonia, towards thinking about the Great Dionysia as a socio-political event, and as a socio-political institution within the new topography of democracy" (369). In so doing, he makes an argument by analogy. He claims that because the *polis* excluded women from its major civic functions, such as the gymnasium, the assembly, and the courts, the *polis* also excluded women from the theatre.

One issue with such synchronic approaches is that they rely on a method of periodization, an organization of historical time, to construct a synchronic identity for a given period. For example, the terms fifth and fourth century serve to organize time, but despite the qualifications of, for example, late and early fifth century, these organizing categories still impose a synchronic identity on each century that implies a seamless unity for an age and designates a point of separation that historians have retrospectively deemed significant. As the philosopher David Carr has commented, "Coherence seems to be a need imposed on us whether we seek it or not. Things need to make sense. We feel the lack of sense when it goes missing."[29] Despite Carr's observation, historians do not always treat periodization as an artificial construct, imposed by them onto the sources when convenient.

Another historiographical issue related to Goldhill's synchronic approach arises from his reliance on a model of discourse in which the subject is the effect of discourse, i.e., a sort of unconscious collective code that speaks through individuals. In such a model, "the author," according to Michel Foucault, "is not an indefinite source of significations which fill a work; the author does not precede the works; he is a certain functional principle by which, in our culture, one limits, excludes, and chooses."[30] Thus, the question of "who really spoke" should not be an issue; instead one should ask, "What difference does it make who is speaking?"[31] Foucault's definition here is opposed to that of Paul Ricoeur's phenomenological model of discourse that challenged Saussure and structuralism in general by making the case for the activity of "*parole*" (an individual, particular message) against "*langue*" (a collective code, often functioning unconsciously) and giving the subject a narrative identity of an individual self that is mobile, fluid, and changing.[32] In a discourse modeled on *langue*, language speaks people, but according to Ricoeur, "Languages do not speak, people do. . . . The utterance meaning points back towards the utterer's meaning thanks to the self-reference of discourse to itself as an event."[33] Thus, Ricoeur's interest rests not only in semantics, the science of the sentence that is "concerned with the concept of sense,"[34] but also in semiotics, "the science of signs that relies on the disassociation of language into constitutive parts."[35] Relying not on this Ricoeurian model but on one in which the subject is dissolved into a repository of discourse, Goldhill constructs a singular identity for the audience as well as for the age. However, the role of individual action and temporal change in history also requires consideration.

As the historian Michael Stanford has stated, "perhaps the most characteristic attribute of history is change,"[36] but in synchronic approaches, the temporal aspects of human events are largely ignored. Drawing on Marshall Sahlins's discussion of structure and event, Thomas Postlewait has commented on this inherent problem: "All too often the ideas of discourse and structure ignore the temporal, developmental nature of human events. Synchronic time displaces diachronic time."[37] Thus, in analyzing institutions in relation to one another, synchronic studies inevitably obscure the diachronic causes and effects of historical change.

Goldhill himself recognizes these problems in part, for he provides a disclaimer: "I have offered a largely synchronic view; but these institutions are not only in relation with each other in the topography of democratic Athens, but also change over time."[38] However, despite his acknowledgment of the critical factor of historical change, his synchronic perspective settles into a singular idea of the Athenian era, and so his article ultimately offers a singular identity for women. Goldhill's 1994 sociopolitical approach to women's attendance is praiseworthy for introducing an expansive perspective on the historical issues, but although he aimed to provide "a stimulus to further research on such social and topographical issues" (369), many basic obstacles in responding to the question of women's presence persist. Such new approaches to the question have enriched historical understanding, but still have not moved beyond the realm of informed opinion.

Roselli's *Theater of the People*:
Individuals versus Target Audiences

One of the most recent studies on women in the fifth-century theatre appears in chapter 5 of David Roselli's *Theater of the People*. The work participates in a new generation of classical scholarship characterized by the influence of cultural studies, an interdisciplinary approach to the study of culture and society that considers topics such as gender, ethnicity, class, and citizenship. Drawing on methods from theatre semiotics as well, Roselli examines fifth- and fourth-century sources such as Plato, Aristophanes, Xenophon, Demosthenes, Plutarch, and Athenaeus. Like Goldhill, he situates the question of women in the theatre within the larger framing institutions of society, politics, and economics, but, unlike Goldhill, Roselli argues that only some elite women were excluded from the event. Despite his distinct approach, even this most recent examination of the issue cannot move beyond the realm of informed opinion. Roselli too must begin his thesis about women's attendance with the all too common disclaimer: "It is probable."

In making his case, Roselli argues against what he calls "Athenocentric" approaches, which he suggests have contributed to the erasure of women from the event. He cites Goldhill's article "Representing Democracy" as an example of such an Athenocentric approach that "views drama in terms of the citizen male population and makes citizen identity a backdrop for understanding the effects of drama."[39] According to Roselli, Athenocentric narratives such as Goldhill's "are not sufficiently sensitive to the possibility of noncitizen agency in the construction of dramatic representations of foreigners" (8). Instead, such studies construct an ahistorical and classless subjectivity of citizens by treating women and foreigners collectively as the "other." Roselli attributes Goldhill's Athenocentric discussion to the influence of works, such as Nicole Loraux's *The Children of Athena*, "that present the *polis* as a 'men's club' and deny any form of citizenship to women" (165). Mindful of these issues, Rosselli suggests that Goldhill depicts the festival in its political terms without due consideration to its combined ritual and cultic function in which women would have exercised a gendered form of citizen rights. Moreover, the festival's religious function would require rather than exclude women's attendance, because "with the theater viewed in terms of a ritual event in honor of Dionysus—for which there is good evidence—the presence of women seems unproblematic" (164). In this way, Roselli questions the assumption of Athenocentric works that relate drama to the "*democratic* polis rather than the broader community" (8) of metics, slaves, foreigners, and women.

Having established that women in general were present, Roselli, like Henderson, then considers which women were present. Although Henderson and Roselli agree that women attended the festival, their distinct views on the ways in which labor practices affected women lead to their disagreement on the types of women who attended. Henderson suggests that working women may not have been able to attend because of their lack of leisure time, but Roselli claims that "women from poorer households who were familiar with the 'vulgar' world of the masses in the agora [marketplace] doubtless were present in larger numbers at unofficial viewing areas" (174) and the few elite women who attended, "were likely prominent in the community and sat in the *theatron*" (174). These opposing speculations are based on distinct assumptions about the influence of class on women's social practices and demonstrate all too clearly one of the central problems of a historical methodology that Hajo Holborn has identified: "An objective knowledge of the past can only be obtained through the subjective experience of the scholar."[40]

A key historiographical issue that underlies Roselli's study is one endemic to audience studies in general: the assessment of audience responses. To deal with this problem, he constructs target audience groups, the social composition of which would influence and shape the semiotic signs produced by the performance, but despite this attempt to address the problem of audience response, Roselli must explain away the importance inherent in recognizing the individual perspectives within the groups that he defines.[41] He states that sufficient evidence does not exist for a study of individual spectators and that such a study would be difficult to conduct on even modern audiences (3).

To support his point about the merits of studying target groups, he cites theatre scholar Susan Bennett's study which explains that "the description of an individual response to a particular production may not be possible or, indeed, even desirable."[42] He further suggests that "there will always be a limitless number of isolated individual responses to a performance. But viewing audience members as individuals does not appear to have been the approach adopted by poets, performers, and officials involved in the city's oversight of the theater" (3). While these points make sense, individuals nevertheless exist within groups, and according to Marvin Carlson, each brings to the theatre "expectations, assumptions, and strategies which will creatively interact with the stimuli of the theatre event to produce whatever effect the performance has on an audience and what effect the audience has upon it."[43] Although the concept of individuality may have been of little or no concern to the fifth-century Athenians,[44] it may be naïve to think that the ancient Greeks did not have divergent individual perspectives and unconventional viewpoints, even if the society as a whole was not concerned with the concept of the individual. Moreover, focusing on culturally constituted target audiences ignores the ways in which individual actions—hissing, gasping, laughing, clapping, walking out—impact the audience as a whole, the performers on stage, and thereby the performance itself. In any case, Roselli does not, and perhaps because of the limitations in methodologies and sources cannot, adequately address the significance of individual responses that shaped and created the meaning of the theatrical event. He simply declares that such responses are limitless.

Even when theatre scholars do recognize and appreciate the importance of individual perspectives, documenting them is a struggle. How can one acknowledge fully the ways in which individual spectators are active participants? What model could recognize, within the diversified demographics and target groups, the individuals whose ephemeral emotions and reactions together with their cultural, historical, and individual positioning create the theatrical event? While constructing a single identity of an audience is inappropriate, reconstructing the range of possible identities and responses of the spectators is quite difficult. The approach of target audience groups is a practical compromise, but the method still overlooks the variety of audience responses that created the theatrical event and its cultural significance in all its historical complexity. David Bain's words seem to have well summarized the problem: "Obviously it is vain to hope to enter the psyche of a fifth- or fourth-century spectator, but anyone writing about Greek drama must at least make the attempt."[45]

The Dressing-up Scene and the Audience

These historiographical issues related to the homogenization of the audience and its responses emerge in various interpretations of *Bacchae*'s dressing-up scene (912–976), such as those of Helene P. Foley, Richard Seaford, and Kirk Ormand, but before discussing these interpretations, a citation of the scene is necessary. Richard Seaford's translation reads as follows:

> DI: (*emerging from the house*) You, who are eager to see what you should not see, and strive for what should not be striven for, Pentheus I mean, come out in front of the house, be seen by me, wearing the equipment of a woman, a maenad, a bacchant, and a spy on your mother and on her band. (*P. emerges from the house, dressed as a maenad.*) You look just like one of Kadmos' daughters.
>
> PE: (*probably looking at a reflecting surface*) And indeed I seem to myself to see two suns, and a double Thebes and seven-mouthed fortress; and you seem to be leading, ahead of me, as a bull, and horns seem

to be on your head. Were you a beast before? For you are certainly changed into a bull.

DI: The god, being previously not well-disposed, is accompanying and at peace with us; now you see what you should see.

PE: How do I look then? Am I not standing like Ino stands or Agaue, my mother?

DI: In seeing you I seem to be seeing them in person. But this lock of hair of yours has come out of its place, not as I fitted it under the sash.

PE: Inside, in shaking it forward and shaking it backward and acting as a bacchant, I dislodged it from its place.

DI: But I, whose concern it is to attend to you, will put it back in position. But hold your head straight.

PE: Look! Adorn me! For on you I depend indeed.

DI: Your belt is loose and the pleats of your robe are not in order where they hang below the ankles.

PE: I think so too, at least by the right foot. But on this side the robe is straight at the tendon.

DI: Certainly you will consider me as first of your friends, when you see the maenads unexpectedly self-controlled [sōphrones].

PE: Shall I take the thyrsos in my right hand or in this one so as to seem more like a bacchant?

DI: You must raise it in your right hand, in time with your right foot. I congratulate you on your altered mind.

PE: Would I be able to carry the folds of Kithairon, together with the bacchants, on my shoulder?

DI: You could, if you wished. Your previous mind was not healthy, but now you have the kind of mind that you should have.

PE: Should we take levers? Or should I tear them up with my hands, putting my shoulder or arm beneath the peaks?

DI: Don't you go destroying the shrines of Nymphs and the abodes of Pan where he plays his pipes.

PE: You are right; it is not by strength that women are to be defeated; I will hide my body under the firs.

DI: You will be hidden in the way that you should be hidden, for one who comes as a cunning spy on maenads.

PE: And indeed I suppose them to be in the thickets like birds, held in the most pleasant nets of love-making.

DI: Are you not sent off as a guardian against this very thing? You will probably catch them, if you are not caught beforehand.

PE: Escort me through the middle of the land of Thebes; for I am the only man of them to dare this deed.

DI: Alone you are toiling for this city-state, alone. Therefore the appropriate contests are awaiting you. Follow: I will go as your escort providing security, but another will bring you back from there . . . PE: Yes, my mother.

DI: Conspicuous to everybody. PE: That is why I go.

DI: You will come carried . . . PE: What you describe is luxury for me.

DI: In your mother's arms. PE: You will compel me to be pampered even.

DI: Pampering in my fashion. PE: I am taking hold of what I deserve.

DI: Amazing you are, amazing, and you are going to amazing sufferings, with the result that you will find glory towering to heaven. Stretch out, Agaue, your arms, and you her sisters, daughters of Kadmos; I bring this young man to a great contest, and the winner will be myself and Bromios. The rest the event itself will show. (*Pentheus follows Dionysos off to the side, to Mt. Kithairon. The Chorus sing and dance.*)

In her *Ritual Irony: Poetry and Sacrifice in Euripides*, Helene P. Foley has imagined a staging of this scene and suggested that the audience sees double in the juxtaposition of Pentheus and Dionysus.

Onstage are two feminine or feminized figures wearing long robes and fawnskins, two figures carrying the same Dionysiac paraphernalia. Each has long hair, although Pentheus' is poorly confined in a *mitra* [feminine headband]. In Aristophanes' *Frogs* (46) and in Pollux (4.116–17) Dionysus wears the *krokōtos*, a garment emphasizing his feminine side and, to the audience, his divinity.[46]

She then relates her version of the scene's staging to the practice of Greek ritual: "If both Dionysus' and Pentheus' costumes were saffron, the audience as well as Pentheus would see 'two suns,' two brilliant yellow costumes moving side by side. The sacrificial victim of the god, here his contemporary and cousin, has visually become almost the ritual double[47] he often seems to have been in religious and literary tradition" (250). Influenced in part by anthropological studies,[48] Foley suggests that the language and action of the play purposefully incorporate references to ritual, for with ritual Euripides "can raise issues that touch the society as a whole, not simply the narrow political sphere" (256). The argument thus offers clear historical insights about the play and recognizes not only the presence but also the customs of its audience. The novelty of Foley's approach in this 1985 work was a meaningful contribution in scholarship on audience studies.

At the same time, the argument cannot avoid the common problem of designating the audience as a singular unit with a unified response. Foley often refers to the audience's "experience," not "experiences,"[49] and she does not present any other possible stagings of the scene. As a result, she inadvertently constructs an ideal audience with a singular perspective, and she projects her own direction of the scene onto the play. On the one hand, this ideal audience could certainly have viewed the performance that she described: two feminine or feminized characters wearing long robes and fawnskins. On the other hand, Pentheus and Dionysus may not exactly be mirror images of each other. As in many modern productions of the play, such as Tadashi Suzuki's (1981–1982),[50] Sir Peter Hall's (2002), and John Tiffany's (2007), the characters' costumes might have been distinct, and the distinctions between the characters and their costumes could have been the entire point of the scene. Many types of stagings are possible, just as there are many possible, individual perspectives and responses of a heterogeneous audience.

Richard Seaford's argument offers another example of the ways in which scholars tend to construct one staging of the scene and posit one possible response to it. He theorizes that the audience would have understood Pentheus's dressing-up as a reference to Dionysiac ritual and that they would not have interpreted the scene as comic, as other scholars have suggested.[51] One of his points to support this claim rests on lines 840–42, where Dionysus states that he will lead the dressed-up Pentheus through the back-streets (literally "desolate" streets) in order to allay the young ruler's fears of being seen by the Cadmeian townspeople and having the maenads laugh[52] at him. Using these lines as evidence together with line 854, Seaford argues that the mockery which Pentheus's dress incurs has ritual as opposed to comic connotations.[53] The audience never sees the Thebans mock Pentheus, and therefore, the scene would not necessarily have had comic undertones.

Perhaps in part because of the absence of sources such as rehearsal notes, marked-up scripts, and interviews, Seaford does not consider or conjecture about how an actor's delivery of line 841 could undermine his point. What if the *didaskalos,* performer, or audience interpreted line 841 as a lie that Dionysus told Pentheus in order to convince him to dress up? So much depends on how the scene was played and how it was received. Even though the audience would not have seen the fictional Thebans mock Pentheus, some spectators, or even a spectator, might have mocked the king. Did Pentheus's array provoke hisses, hoots, whispers, and chuckles? Or was there silence instead? Or a mix of responses? In what ways would the audience's heterogeneous reactions have created multiple experiences of this scene? Instead of becoming the laughingstock of Thebes, could the actor playing Pentheus have played the scene to try to become the laughingstock of the performance, i.e., the audience? Would the various members of the audience have responded to that representation with laughter, tears, or some other response? Would they have thought of the mockery as having ritual undertones? Perhaps because the limited sources do not allow for an investigative analysis of such questions, Seaford must focus on a single interpretation of the scene with a singular audience response.

Kirk Ormand, in his "Oedipus the Queen," a study of cross-dressed roles, also constructs a singular audience response in his interpretation of *Bacchae.* Influenced by Stephen Orgel's *Impersonations,*[54] he begins his discussion with a focus on performance asking: "What does the tradition of transvestite theatre in Athens reveal about Athenian notions of gender, and of the mode of representing it on the Athenian stage?"[55] To address such questions, Ormand first draws on previous studies of fifth-century gender, such as those of Sir Kenneth Dover, David Halperin, and John J. Winkler,[56] to argue that Athenian gender is expressed in nonsexual terms: "In this system, male femininity does not necessarily imply sexual submissiveness to men, let alone homosexuality."[57] Moreover, he explains, "the ancients did not think of men and women as hetero- or homosexuals. In so far as they developed categories of sexual actors, they thought of players as either active or passive, or more precisely, penetrating and penetrated" (6). If, as he states, Athenian gender is expressed in nonsexual terms, then cross-dressing does not "challenge the binarism of Greek gender" (10), for episodes of cross-dressing in fifth-century drama do not "interact with notions of sexuality in the same way as they do for us" (6). After explaining the Athenian construction of gender in these terms, Ormand applies these ideas to his discussion of male gender slippage in certain plays, i.e., when male characters acquire "a feminine identity—to their shame and disempowerment" (3). Using *Bacchae* as one of his examples, Ormand challenges suggestions found in the studies of William Poole, E. R. Dodds, and R. P. Winnington-Ingram that Pentheus's cross-dressing reveals "a subconscious reality to be drawn out" (12), a latent homosexual desire or feminine sensuality (13). He instead argues that the triumph of Dionysus is expressed in terms of his public humiliation of Pentheus as feminine (13) and posits that "Pentheus' feminization is the primary vehicle and onstage expression of his downfall" (13). He continues: "In sum, when Pentheus desires Dionysus [whom Ormand earlier describes as having attributes of femininity (10–11)], he is masculine, not feminine; and when he is feminized, he expresses no desire, sexual or otherwise, for Dionysus. It is the totality of his fall from power that motivates a reversal of gender, which is for the Athenians a powerful expression of Pentheus' undoing" (13). In this way, Ormand attempts to identify the ways in which modern notions of gender identity have influenced scholarship on the play, and he aims to correct such anachronisms with an interpretation that he suggests is more in accordance with fifth-century practices.

However, in making this argument, Ormand imposes onto *Bacchae* a neat theory of the audience's concepts of gender, and in the process he assumes a singular audience response as opposed to responses. Because a play and its performance do not provide a mirror image of Athenian men and their gender identities, scholars cannot be certain that the play represented the gender codes he posits. Nor can we know if the actors interpreted them as such, nor if the audience—any of them—held the ideas he posits and perceived them accordingly. Moreover, how can we know if, as Ormand claims, Pentheus "desires" Dionysus when he is masculine and expresses no desire when he is feminine? The dramatic representation is open to various possible meanings, but Ormand seems to reduce it, at times, to a historical reality. In the process, the audience becomes a collective of homogeneous passive recipients of ideology rather than active, diverse, thoughtful, questioning heterogeneous participants in a theatrical event.

Even though these scholars surely understand the many possibilities for a scene's performance and for the audience's responses to the scene, Foley, Seaford, and Ormand have all tended to focus on a singular audience with a singular interpretation of the play, and such a viewpoint may likely result from the influence of the traditional model of scholarship. In this model, one typically begins by criticizing previous studies before attempting to offer a superior interpretation. The method often calls for the imposition of a dominant meaning onto a performance of a scene, for the model is not particularly conducive to the recognition of the multiple possibilities and receptions of a theatrical staging, which are difficult to determine in any case. According to historian Keith Jenkins, "change the gaze, shift the perspective and new readings appear. Yet although historians know all this, most seem to studiously ignore it and strive for objectivity and truth nevertheless."[58] Despite these issues, studies of the play-text are crucial for conjuring the play's performance, but a play-text alone cannot fully capture or indicate the theatrical event that was the historical event. The unknown, absent performance context presents persistent challenges to conclusions that necessarily rely on the known and present, extant text.

One such challenge arises from women's possible presence at the theatre, for even if the dramas were directed at male citizens, the presence of women, any women—priestesses, prostitutes, privileged, or poor—would have influenced the historical meaning of *Bacchae* in several ways. For example, women would have likely interpreted and responded to the costume and comportment of Dionysus and Pentheus in distinct ways from men. While an effeminate Dionysus, if he was effeminate,[59] may not have felt threatening to women in the same way he may have to some males, civic women, who participated in or had knowledge of the Dionysiac cult, may have felt threatened by the male chorus members' appropriation and misrepresentation of their rituals.[60] And as Aristophanes joked in his comedy *Women at the Thesmophoria*,[61] some women may have detested Euripides. They may have been angered by the depiction of Agaue, by the use of female dress as a means for humiliation, or by Pentheus's impersonation of them in the dressing-up scene, for it would be naïve to think that women in oppressive societies cannot think outside the box.

At the same time, other women may have been impressed with the play and its performance. They may have enjoyed the artistry of the maenad chorus, been amused and laughed at Pentheus's awkward impersonation of their gender, and thought Euripides was poking fun not so much at them but at male fantasies, including his own, about who women are. For if *Bacchae* was a response to *Women at the Thesmophoria*, as Daniel Mendelsohn has suggested,[62] Euripides, unlike Aristophanes, had the women kill the male who imitates them inappropriately instead of letting him escape.

On the one hand, women's presence at the fifth-century theatre could have fomented women's feelings of resentment. On the other hand, the performances could have served as a sort of inoculation or safety valve against women's frustrations. But whatever women's specific responses, their simple |

presence in the auditorium would have undoubtedly influenced, in some way or other, the poets' composition of the plays, the actors' interpretations of the characters, the male audience's responses to the performance, and thereby the cultural and historical meaning of the performance.

Despite women's possible attendance at and thereby influence on the meaning of the plays and their theatrical events, scholars have avoided speculation on the matter. Such avoidances have then inscribed themselves within the methodologies upon which scholarship depends, and consequently, methodological approaches may inadvertently obscure perspectives and insights on historical events. For these reasons, discussions of women's presence and their responses may not be unproductive speculations, but may instead point to historical descriptions and understandings of the dramas that move knowledge beyond what may only be other types of conjectures and propositions.

3 | THE CHORUS, MUSIC, MOVEMENT, AND DANCE

From mourning and initiation rituals to the dithyrambic and dramatic competitions, choral performance was a tradition that, according to Plato, educated citizens.[1] Although Aristotle's *Poetics* implies that the role of the chorus in tragedy was marginal,[2] other sources, such as the epigraphic records commonly known as the Fasti, demonstrate that the fifth-century chorus played a crucial role in the festival. In commemorating the dramatic competitions, the Fasti referred to the choral performances as tragedies (*tragōidoi*) and to what the western theatrical tradition calls a playwright as he who "trained the chorus."[3] While the chorus clearly played a major role in theatre and society, many basic questions about the dramatic chorus, concerning their costuming, dances, manner of delivery, and relationship to the audience, are still difficult to answer.

Addressing such questions, scholars have relied for information on key literary sources, such as the dramatic corpus, Plato, Athenaeus, Pollux, and Plutarch, and iconographic sources such as the Pronomos Vase (figures 1, 2, 3), the Basel Dancers (figure 6), and the Attic pelike from Cerveteri (figure 10). Plato's *Laws* (ca. 350 BCE) mentions various types of ancient dances such as the satiric *sikinnis*, the comic *kordax*, the warlike *pyrrichē*, and the harmonious *emmeleia*.[4] Athenaeus (ca. 200 CE)[5] and Plutarch (ca. 115 CE)[6] describe the chorus's use of hand movements, and Aelius Aristides (ca. 150)[7] suggests that the chorus's dances were rectangular and organized according to the formation of a hoplite battle line in a manner such as depicted on figure 6. However, as Pickard-Cambridge has commented, these sources are "sketchy" and "couched in highly abstract and uninformative language."[8] While the ancient authors would have had access to a library of resources that no longer exists, scholars still cannot depend upon these later authors to have quoted and referenced their sources accurately.

Debating over such sources and their reliability,[9] scholars have studied topics such as the nature of the dramatic chorus's music[10] and dance,[11] its function within the fictive world of the plays,[12] and its relationship to the larger framing institutions of civic and religious life.[13] These topics further subdivide into distinct approaches and specializations. On the subject of dance, for example, scholars study meter and images in their attempts to reconstruct ancient dance, conduct comparative analyses with modern dance, and explore dance's social and religious functions.[14] The subject of music, which joins with dance through the terms *moysikē* (poetry, music, and dance) and *molpē* (song accompanied by movement), has many facets as well. Sources such as musical notation on papyri, meter, and depictions of musicians and their instruments, especially the aulos (an instrument typically consisting of a double-reed pipe played in pairs), have become the basis for investigations of instruments and their reconstruction, harmonics and acoustic theory, the status of the musicians, and music's social function within the *polis*.[15] Despite the variety of these specializations and approaches related to a study of the chorus, most works tend to focus either on the performance aspects of music and dance or by contrast on the words of the chorus within a play. Few studies have attempted to combine the knowledge developed from both of these approaches and consider simultaneously the words, music, and choreography of a chorus during a historical performance set in space and time.[16]

In this chapter, I concentrate specifically on historiographical topics that affect studies of dance, music, and choral voice, e.g., overreading the significance of sources, studying a multidimensional subject in a two-dimensional print system, the political bias of sources, constructing cause and effect relationships, and the influence of distinct types of evidence on an argument's conclusion, a topic which I explore in relation to John Gould and Simon Goldhill's 1996 debate over the status of the tragic chorus.[17] After demonstrating these issues in the first sections of the chapter, I then present a method for identifying the traces of choral movement inscribed in Euripides's *Bacchae* by considering the play's theme of *sōphrosynē* (moderation, balance). My aim is to illustrate that textual analysis can reveal traces of ancient choral movement, while also acknowledging that the polysemous meanings of the text are not the same as those of a performance.

Overreading the Sources

In their attempts to reconstruct fifth-century choral dance, scholars have relied on both literary and visual sources, but the limited supply of these sources has resulted in methodological problems. While Lillian B. Lawler, Sir Arthur Pickard-Cambridge, and John J. Winkler all use later literary sources to argue that dramatic choral dance was rectangular,[18] Wiles and theatre historian Graham Ley dismiss those sources as late and suggest a circular dance instead (a point which Wiles uses to reinforce his argument about the circular shape of the *orchēstra*[19]). Thus, some scholars reject anachronistic sources for their possible misleading claims, but others use these sources, as Winkler suggests, to persuade through an "ensemble of many details."[20]

Included in this ensemble on the fifth-century chorus are the fifth- and early fourth-century visual sources, such as figures 1, 2, 6, 10, and 11, but these are no more reliable than the literary record. Although fourth-century vases from the Greek West (i.e., modern day southern Italy and Sicily) that depict tragedy-related scenes are relatively ample, fifth-century Attic vases connected to tragedy are in small supply, for this period of Attic art focused primarily on mythical representations without making a dramatic context clear. Oliver Taplin, a pioneer in the study of visual images of ancient performance, has explained this problem of supply.

> Throughout the world's museums and galleries there must be something of the order of 100,000 Athenian decorated vases from the canonical "golden age" of tragedy (say 499 to 406 BC)—and those presumably represent well under 1 per cent of the total produced. . . . [Of these] I know, in fact, of only two fifth-century paintings that can plausibly be claimed to show a play in performance [the Basel Dancers[21] (figure 6), and five fragments of Attic pottery ca. 460s[22]].[23]

While Taplin concedes, "there *may* be all sorts of other tragedy-related paintings," he cautions that "they do not seem to call on the viewer to bring to bear on them an acquaintance with a tragedy; and they do not seem to include signals of their connection with drama."[24] Because of their scarcity, the extant Attic fifth-century images related to theatrical performance have acquired great significance.[25]

The significance granted to these pieces can be problematic for the process of historical interpretation. Because the images have survived by chance, scholars have no means by which to contextualize them within the larger market, and their rarity can cause an overreading of their significance. A desire to see theatre in these images can result in distorted views of them and the creation of meaning where none exists. According to Peter Burke, "Images are mute witnesses and it is difficult to translate their testimony into words. They may have been intended to communicate a message of their own, but historians not infrequently ignore it in order to read pictures 'between the lines,' and learn something that the artists did not know they were teaching. There are obvious dangers to this procedure."[26] Images present problems to historians of all subjects, but for the historian of fifth-century theatre the dangers are especially pronounced because of the scarce supply of sources.

The so-called Basel Dancers Vase (figure 6), for instance, presents difficulties for the reconstruction of choral dance, for the static image is problematic evidence in the reconstruction of kinetic movement. The vase appears to suggest that choruses sang and danced in unison, but this particular chorus of young men in military-style costume could have been imitating hoplite formation, whereas a chorus of women, who often appear dancing one before the other as in circles (figure 7), may not have danced in rows. Moreover, if as Fritz Naerebout suggests, one "sees real movement as something continuous in time," then images "cut up" movement and depict only a snapshot or "an initial or final moment or a sustained pose."[27] For this reason, a single image may indicate little about a dance's style and form, let alone about an entire dance tradition. Thus, even if viewers accept that the Basel Dancers Vase represents a scene from an actual performance, it is difficult to use it to make assumptions about choral performance in general.

Reading Dance in Two Dimensions

Although the sources leave little certainty about the appearance of choral performance, in *The Theatricality of Greek Tragedy* Graham Ley has taken an innovative approach to the reconstruction of a chorus in terms of its music and choreography. Exploring the relationship between movement, gesture, and dance, he attempts to demonstrate movement through its absence. In other words, he uses the presence of altars, tombs, and shrines "to trace the disposition of actors/characters and *choros* in scenes or sequences in the scripts" (203). Mindful of the role of performance in his aim to appreciate "on its own terms" (206) the theatricality of Athenian tragedy, which he argues was both music theatre and dance drama (206), Ley provides a series of diagrams to aid with the visualization of the scenes or sequences in certain tragedies.

For example, he argues that sequences with a tomb as a focus, such as in Euripides's *Helen*, provide evidence that "in other tragedies (e.g., Euripides' *Suppliants*, Sophocles' *Oedipus at Colonus*), the *skene* is marginal to the action" (203). Vehicles too help to "give a vivid picture of composition for the open ground and indications of the disposition of performers, actors and extras alike" (203). He also considers the vocal delivery of the actors and the role of anapestic meter (also known as marching anapests) to question whether such rhythms always express movement. His attempt to reconstruct tragedy's theatricality, however, cannot surmount inevitable interpretive problems.

Because dance is an embodied discourse, *writing* the history of physical performance presents a problem with which dance historians continue to struggle. How can scholars notate kinetic movement and memory in words and diagrams? Mary-Kay Gamel has raised this issue in her review of Ley's work. According to Gamel, the inadequacy of Ley's diagrams indicates "a tremendous problem for scholars working in performance studies: the use of the two-dimensional print system to discuss a phenomenon which exists in four dimensions. . . . It is time for performance studies scholars to develop a medium which can more effectively communicate the full range of our ideas."[28] Even if a better medium of communication is developed and employed, theatre historians will continue to grapple with the two-dimensional ancient sources, the static remnants of a multidimensional, kinetic experience.

Biases in Sources and Cause and Effect Relationships

Music presents a problem with medium as well. Because no recording of sound from the fifth century exists,[29] scholars have tried to understand the sound of ancient music by studying a controversy in the philosophical commentary over the so-called "New Music," whose "main characteristics were a large increase in music's range and complexity and a wide-scale rejection of traditional music's conventional restraints."[30] Musical notation from Euripides's *Orestes* (338–44)[31] and Euripides's *Iphigenia at Aulis* (784–92)[32] has survived on papyrus, and the *Orestes* papyrus shows a doubling of syllables that is a good example of New Music's imitative expressionism similar to that parodied in Aristophanes's *Frogs* 1301ff.[33] This so-called New Music was, according to the comic and philosophic commentary, prone to "self-indulgence and spiritual degeneracy,"[34] but this commentary should not necessarily be trusted. Csapo and Slater explain that for the most part "the music seems to respect the linguistic norms and does not reflect the kind of wild abandon projected by the conservative theorists."[35] As a result, the modes of ancient Greek music may be, as Ley suggests, invariably "obscured by an ideological debate about the 'proper' form of music that dates back to the time of Plato and, beyond, into the end of the fifth century BCE."[36] These scholars' comments thus demonstrate what historian Georg G. Iggers has called a more cautious approach to the sources which "do not directly convey reality but are themselves narrative constructs."[37] Although ancient authors present biased interpretations of music's sound and reception, the shared testimony to a controversy over music does strongly suggest that a new style of music did in fact develop.

Scholars have explained this change by linking theories regarding the causes and effects of the introduction of the New Music to theories about the decline of the chorus in the fourth century. Csapo and Slater in *The Context of Ancient Drama* have proposed that "the complexity of the New Music was a major factor in the diminution of the chorus' role in drama, since it was better suited to delivery by soloists with professional training than by a nonprofessional citizen chorus" (333–34). They also posit other causes for choral decline, such as "the growth of professionalization in the theater and the development of new standards in acting, music, and dance, rather than changes in the constitution of the chorus itself" (351). Many other possible factors could have also led to choral decline. Perhaps the performance of the amateur chorus could not compare to that of the trained principal actors, or perhaps a subsequent change in performance style was responsible for the chorus's marginalization (351). While these causes are certainly possibilities, the causes of the changes in music are still as uncertain as their effects.

Despite the uncertainty, historians often construct such cause and effect relationships in order to make sense of the past, for linking causes to effects helps to develop a narrative that organizes human time and events. Hayden White has discussed this role of narrative in the development of historical arguments and characterized "historical discourse as interpretation and historical interpretation as narrativization."[38] Although his views have been controversial for their apparent implication that recognizing the role of narrative in historical writing precludes the scientific nature of history, White has stressed that his study focuses not on methods of research but on a theory of historical writing. He maintains that the "principal problem for any theory of historical writing, then, is not that of the possibility or impossibility of a scientific approach to the study of the past but, rather, that of explaining the persistence of narrative in historiography. A theory of historical discourse must address the question of the function of narrativity in the production of the historical text."[39] The problems of narrative in historical writing, which White identifies, relate to the construction of cause and effect relationships.

For example, the narrative developed by scholars to explain the trend of the New Music begins with the near certain fact that a change in the style of music occurred. Historians then may consider possible causes and effects of the advent of New Music, such as the possible effect of the diminution of the role of the chorus. In connecting ideas about the causes and effects, a narrative develops that creates an historical understanding that is contingent upon the chain linking the sequence of events.[40] However, because the historian has constructed or imposed cause and effect relationships, the chain linking the sequence of events in the narrative may inevitably be nothing more than a function or by-product of the historian's narrative. In this way, historical understanding can reflect the narrative process.[41]

Gould and Goldhill: The Fictional Event versus the Historical Event

Another historiographical issue related to the study of the chorus arises in a key debate over the status of the choral voice in Simon Goldhill's "Collectivity and Otherness — The Authority of the Tragic Chorus: Response to Gould" and the late John Gould's "Tragedy and Collective Experience." Gould, known for his interest in anthropological approaches to the study of Greek drama as well as his extensive revision with D. M. Lewis of Pickard-Cambridge's *The Dramatic Festivals of Athens*, argues that the chorus has a marginal position; Goldhill, in the same volume, challenges Gould's claim. Their articles build on and against each other as the scholars attempt to move forward the discussion of the role of the chorus in tragedy.

Although they take distinct viewpoints on the question, Gould and Goldhill also share points of agreement, such as finding fault with the so-called "Vernant model." This model, posed by Jean-Pierre Vernant, constructs the "chorus as the collective on stage representing the collective of the audience."[42] Recalling examples from the tragic corpus and other records, Goldhill argues that Vernant's view "is not merely insufficiently sensitive to the different and often liminal roles of the chorus, but also distorts the complexities of the relation between the audience, the chorus, and the action" (244–45). Gould and Goldhill agree that the chorus is not an ideal spectator of the drama, nor does the chorus represent the poet's voice or the feelings of the spectators. Goldhill also concurs with Gould that "when the chorus *qua* collective stands in opposition to, or in judgment on, the hero of the drama, this formal tension between group and individual, integral to tragedy, speaks to the tension between individual and collective which is integral to democratic theory and practice" (248–49). While the two agree on these points, Goldhill states that Gould's "rejection of *any* authority or privileged presence inevitably distorts the way that tragedy engages with the question of authority and the collective" (253). In this respect, the two disagree about the status of the tragic chorus.

Focusing on the "dramatic role of the chorus within the fictional world,"[43] its constant presence on the stage, and its essential role in the fiction, Gould argues that "the chorus exists wholly within the tragic fiction and its imagined world, and that its 'otherness' does not entail any ability to stand outside that fiction" (232). He defines the "marginal" status of the chorus as "a sort of 'social' marginality within the imagined social structure implicit in the world created by the tragic fiction" (220–21). Because the chorus in the fictive world of the play embodies the identities of old men, women, slaves, and foreigners, Gould finds it "surely hard, if not . . . impossible, to imagine a 'civic discourse' which is perceived as giving authoritative voice to the democratic *polis* and its values through the collective utterance of such groups" (220). Gould's focus on the dramatic texts and their fictional worlds leads him to conclude that the chorus's marginal position within the plays excludes it from the tragic action and that such exclusion "in turn rules out any reading of the chorus's role as that of expressing the authority of the democratic *polis* and its dominant values in opposition to an alternative and competing value-system, that of the heroic, 'excessive,' protagonists" (221).

Like one dancer reading the choreography of another, Goldhill internalizes and then plays back Gould's moves, editing and sharpening the steps rather than beginning a new dance entirely. Throughout his discussion, he rebuts four of Gould's claims: "[First,] the ritual dance-song of the chorus is said to antedate the democratic city. Second, the city funds the actors but not the chorus. Third, the speech of the chorus, with its Doric lyricism, is removed from the language of the city. Fourth, the chorus is marginal and 'other' in status and thus cannot speak with authority to or for the city."[44] Goldhill responds to Gould's first and second points, not by focusing on the fictive world of the play, but rather by drawing on a variety of examples from the larger context of the Dionysian festival, e.g., the dithyrambic events, the seating of the audience, the competitive nature of the festivals, and the theatrical convention of masking. He also draws on historicized studies, such as Claude Calame's study of women's choruses and Peter Wilson's study of the Athenian *chorēgia*, which consider the performance of the chorus not as a singular, aesthetic entity but as a participant in a complex set of social, religious, political, educational, and economic practices. In response to Gould's third point, Goldhill also reflects on issues of social context, culture, and class. While Gould claims that the Doric dialect, in which choral lyric was written,[45] would register to the audience as an "alien and strangely 'distant' tongue"[46] and contribute to the chorus's marginal status, Goldhill counters this point by looking to extra-tragic sources to claim that Doric registered as a competing tongue, not a marginal one.[47] He argues against Gould's fourth point by appealing to both the political and ritual functions of tragedy, stating, "Attic fifth-century tragedy is played out as 'the drama of the other': there are very few Athenians on stage, and only the *Eumenides* of our extant tragedies reaches the city itself" (253). Furthermore, he contends that the "ritual role of the chorus, especially when so many choral lyrics return to the resource of the traditions of myth, stands against marginal status" (253). After making these various points, Goldhill concludes that the ability of the chorus to "speak with the full weight of a collective authority is crucial to tragedy's explorations of authority, knowledge, tradition within the dynamics of democracy's ethics of group and individual obligations" (253).

Despite Gould's explanation that his position on "the issues of 'civic discourse' and 'ideology' raised by Goldhill is very much closer to his own than it is, say, to that implicit in the characterization of the Dionysia offered by Oliver Taplin in 1978,"[48] Goldhill's conclusion and methodology differ significantly from Gould's. Gould's argument derives from his discussion of the roles of choruses in various extant plays, but Goldhill draws his conclusion primarily from evidence related to the framing institutions of the festival and its engagement with myth, religion, and politics, even though he reinforces his conclusion by ending his discussion with brief examples from Aeschylus's *Eumenides* and Euripides's *Hippolytus*. In other words, Gould presents sources as evidence in considering primarily the fictive world of the plays; Goldhill uses the sources to construct a social, political, religious, economic, archaeological, and geographical context, in which to position the tragic chorus.

In this way, their debate is over a play-text's double identity as both a representation of a fictional event and a representation of a historical theatrical event in which that fiction was performed. Eli Rozik has described this gap as having a twofold distinction: "first, between a descriptive performance-text and actors (in the wide sense) as both performers of descriptions of fictional entities and denizens of the real world (W_0); and second, between such a text and characters (in the wide sense) as both fictional referents of textual descriptions and denizens of fictional world (W_1)."[49] Both Gould and Goldhill recognize this dual nature of the text, but each primarily emphasizes one side. Gould focuses on the fictional action, such as the characters and plot of the play, a characteristic method of an aesthetic approach; but Goldhill emphasizes the sociopolitical aspects of the real-life historical festival, a method typical of cultural historians. The text's dual function allows for these two distinct methodologies and competing conclusions, so although Goldhill attempts to parry Gould's points, he cannot disengage from them entirely.

Bacchae's Chorus

Bacchae is arguably the best resource for reconstructing a choral performance, especially because many of the play's descriptions of the appearance and movement of the chorus correspond to those of depictions of maenads on late fifth-century vases. From fawnskins, to tympana, to thyrsi, to leaping feet and lifted throats, the chorus describes in detail the visual images that vases depict (figures 7 and 8). This correspondence between the textual and iconographic representation of maenads puts the performance historian on relatively secure ground, for with corresponding descriptions from both text and iconography, the chances increase that the performance reflected a similar version of the costumes and gestures.[50] In comparing the depictions of maenads in iconography to the descriptions of them in *Bacchae*, an interesting point emerges. Just as images of peaceful maenads, such as those on the so-called Lenaia Vases,[51] may reflect the ritual activity of real-life civic women, so the violent and fantastic representations of maenads (figure 8) may derive from the mythical tradition. Likewise, the cultic practice of real-life maenads, if they existed,[52] may have inspired the characterization of the Euripidean chorus of Asian maenads, while the depictions of wild and violent maenads of myth correspond more closely to the descriptions of the Theban maenads. If this observation is correct, real-life maenads may have danced, beat drums, worn fawnskins, and even eaten raw flesh,[53] but it is not likely, as with the Theban maenads, that snakes licked their cheeks, animals suckled their breasts, or children fell victim to their violence (677–774). Mindful of the portrayals of these two types of maenads, I will here argue that the Asian chorus of Dionysus's true followers in *Bacchae*'s 405 BCE production was *sōphrōn* (balanced, moderate). Moreover, contrary to their typical depiction in various modern productions, they did not depict the wild, maddened, or frenzied movement that the text associates with the Theban maenads whom Dionysus possessed as punishment for their insults against his mother (26–42).

The assumption that the chorus was frenzied may have been influenced in part by E. R. Dodds's influential, classic 1944 commentary on the play.[54] Like the philosopher Friedrich Nietzsche, who in his *The Birth of Tragedy* concentrates on the "barbaric" or irrational modes of Dionysus,[55] Dodds focused on the god's effect of disrupting the psyche. Interpreting the Bacchic rituals through the comparative lens of Christian ecstatic rites such as those of St. John's and St. Vitus's days, he interprets *Bacchae* as informed by real-life fifth-century maenadism (if it existed[56]) while also using the play, in a circular way, to provide evidence for what real-life maenadism was. While he clarifies the distinction between maddened Theban maenads and the god's true devotees in the chorus, he ultimately concludes that Dionysus causes the "hysteria" present in both types of maenadism, the Theban women's "hysteria in the raw" and the chorus's "hysteria subdued to the service of religion."[57] Dodds's association of Dionysus and his chorus's music and dance with "hysteria" reflects a stereotype of the dancing body, particularly the female dancing body, as a locus of irrationality that may not have been shared by the late fifth-century Athenians, for whom choral dance was an integral part of their culture.

I will now suggest one way to reconstruct choral performance by arguing, in contrast to Dodds, that the chorus was not hysterical or frenzied but rather *sōphrōn*. *Bacchae* poses the questions of who is *sōphrōn* and what does their comportment (*schēma* and *morphē*) look like, and through the presentation of this theme,[58] the text, despite its static nature, provides rich information about choral performance. *Bacchae* presents varying descriptions of *sōphrōn* behavior or the lack of it and, in the process, offers traces of movement cues that can help to develop general perceptions about the choreography.[59]

Teiresias first introduces the theme of *sōphrosynē* in response to Pentheus's rant against the maenads (2125ff.): "Dionysos does not compel women to be moderate (*sōphronein*) in the affairs of Aphrodite (the goddess of sexual love) but this behavior depends on their nature. . . . For a woman who has moderation (*sōphrosynē*) will not be corrupted in bacchic revels" (314–18). At the end of this speech, the chorus then congratulates Teiresias for showing himself to be *sōphrōn* (328–29). In 504, Dionysus tells Pentheus, who is about to bind him, that "I who am *sōphrōn*, tell you who are not *sōphrōn* not to bind me." Then Dionysus, expecting Pentheus's blustering entrance upon the god's escape from prison, states, "A wise man exercises *sōphrōn* gentleness of temper" (641). The word is later used in the messenger speech to describe the Theban maenads' appearance while they were sleeping, i.e., before they attack the villagers in a frenzy (686), and Dionysus also uses it ironically when he says to Pentheus in the dressing-up scene, "You will consider me your best friend, when, to your surprise, you see the *sōphrones* bacchae" (940). Then in the third stasimon, the chorus states that death is a teacher of *sōphrosynē* (1002); and the third messenger ends his speech about the brutal death of Pentheus by saying, "To be *sōphrōn* and to honor the things of the gods is the best" (1150–51). Finally, Dionysus tells Cadmus and Agaue that if they had *sōphrosynē*, they would have been fortunate (1341–43). In all cases, the acquisition or possession of *sōphrosynē* is contingent upon the appropriate worship of Dionysus, for one consistent use of the term throughout all of Greek literature and especially in *Bacchae* is to honor the gods.[60] To honor the gods is to be *sōphrōn*, and being *sōphrōn*, one honors the gods.

Through this primary meaning of *sōphrosynē*, i.e., to honor the gods, the play offers an ironic twist on the theme. *Sōphrosynē* is elsewhere associated in Greek literature with quiet, reserved (*hēsychia*) behavior,[61] but in *Bacchae*, performing for Dionysus is *sōphrōn*. Only through performing gestures that are not typically characterized as *sōphrōn* can the chorus and the characters embody *sōphrosynē*. Being *sōphrōn*, the chorus honors the god, and honoring their god through ritual song and dance keeps them *sōphrōn*. In this way, *Bacchae* challenges the typical association of *sōphrosynē* with proper Greek women who stay in the house and associates the term with the dancing, foreign chorus and their god of liberation.

The text also suggests that the performances of maenadism by the principal characters visually and aurally contrast with those of the chorus, just as the representation on vases of frenzied maenads (figure 8) differs from those of the peaceful maenads (figure 7). For example, Cadmus and Teiresias (170ff.), the raving Theban women on the mountain (677ff.), Pentheus in the dressing-up scene (912), and Agaue (1167ff.) all attempt, unsuccessfully, to perform maenadism. Dionysus has stung the women, Pentheus, and Agaue with his madness (32, 850, 1123), and Cadmus is a suspicious convert, who waffles in worship (191, 195), is embarrassed by his garb (205) (even though he is bold enough to wear it), and begs Pentheus to at least pretend that Dionysus is a god, if for no other reason than to counter the rumors that his Aunt Semele had an illicit affair that produced a child out of wedlock (333–36). In this way, the juxtaposition of the perverse performances of maenadism, such as that of Pentheus in the dressing-up scene or Agaue on the mountain, with the appropriate performance of the chorus provides critical commentary on choral performance itself.

The play's choreography should distinguish the movement of Agaue and the dressed-up Pentheus from that of the Asian maenads, because even though Agaue is the only Theban maenad who appears on stage, the messenger speeches offer verbal cues that serve to contrast the movement of the offstage Theban maenads with the onstage Asian maenad chorus. The frenzied descriptions of the Theban maenads contrast with those of the sweet chorus, and the two maenadic behaviors correspond to the two sides of Dionysus, the sweet joy of his rightful worship and the stinging frenzy of his punishment for *hybris*. The whirlings of the joyful choral dances (*heilissomenas mainadas*, 569–70) have an inverse in the whirlings of Agaue's maddened eyes (*diastrophoys koras, helissoys* 1122–23). Agaue's upward gaze, which returns her to sanity, mirrors the chorus's ecstastic lifted throats, and the image of Pentheus's tragic human face/mask (*prosōpon*) on Agaue's stake may have an inverse in the "smiling" divine mask of the god (if it was smiling[62]). Where one figure (*schēma*) ends and the other begins relates to the theme of *sōphrosynē*. Who has it? Who doesn't? Through this contrast of appropriate versus inappropriate performance, the text points to a general idea of its choreography that should visually contrast the movement of the Theban characters from that of the Asian chorus.

But what meaning did the performance of the chorus give to its words? Was its dance as *sōphrōn* as the text suggests? The exact nature of the chorus's song and dance remains uncertain, but one important clue suggests that the choreography of the chorus did reflect the calm of *sōphrosynē*. The chorus, unlike Pentheus, Agaue, and Dionysus himself, is never violent. The women recognize, witness, and understand both their god and his violence, but they do not literally participate in it. Nor do they threaten violence as does the chorus in Sophocles's *Oedipus at Colonus*, who threatens Creon for terrorizing Antigone, and the chorus in Euripides's *Heracles*, who gladly celebrates the death of Lycus (755ff.) and who states that if they were not so old they would surely raise a spear against the tyrant for calling them slaves.[63] In *Bacchae*, Pentheus does not just call the chorus slaves, he threatens to make the women literally so (511–14), but despite their vigor and collective strength, they never once threaten Pentheus directly. Instead, the chorus fears Pentheus. The women are "afraid (*tarbō*) to speak their mind" in his presence, despite having just heard the messenger's description of the ferocity of the Theban maenads on Cithaeron (775–76). They later indicate that they hurl their frightened "trembling" (*tromera sōmata*, 600–1) bodies to the ground during Dionysus's earthquake, so if the chorus is vengeful, it is not violent. Although the chorus does celebrate the death of Pentheus, within the terms of the ancient Greek maxim of "helping friends and harming enemies,"[64] this attitude may be justified, as with the chorus of Trojan women in Euripides's *Hecuba*, who find Polymestor well deserving of Hecuba's gruesome blinding of him (1085).[65] Moreover, despite its bitter and righteous anger with Pentheus, the *Bacchae* chorus still expresses pity for Agaue and Cadmus. The women call Agaue wretched (*talaina* 1200 and *tlamon* 1184), and although these words may be ambiguous and ironic (depending on the performance), the chorus undoubtedly later sympathizes with Cadmus (1327–28). The Asian maenads may shock the messenger with their vindictiveness (1039–40), joyfully celebrate Pentheus's death (1153ff.), and perhaps even revel in their repulsion of Agaue's proud display (*epideixis*) of Pentheus's freshly cut "head" (1165ff.), but the chorus has avoided the characters' predicament by being *sōphrōn* and honoring the god. Perhaps the maenads' ritualized songs and dances have afforded them a *sōphrōn* balanced perspective,[66] for in the midst of all the madness, they are the only bodies who never once go to Cithaeron.[67]

By comparing the chorus's movement to that described of the Theban maenads, one can attempt to excavate their songs and steps from the text. Unlike the Theban maenads who literally hunt and kill, the songs and dances of the chorus imagine Dionysus's violence. They ritualize it through dance.

The fourth ode,[68] with its presumably turbulent meter of dochmiacs[69] and violent ritual refrains, gestures to violence instead of literally enacting it, imagines it, sees it, and ritualizes it rather than executing it.[70] The meter, i.e., the rhythms that mark their steps, contains the violence, moderates it. The fourth stasimon of *Bacchae* juxtaposes the chorus's *imagined* murder of Pentheus in the song and dance with the Thebans' *actual* murder of Pentheus reported by the messenger in the following scene. In this case, choral song and dance, i.e., the ritualized comportment of the body, mediate the violence within the fictive world of the play, just as it might within the historical world of Athens. The text of *Bacchae* makes clear that to dance is *sōphrōn*, if for no other reason than because it is part and parcel of worshipping Dionysus, for honoring gods is always *sōphrōn*,[71] as Pentheus has unfortunately learned the hard way.

Therefore, while E. R. Dodds has argued that the chorus manifests hysteria subdued, its choreography could be as *sōphrōn* and balanced, as the chorus itself claims. Although the stasimon's dochmiacs may suggest a less controlled or more emotional ethos,[72] the irony is that to dance and sing in complex meters requires training and physical harmony in order to execute the complex movement. Vigorous dance movements demand an ease and flow and skill and control that would placate the force of the disruptive emotion expressed in the ode.[73] As Dionysus earlier demonstrated, *sōphrosynē* is bearing someone or something easily, even when it comes in full force (641). Furthermore, according to Teiresias, Dionysus has nothing to do with *sōphrosynē*, which is inherent in a woman's body-mind (*physis*).[74] Instead what determines *sōphrosynē* is how individuals behave in the midst of "heavy breathing" (*pneōn mega*), whether it be Pentheus's blustering entrance (642) or the god's grips of revelry, and the chorus consistently embraces Dionysus through song and dance, while the Theban maenads move to violence. In this case, the chorus's dancing is not a subdued hysteria, or the wild, ecstatic frenzied abandon that Nietzsche associates with Dionysus, but rather *sōphrōn*, a mean between the extremes.

While Helene P. Foley's sophisticated study of the play has influenced my interpretation of the chorus's ability to imagine violence instead of participating in it, her argument also emphasizes the chorus's vindictive desire for revenge against Pentheus. Like Marylin B. Arthur, she argues that, while the earlier odes represent the peaceful nature of Dionysus, the later odes show the manipulation of the language of popular Greek morality, i.e., *sōphrōn, sophos* (wisdom), and *mēden agan* (nothing in excess).[75] According to Foley, "though voicing uncannily familiar Greek ethical sentiments, they [the chorus] are ultimately a voice alien to the community and use the language of *sōphrosunē* (self-control and moderation) and *hēsuchia* (apolitical quiet) to serve their passionate desire for revenge" (222). She suggests that the play emphasizes "the possibility that Dionysus may be safely incorporated into civilized life," because "the sacrifices made by art and ritual substitute for actual violence" (245). But at the same time, "Euripides seems to subvert this claim. The chorus, as spectators who identify too closely with the divine revenge and who travesty the language of ethical moderation, are clear reminders of continuing contemporary excesses in the Athenian political scene" (245). She thus finds the chorus unable "to move fully toward a tragic perspective (to feel pity and fear over the fate of Pentheus)" (233).

However, a silence of about fifty lines, beginning at line 1329 and resuming with the appearance of Dionysus *ex machina*, limits scholars' understanding of the chorus's final position. Based on a Christian version of *Bacchae*, the *Christus Patiens*,[76] the author of which would have had access to a complete manuscript of the play, many critics have suggested that this lacuna would have included a lament by Agaue. Knowledgeable of this text, Colin Teevan's translation of the play, performed in 2002 by the Royal National Theatre of Great Britain, in fact includes a solo lament. However, because *Bacchae*'s amoibaion (1168–99), or standard, lyrical exchange between a principal character and the chorus,[77] is not a lament (*thrēnos*) and because an *amoibaion* in Euripides is usually a *thrēnos*, the lacuna may have included a second *amoibaion* that was a lament between the chorus and Agaue. Even if the chorus would have been unlikely to mourn Pentheus (1327–28), Euripidean choruses usually reserve the *amoibaion* for the chorus's display of compassion for a grieving principal character, such as perhaps Cadmus or Agaue. In a play as unusual as *Bacchae*, anything could happen. The absence of an *amoibaion* that is a *thrēnos* (lament) might be another aspect of an already unusual play, or possibly the typical lament scenario was restored with a second *amoibaion* where there is now a lacuna. In any case, the lacuna is a very literal hole in the historical record that complicates any and every view of the chorus in this important play, which is crucial for understanding both Athenian performance and the god who presides over the event.

Because the chorus's words are ambiguous, their performance of those words is crucial to understanding their position. Would the movement of the chorus have suggested a synchronicity with that of the crazed Theban maenads, as interpreted by modern productions such as the Performance

Group's *Dionysus in 69* (1968–1969), in which a crowd of actors chase after Pentheus? Or would it instead have contrasted with the movement of Agaue, as in Bill T. Jones's workshop of the play (2002), in which a chadoor-clad chorus performed sophisticated, fluid choreography in contrast to the disjointed movement of the ball-gown–adorned Theban women?[78] What views about the chorus would the performance have elicited from the audience? Were the Asian maenads hysterical, *sōphrōn*, vindictive, or did they show all of these characteristics? Many possibilities exist.

In all of these cases, the ideas and assumptions of scholars and artists influence their interpretations of the *Bacchae* chorus. Influenced by my own viewings of modern *Bacchae* choruses, I have demonstrated the ways in which the textual details indicate a *sōphrōn* choreography of the chorus. However, the literal music and choreography of the 405 BCE chorus remain in part a mystery. Thus, although I have attempted to demonstrate the rich historical information about the chorus's movement, the unknown specter of performance, with its many absent variables, threatens to undermine that information and makes any approach to *Bacchae* an especially complex endeavor.

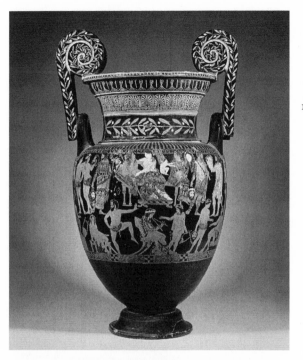

1. Dionysus and the Cast of a Satyr Play (side A). Attic red-figured volute krater attributed to the Pronomos Painter, ca. 400 BCE. Naples, Museo Archeologico Nazionale, inv. 81673 (H3240). Photo by L. Pedicini. All rights reserved. Reproduced by kind permission of the Ministero per i Beni e le Attività Culturali–Soprintendenza Speciale per i beni archeologici di Napoli e Pompei.

2. The Cast of a Satyr Play and Two Satyrs (detail side A/B, handle area). Attic red-figured volute krater attributed to the Pronomos Painter, ca. 400 BCE. Naples, Museo Archeologico Nazionale, inv. 81673 (H3240). Photo by L. Pedicini. All rights reserved. Reproduced by kind permission of the Ministero per i Beni e le Attività Culturali–Soprintendenza Speciale per i beni archeologici di Napoli e Pompei.

3. Dionysus with Satyrs and Maenads in *Thiasos* (side B). Attic red-figured volute krater attributed to the Pronomos Painter, ca. 400 BCE. Naples, Museo Archeologico Nazionale, inv. 81673 (H3240). Photo by L. Pedicini. All rights reserved. Reproduced by kind permission of the Ministero per i Beni e le Attività Culturali–Soprintendenza Speciale per i beni archeologici di Napoli e Pompei.

» 4. (*Top*) Theatre of Dionysus at Athens. Photo by Ilse Kleemann ©DAI Athens (Neg. no.: D-DAI-ATH-Kleemann 540). All rights reserved.

»» 5. (*Bottom*) Theatre at Thorikos. Photo ©DAI Athens (Neg. no.: D-DAI-ATH-Attika 79). All rights reserved.

6. A Tragic Chorus Approaching a Tomb Monument. Attic red-figured column krater attributed to an unidentified Mannerist painter, ca. 500–490 BCE. Antikenmuseum Basel und Sammlung Ludwig, inv. BS 415. Photo by Andreas F. Voegelin. All rights reserved. Reproduced by kind permission of the Museum.

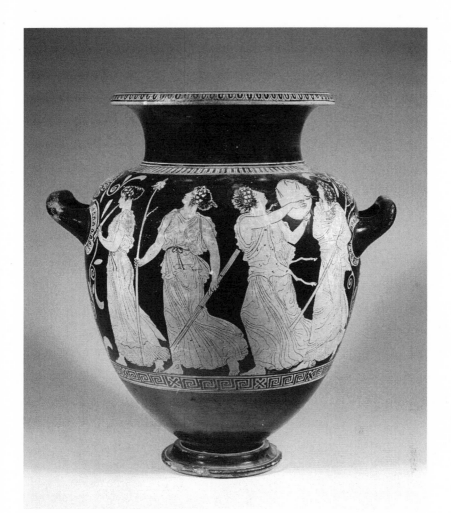

7. Dancing Maenads. Attic red-figured stamnos attributed to the Dinos Painter, ca. 420 BCE. Naples, Museo Archeologico Nazionale, inv. 81674 (H2419). Photo by L. Pedicini. All rights reserved. Reproduced by kind permission of the Ministero per i Beni e le Attività Culturali–Soprintendenza Speciale per i beni archeologici di Napoli e Pompei.

8. The Madness of Lycurgus or an Armed Pentheus Fighting Maenads. Attic hydria attributed to the Painter of Louvre G 433, ca. 425–400 BCE. Rome, Museo di Villa Giulia, inv. 55703. Reproduced by kind permission of the Soprintendenza per i Beni Archeologici dell'Etruria Meridionale.

9. *Phlyax* Scene of a Tragic Actor (Aegisthus) On-stage with Three Comic Actors (*Chorēgos*, Pyrrias, *Chorēgos*). Apulian red-figured bell krater, name vase of the Choregos Painter, ca. 380 BCE. Naples, Museo Archeo-logico Nazionale, inv. 248778 (formerly J. Paul Getty Museum, 96.AE.29). Reproduced by kind permission of the Ministero per i Beni e le Attività Culturali–Soprintendenza Speciale per i beni archeologici di Napoli e Pompei.

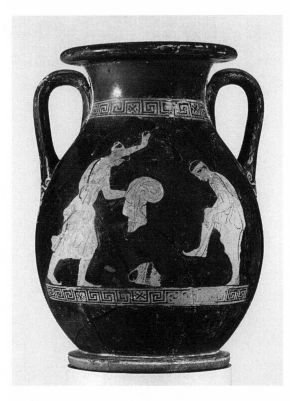

10. Actors in Female Costume Preparing for a Performance. Attic red-figured pelike attributed to the Phiale Painter (also known as the Boston Phiale Painter), ca. 440–430 BCE. Museum of Fine Arts, Boston, Henry Lillie Pierce Fund, inv. 98.883. Photo ©Museum of Fine Arts, Boston.

11. Actor (Possibly Pentheus) and a Dancing Chorus Maenad. Attic red-figured bell krater, ca. 460–450 BCE. Ferrara, Museo Archeologico Nazionale, inv. T173C. Reproduced by kind permission of the Ministero per i Beni e le Attività Culturali.

12. An Actor in a Comedy or
Phallic Mime Performing
before Man and Youth. Attic
red-figured chous, name vase
of the Group of the Perseus
Dance, ca. 420 BCE. Athens,
National Museum, Vlastos
Collection (see drawing by
E. R. Malyon in Hart, *The
Art of Ancient Greek Theater*,
105). Photo by Herman
Wagner ©DAI, Athens (Neg.
no.: D-DAI-ATH-Athen Varia
1088). All rights reserved.

13. A Piper with Two Actors
or Chorus Members
Costumed as Birds. Attic
red-figured calyx crater,
ca. 415 BCE. Naples, Museo
Archeologico Nazionale,
inv. 205239 (formerly J. Paul
Getty Museum 82.AE.83).
Reproduced by kind per-
mission of the Ministero per
i Beni e le Attività Culturali–
Soprintendenza Speciale per
i beni archeologici di Napoli
e Pompei.

14. Two Comic Actors, One (left) Costumed as a Woman, the Other (right) as a Dancing Man. Attic red-figured bell krater, ca. 390–370 BCE. University of Heidelberg, Museum of Antiquities, inv. B 134. Photo by Hubert Vögele. All rights reserved. Reproduced by kind permission of the Museum.

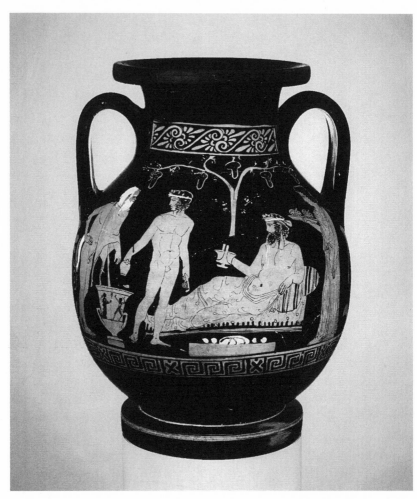

15. Bearded Dionysus Banqueting. Attic red-figured terracotta pelike attributed to the Somzée Painter, ca. 420–410 BCE. Metropolitan Museum of Art, Gift of Samuel G. Ward, 1875, inv. 75.2.7. Photo ©The Metropolitan Museum of Art, New York. Image source: Art Resource, New York, NY.

4 PERFORMANCE STYLE

Theatre historians struggle with the subject of fifth-century performance style for several reasons. For one, many components factor into the subject. Performance style begins with the body, but the space of the theatre, the audience, and the actor's physicality, training, and costume all inform styles of movement. Second, although the theatre semioticians have made some attempts,[1] theatre historians still have no systematic method for observing and interpreting acting;[2] and third, while the distinct writing style of Aeschylus, Sophocles, and Euripides bears the imprint of performance style, limited commentary exists on fifth-century acting in particular. Aristophanic comedy,[3] an anecdote in Aristotle's *Poetics*,[4] and a few fifth-century vases[5] provide dubious information.[6] Perhaps on account of these difficulties, few studies have directly addressed fifth-century actors and their performance styles.[7]

Of the extant sources on performance style, the anecdote[8] in *Poetics* well illustrates some of the relevant interpretive issues. According to Aristotle, with an utter lack of subtly, the actor Mynniskos called his younger rival Kallippides an ape, for apparently the young Kallippides's style was seriously over the top (*lian hyperballonta*). The anecdote, like Sir Laurence Olivier's alleged gibe at Dustin Hoffman,[9] is somewhat apocryphal. While it provides information about performance style, it also raises many questions about that information. What might it mean for fifth-century acting "to go too far"? Is the anecdote a bona fide fifth-century description about acting, or is it only an Aristotelian fourth-century invention? What are the values, judgments, and motives behind this comment? Such questions indicate the inherent difficulty in studying performance style. When the sources indicate little certain information about fifth-century actors, their bodies, their training, and their movement, how can historians then begin to describe performance style?

In this chapter, I focus on the innovative ways in which scholars have managed such questions and some of the interpretive problems that arise in the process. I begin by addressing one point on which most scholars agree: that a transition in performance style took place beginning in the late fifth century BCE. I then consider the application of modern terms for performance style to describe this transition before I take a closer look at two critical articles on the subject: Eric Csapo's "Kallippides on the Floor-Sweepings: The Limits of Realism in Classical Acting and Performance Styles" (2002), which has recently been revised,[10] and J. Richard Green's "Towards a Reconstruction of Performance Style" (2002). Through an examination of such topics and discussions, I explore historiographical issues, such as the anachronistic application of modern terminology in describing ancient performance style, the use of neat dualisms and disclaimers, the strategy of deriving general perceptions from the sources as opposed to specific historical truths, and the use of comedy as evidence. I then turn to my case study of Euripides's 405 BCE tragedy *Bacchae* in order to illustrate both the information that the play's dressing-up scene provides about performance style and the methodological problems that arise in relying on that information as evidence. I conclude by demonstrating the ways in which the uncertainty over late fifth-century performance style complicates any interpretation of the play, particularly those that address *Bacchae*'s possible political commentary.

Modern Misnomers and Neat Dualisms

Most scholars agree that a transition in style took place on the Attic stage beginning in the late fifth century BCE, and many refer to the new style as realism. J. Michael Walton, for example, has explained this apparent transition toward realism as follows: "In later times drama tended to be described as realistic when it was presented in conditions that replicated the physicality of life. . . . If Euripides was the pioneer of such a tendency in his tragedies when he made his mythical characters behave like real men and women, Menander was the Greek playwright to hone the method."[11] Eric Csapo has argued that "in the late fifth century BC there occurred a signifi- cant movement toward something we may provisionally call 'realism,'"[12] and E. R. Dodds has stated that lines 453–59 of *Bacchae*, when Pentheus de- scribes the costume of Dionysus, "belong to a time when mask and costume were being made more individual and realistic."[13] Kostas Valakas replaces realism with mannerism when he describes *Bacchae*'s dressing-up scene as "a fine example of mannerism in acting: the emphasis on sophisticated details in the actor's use of the body and costume aims first and foremost to make him look theatrical."[14] Richard Green has used the term naturalism in stat- ing that "tragedy of the fifth and fourth centuries seems to have become, for a while, more naturalistic in its presentation."[15] Ismene Lada-Richards has avoided the term realism as well and has instead argued that comedy expressed elements of Brechtian performance, and tragedy more Stanis- lavskian. At the same time, she hedges her claim by stating that she uses these terms as "landmarks" or "a set of guidelines."[16] Taplin also avoids the description of realism and asks instead, "Can we settle at any point between the two extremes of broad realism and of the totally non-naturalistic for- mality of the Nôh?"[17] Taplin leans more toward the former and assumes that "the actions were generally performed in a large and formal yet fairly fluid and naturalistic manner" (19), but he readily admits that "these as- sumptions are unprovable" even if the admission does not cause him any "serious misgivings" (19). As these examples illustrate, scholars have had to identify and describe changes in fifth-century performance style with few extant sources to aid them in understanding that style.

In their descriptions, these classical scholars, like many theatre histor- ians, have followed the practice of art historians who use taxonomic ter- minology, such as realism, mannerism, and naturalism, as a generalized shorthand for describing trends in art. These categories often form the basis of making neat dualisms that emerge in descriptions of one style versus another. Lada-Richards's opposition of Brecht/Stanislavski and Taplin's opposition of broad realism/Noh are two such examples. However, art his- torian Svetlana Alpers has suggested that such oppositions are problem- atic: "Categories [of style] are developed in the interest of externality and objectivity, freeing the observer from any responsibility for them. These presumably objective categories of large historical classifications are then (silently) treated as aesthetic properties of each object. Style, designated by the art historian, is treated as if it were possessed by each object."[18]

Citing Alpers, Thomas Postlewait has cautioned that theatre historians might be wise to resist the trends in art history that make "dualistic systems for identifying and differentiating styles, motifs, and forms."[19] Apart from the risk of imposing reductive labels, modern theatrical styles, such as realism/symbolism and epic/method, are not necessarily styles in antithesis,[20] so when scholars impose these categories onto the source material in an effort to make sense of it, this mode of analysis, this imposition of dualisms, this process of categorization related to historical thinking may force onto the sources a preconceived idea of style that obscures the complexity of a specific style in a specific performance at a certain time.

Moreover, terms such as realism, naturalism, epic, and method may be applied inappropriately in descriptions of Athenian performance because the terms evoke traditions of theatrical style with their own historicity. These terms refer to performance techniques that cannot easily be divorced from their historical, cultural, social, and psychological foundations and then be applied to an altogether different historical situation and performance. Aware of this problem of mixing and matching period style terminology, scholars often qualify their use of realism as a metaphor by encasing the term in quotation marks, otherwise known as "scare quotes," but even employing these terms as metaphors may not be suitable. They still risk ahistoricism by describing in modern terms a system of ancient acting inscribed with its own historical and ideological attitudes that were informed by the ancient Greeks' unique conception of the mind-body relationship.[21] Nevertheless, while naturalism, mannerism, realism, or "realism" may not be the most appropriate metaphors to describe the fifth century's masked theatrical tradition with stylized conventions such as the *ekkyklēma* and *mēchanē*,[22] scholars may have no choice but to rely on these generalized terms of style until they are able to develop a vocabulary specific to Athenian performance.

Csapo and Green: Approaches to Performance Style

Two scholars who have made significant contributions to the development of such a vocabulary are Eric Csapo and Richard Green. Both Csapo and Green are currently situated at the University of Sydney, with Csapo residing in the Department of Classics and Ancient History and Green as an Emeritus Professor in the Department of Archaeology. The two are well known for their innovative approaches to the material, and John Jory has even referred to Csapo as "the most innovative and stimulating iconoclast among historians of classical drama."[23] In their articles in the volume *Greek and Roman Actors*, the encyclopedic knowledge of both scholars is evident as they examine a wide range of evidence related to the study of ancient theatre.

Although Csapo begins his article by immediately forewarning readers about the lack of sources related to performance style, he quickly turns the limitations to his advantage. He supports his argument with two of the few direct references to fifth-century performance style: Aristotle's anecdote about Kallippides and the contest (*agōn*) in *Frogs* between "Aeschylus" and "Euripides."[24] He combines these resources with a study of sociolect in Athenian drama in order to argue three distinct points: (1) the actor Kallippides used nonelite gestures to represent heroic characters, (2) Euripides dressed kings in rags, and (3) Euripides and Aristophanes attempted to present the aristocrats and the *dēmos* as equals by not using speech to distinguish class. Based on these observations, he concludes that "in the late fifth century BC there occurred a significant movement toward something we may provisionally call 'realism.'"[25] However, he continues, "the debate surrounding Kallippides can now be seen to have less to do with an opposition between 'realist' and 'idealist' aesthetics, than with two opposed concepts of the real, one belonging to a conservative, residually aristocratic-hierarchic mentality, the other to an emergent democratic-egalitarian mentality" (146). In this way, Csapo attributes a social cause to the change in aesthetics. He posits that the movement toward realism, which he recognizes in the plays of Euripides and Aristophanes, was part of a class warfare that was taking place over the politics of aesthetics "during the time of the 'radical democracy' in Athens" (146).

While Csapo focuses on the literary material, Green relies on material evidence. He observes and describes images with the acuity of a facial recognition monitor by registering patterns in various corporeal signifiers (e.g., beards, hairstyles, gestures, facial expressions, the length of costumes). He then interprets these signifiers in relation to one another on vases from different time periods (e.g., fifth and fourth century), styles (Rich Style, early classical period), and painters (Pronomos Painter, Phiale Painter); and he categorizes the signifiers in relation to the specific subjects represented in scenes from comedy, tragedy, satyr play, myth, and everyday life. In the process, he aims not necessarily to make a new argument about performance style, but rather to develop a system for further study. He does so, he argues, because in order to "attempt to understand what is represented in the images of theatre, one has to understand the background of expectations, the norm, against which stage behavior might be judged."[26] Green's system of observing, recognizing, and categorizing visual patterns develops a sort of database of designs from which new observations about performance can be extracted, but despite the successes of his and Csapo's works, several issues inevitably arise in their arguments.

Disclaimers

One such issue is disclaimers. While many articles on fifth-century performance begin with a disclaimer about the limitations of the sources, the subject of performance style especially calls for such qualifications. Csapo opens his article by stating: "If we omit the schematic and dubious claims, mainly in the scholia and poets' biographies, which are derived from Hellenistic and later authors, and confine ourselves to classical authors, we are left with a few comments by Aristotle, many anecdotal, and some extended by distorted descriptions in comedy."[27] Richard Green begins with a disclaimer as well, identifying two key problems related to his study: limited source material and separating the painting and the painter's style from the theatrical subject of the vase. He further explains that "all too few pictures survive of classical Greek actors acting tragedy. There are good reasons for this, the principal of which is the convention that vase-painters . . . were governed by the sense of the story conveyed by the performance. Thus what is usually depicted on vases is not the process of performance but what the audience was persuaded to see."[28] Csapo's and Green's disclaimers operate as rhetorical tools that alert readers to the common problems that derive from the limited historical record.

Such disclaimers allow scholars to argue their points even though they cannot always offer solid proof for them. Presenting evidence while acknowledging its inherent fallibility, they can speculate while acknowledging their awareness of that speculation. In this way, Green and Csapo try to avoid the speciousness of possibility while attempting to make arguments based on probability.

For example, much of Csapo's case rests on Aristotle's fourth-century anecdote about which he states: "Mynniskos probably delivered his insult, if at all, in the 420s BC."[29] Attempting to persuade his readers that the remark cited in *Poetics*, a 330 BCE text, refers to a debate nearly a hundred years earlier, Csapo argues that the anecdote "gives direct testimony to a controversy already within the second or third generation of 'professional' actors" (127). However, he does not disclose other possibilities for the anecdote's appearance in *Poetics*. The remark could have been a fourth-century invention that has nothing to do with fifth-century practice, or Aristotle might have revised the anecdote to some extent or taken it out of context. Instead of disclosing such alternatives, Csapo exhibits the historian's split personality of artist/scientist by creating a narrative that depends in part on the anecdote's delivery in the 420s but simultaneously hedging that date with an "if at all." Csapo also hedges his bets at the end of his section on vocal mimicry. He not only acknowledges the deficiencies in his evidence, he almost apologizes for it: *"slight and unevenly scattered as it is, the evidence shows* [italics mine] an overall growth of interest in vocal mimicry among comic actors from the later fifth to the fourth and third centuries BC" (137).

This oscillation between near apology and bold assertion is not unique to Csapo but is symptomatic of the discipline, for this trend appears in Green's work as well. He, too, practically apologizes for one of his claims. After asserting that the "tragedy of the fifth and fourth centuries seems to have become, for a while, more naturalistic in its presentation,"[30] he then calls his claim "a gross oversimplification" that overall "appears to hold true" (111). Like Csapo, Green seems uncomfortable at times with his claims. With only "slight and uneven evidence" to work with, they are caught between a field that demands precise, analytical rigor and a subject riddled with conjecture.

Like good trial lawyers, Csapo and Green face the challenge of remaining as honest as possible while manipulating the game to their advantage, but unlike lawyers, historians rarely have sufficient evidence. And even when they do, the evidence, according to Stanford, "can never be conclusive. It can at best achieve a very high degree of probability."[31] For theatre and performance historians especially, the infamous "hole in the case" is often a given and not necessarily a reason to acquit. Disclaimers help with these issues in the aim of persuasion but also serve as bold reminders of the problems with managing facts, truths, and objectivity. Fortunately, for historians, their aim is to convince, not convict.

Deriving "General Perceptions" versus "Specific Truths"

As Csapo and Green acknowledge the scarce supply of sources and the related problems, they also develop strategies to circumvent such problems. One such strategy is posing general perceptions instead of specific truths. Inferred from the limited sources, these general perceptions sometimes involve a move from citing limited evidence on the theatre to an expansive generalization about social context.

Csapo uses the sources to develop general perceptions about the ways in which fifth-century society perceived performance style, for he explains that "the value of the [Aristotle's] anecdote does not depend on its historicity. Whether Mynniskos really called Kallippides an ape is beyond proof. Though anecdotes (and comedy) are not reliable as concerns specific truths, they usually owe their survival to success in expressing general perceptions."[32] Through this approach, he infers a class bias in part from the comments of Mynniskos against Kallippides and "Aeschylus" against his rival "Euripides." This inferred class bias then serves as evidence to reinforce his claim that a transition was taking place which resulted in the development of those biases and rivalries over the aesthetics of performance. In this way, Csapo interprets sources, such as *Poetics* and *Frogs*, that relate to the theatre (event) in relation to the political environment of the so-called "radical democracy" (context). He then infers from the sources a class rivalry (context) to reinforce his point that a transition took place in the aesthetics of performance style (event). The circular strategy of his argument thus shifts from event to context to event. He uses the sources about the event to help with the construction of a context for the event.

Green too employs this strategy of drawing on general perceptions as opposed to specific truths in his attempt to overcome the problem of separating the painting and the painter's style from the theatrical subject of the vase. He first searches for patterns in five painters' representations of a similar theatrical scene from Sophocles's lost play *Andromeda*, for as historian Peter Burke has suggested, "a series of images offers testimony more reliable than that of individual images, whether the historian focuses on all the surviving images which viewers would have seen in particular places and times . . . or observes changes in images of purgatory (say) over the long term."[33] Through this method, Green suggests, "it is possible to gain some reliable idea of what the performance looked like on stage, despite the way the scenes are shown, as usual, as mythological reality."[34] His strategy is thus similar to that in an earlier article, "Messengers from the Tragic Stage," where he identifies forty-nine depictions of *paidagōgos* or messenger scenes on southern Italian vases from the mid-fourth century BCE, but here he argues that five scenes of *Andromeda* "seem to reflect independent observations of a single performance. They share many elements of character, costume, and action" (107), such as Andromeda's dress, her being tied to stakes, and the presence of Ethiopian attendants with their wedding/funerary gifts. While Green seems confident in the approach, his disclaimer of "seem to reflect" demonstrates the inevitable uncertainty inherent in the endeavor. Continuing with further disclaimers, he cautions that "we have to be wary of interpretation by the vase-painter into the parts played, beyond the actuality of the performance" (107). The five vases may still reflect the conventions of painting rather than those of the theatre, or their painters may have simply all shared a similar artistic vocabulary in painting the subject. Green cannot be certain that each painter interpreted the same performance, nor can he know the extent to which the conventions of vase-painting influenced the representations of performance. Green wants to indulge in the sources, but he is cautious. He knows that the vases cannot offer specific truths, so he focuses on general perceptions while hedging his claims.

The Use of Comedy as Evidence

Applying comedy as evidence also involves the practice of deriving general perceptions as opposed to specific truths, and Csapo employs this technique by drawing on several examples from the *agōn* (contest) between "Aeschylus" and "Euripides" in *Frogs* to offer general perceptions about performance style. Some such examples include: Aeschylus's objections to Euripides's practice of dressing kings in rags (*Frogs* 842, 1066; cf. *Arch.* 404–34), using colloquialism and degrading "high" style (*Frogs* 841 [cf. *Arch.* 398], 843, 943, 949–52, 1297), choosing themes concerned with reality (*Frogs* 959–61), introducing sophistic arguments (*Clouds* 1353–72), and representing more "democratically"[35] the speech of servants and masters, women and men (*Frogs* 779, 952–53).[36] On the one hand, the *agōn* and its many inflated exaggerations cannot be interpreted too literally. On the other hand, the parody must be based on an aspect of social reality in order for the comedy to work and produce its intended effect of laughter. For example, regarding the depiction of Socrates in *Clouds*, Jeffrey Henderson has suggested: "The fact that a real person was thus turned into an exaggerated stereotype for the purposes of ridicule does not mean that the ridicule was mere jesting and without effect. The stereotype embodied real social hostility and Sokrates seemed to fit it."[37]

Following Henderson's suggestion, scholars can use their knowledge of *Frogs* winning first prize at the Lenaia Festival in 405 to assume that the parody succeeded. Some of the audience (or the judges at least) got the joke, but to claim that the parody proves Aeschylus to be an elitist conservative and Euripides the *enfant terrible* would oversimplify the matter. One could, however, assume that Euripides must have been both popular (despite his winning few prizes in the tragic festivals' contests) and controversial for him to play this major role in Aristophanes's comedy. One could also assume that the judges who voted for the comedy found this parody to be funny, but exactly why is unclear. Comedy sometimes provides the luxury of specific information about performance practices, such as through deictics and metatheatrical references to costumes, properties, and audience address, but one cannot interpret Aristophanic jokes about Euripides and his performance style too literally. Scholars still use these jokes to construct general perceptions about performance style, but they often do so with caution.

Performance Style in the Dressing-up Scene

Bacchae arguably offers more information on the subject of performance style than any other tragedy,[38] for the play stages a dressing-up scene (912–76)[39] that includes many "metatheatrical" or "metatragic" dimensions, a term which Charles Segal has defined as "the self-conscious reflection by the dramatist on the theatricality and illusion-inducing power of his own work, on the range and the limits of the truth that the dramatic form can convey."[40] Such allusions appear in the depiction of Pentheus as he attempts to disguise himself as a maenad so that he can spy on his mother and the other Theban women on Mt. Cithaeron. The scene opens with a dazed Pentheus entering the stage dressed like these women. His double vision causes him to see two suns and Dionysus as a bull. Pentheus now sees "the things which he ought to see" (924), and the presumably still disguised god proceeds to direct the young ruler in his new role. In the process, Pentheus tries to look and act not like the chorus of Dionysus's true followers, but like his possessed mother and aunts (26–42), and his attempt to perform like these crazed and not *sōphrōn* maenads (925–26) offers vital information about fifth-century performance style.

However, the reliability of this information is suspect for several reasons. First, Pentheus's approach to performance is that of a character, not an actor. The character's fictional performance of preparing to impersonate a maenad, which on the stage is the result of the mediation between actor, character, and text,[41] has an uncertain relation to an actor's methods. Another issue is that Pentheus is not preparing for a role in a play. He is attempting to disguise himself to spy on the offstage Theban maenads. Nevertheless, the metatheatrical references in the scene are still valuable, because, like an actor, Pentheus wants desperately to convince his audience (i.e., the Theban maenads) of his new image.[42]

In the process, the young ruler thinks about his outer physicality, not his inner psychology. No method actor, he asks Dionysus, "How do I look? Do I not have the stance of Ino or my mother Agaue?" (925–26). Aiming for the right posture, he prompts his director to comment, "Seeing you, I seem to see those very women" (927).[43] Although in a daze, Pentheus is not exactly channeling his inner maenad. He is under the god's spell, but he still wonders if he looks the part, is properly dressed, and holds his thyrsus correctly. He is still conscious of his acting and impersonation and is not ritually immersed in a new identity. He is mad. He is, as Dionysus states, "seeing as he ought to see" (924). He is mad enough to think he can carry mountains on his shoulders (945–46), but as confused as he is, Pentheus still realizes that he is pretending to be a maenad. He is conscious of his craft, not ritually transformed in character.[44]

This self-consciousness may be due to his lack of a new maenad mask. An actor of course dons a mask to transform into a character's identity, but Pentheus does not appear to have a new mask together with his new costume. His attempt at disguise clearly differs from an actor's art of transforming into a character, yet with the god of mask and theatre present, the scene nevertheless makes clear allusions to the process of acting.

These allusions raise various questions. Could Pentheus's dressing-up perhaps have served as a way for the poet or the *didaskalos*[45] to comment on a transition that was taking place in late fifth-century performance style? *Bacchae*'s text employs several formal components that are characteristic of early fifth-century tragedy, so perhaps the chorus may have acted in a more traditional style as well. If so, Cadmus and Teiresias, in their scene, and Pentheus, in the dressing-up scene, could have performed in a new type of acting style that contrasted with the style of the chorus. Or perhaps the style of Cadmus and Teiresias contrasted with that of Pentheus in order to illustrate the distinction between their (presumably funny yet somewhat earnest) attempt at a proper performance of Dionysiac worship versus the maddened young ruler's delusional performance. Could the performance have experimented with genre in this way or even parodied the latest styles in performance?[46] Could, as Mendelsohn has suggested, Euripides or the director of *Bacchae* have included the scene in response to the parody of the tragedian in Aristophanes's *Women at the Thesmophoria*?[47]

Even if these questions could be answered, perhaps, frustratingly, all of the information that this scene offers is actually the reverse of typical practice. This is just one of the dressing-up scene's interpretive problems. Although the scene provides rich commentary on performance style, scholars must approach it with caution, for a play-text describes a fictional and not a real world.

Without a clear understanding of *Bacchae*'s performance style, information that is crucial to any interpretation of the play is missing, for performance style is not only an aesthetic choice but is also inscribed by political and social connotations[48] that can evoke powerful emotions from audiences. The rivalry over how to perform Shakespeare between the American actor Edwin Forrest and his English nemesis William Charles Macready even led to violence with the eruption of the Astor Place Riots on May 10, 1849.[49] Because of the connection between politics and performance style, lacking such critical information about the actors' style(s) in the 405 BCE *Bacchae* presents interpretive problems for any examination of the play's political commentary.

For example, Paul Woodruff has argued that Euripides presented prodemocratic sentiments in the play. He states that "in writing as if lawful democracy is a real possibility, Euripides is squaring off against those enemies of democracy who slander it as a lawless tyranny by the lower classes over everyone else."[50] However, without knowing *Bacchae*'s performance style, making such a claim is difficult.

On the one hand, one could argue that Woodruff's and Csapo's studies complement each other. If a movement toward realism with its associated class connotations did take place, as Csapo suggests, and if *Bacchae* participated in this movement, then Woodruff's argument that Euripidean tragedy suggests prodemocratic sentiments would have more authority. In return, Woodruff's interpretation adds fuel to Csapo's theory of a movement toward realism, for his suggestion of *Bacchae*'s implicit political sentiment agrees with Csapo's argument for the dramatist's prodemocratic use of sociolect and Aristophanes's parody of the playwright as a prodemocrat.

On the other hand, while Woodruff has suggested that the chorus objects to Pentheus's autocratic rule[51] and champions the *dēmos*, Foley, whose argument I have also discussed in chapter 3, has argued that the chorus's position is more complex.[52] She posits that while the chorus shows that "Dionysiac rite and myth can complement the political aims of a democracy and guard against the institution of tyranny,"[53] at the same time, "in a city under pressure, pushed to excess, he [Dionysus] appears behind the corrosive pressure of the democratic majority for revenge and for the destruction of outstanding men" (240). Foley further suggests that the Asian maenads present no simple position but instead "press the audience to make complex connections and comparisons between the ritualized spectacle of Pentheus' failure to accept the god and the festivities and excesses of contemporary Attic democracy" (239). If Foley is correct, then the text of *Bacchae* provokes discussion on not solely the merits of a democracy, as Woodruff suggests, but also its inherent dangers.

But what about *Bacchae*'s performance? If Euripidean performance style had political connotations inscribed in it, as Csapo suggests, how could this style have been reconciled with the content of *Bacchae*? Did the *didaskalos* employ a style that had what Csapo refers to as "democratic" connotations? Would the implementation of this style impose a political reading on the play? Would the style prompt a prodemocratic interpretation, such as Woodruff's? Or would the *didaskalos* have resisted employing a performance style that may have limited a variety of potential interpretations by the audience? If scholars could know the style of *Bacchae*'s performance, the play's and its poet's relationship to Athenian politics would be more clear.

Because a fifth-century play's historical signification depended not on its function as a literary work to be read but on its cooperative role with the variable and ephemeral conditions of performance, answering these questions depends in part upon an understanding of the play's performance style. If scholars could know more about a play's historical performance conditions, then these discussions of the politics of Euripides and his *Bacchae* would be more complete. Instead, the study of Athenian performance will continue to generate partial truths that perpetually generate new ones, stimulating a synergistic effect that occurs from identifying and developing historical interpretations, even those created from moth-eaten material.

5 | COSTUMING AND PROPERTIES

Because no material remains of ancient Athenian costumes or clothing have survived, visual and literary artifacts serve as evidence in the reconstruction of fifth-century theatrical costuming conventions. Representations of performers in tragic costume on fifth- and early fourth-century vase-painting, for example, depict principal actors as having covered arms and legs and wearing a whole-headed mask with proportionate features (figures 1, 2, and 9). These characteristics starkly contrast with representations of comic actors who wear body padding, short *chitōns*, a phallus or padded breasts, and a grotesque mask, all of which conceal the actors' bodies and create a disproportionate effect (figures 9, 12, and 14).[1] In addition to these visual artifacts, the tragic texts include various references to costuming and properties, such as footwear, headgear, veils, masks, lionskins, tapestries, and bows; and Aristophanes's 405 BCE comedy *Frogs* stages a contest (*agōn*) between the famous fifth-century tragedians Aeschylus and Euripides in which the comic characters comment on tragic costuming. Apart from these key fifth-century literary sources, Pollux's second-century CE catalogue the *Onomasticon* is another critical reference that offers descriptions of ancient costume, but the work, composed nearly six hundred years after the so-called golden age, may not accurately reflect fifth-century theatrical trends.[2] While these various sources offer the best indication of the conventions of fifth-century costuming and properties, the mediated lenses of iconography and literature may idealize their subjects instead of reflecting actual costuming practices in the theatre.[3] In the reconstruction of the sensorial experience of wearing, feeling, and seeing costumes and properties, the distance between the extant artifacts and fifth-century cloth and material, between ideal representation and actual practice, leave scholars asking several basic questions about the feel and texture of material, its style,[4] makers,[5] and designers.

Just as critical studies of theatrical costuming in general are limited,[6] so classicists have produced few studies of Athenian costume, with Rosie Wyles's *Costume in Greek Tragedy* being the first comprehensive study in over fifty years.[7] Studies of comic costuming are more prevalent, perhaps because vases that depict comic costume are easier to identify and in better supply than representations of tragedies in performance, which can often be confused with scenes from myth.[8] Whatever the reason, few recent studies have addressed tragic costume specifically[9] and studies of properties are also infrequent,[10] even though the subject does arise organically in commentaries on individual tragedies.[11] On the contrary, several recent works have studied ancient dress, and the subjects of dress and costume are inextricably related.[12] Costume participates in the larger cultural significance and language of dress, for the conventions of theatrical costume, everyday dress, and even the nude body all signify in relation to one another.[13] For example, nudity in classical art (not drama) can function as a form of costume,[14] and in contrast to these depictions of the heroic male nude, the costumed male actor may have appeared feminized.[15] Like dress, costume identifies the characters visually, influences their movement and gesture, and responds to the larger environment such as the theatrical space and its location within the fifth-century Athenian *polis*.

Because of this critical connection between costume and dress, I narrow my discussion in this chapter to a few topics and scholarly works that best illustrate the inherent problems with studying each of these two subjects. I begin with a discussion of a critical piece of visual evidence on costume: the so-called Pronomos Vase (figures 1, 2, and 3). The limited accessibility of the vase, the reliance on reproduced illustrations of it, and the discrepancy between its visual appearance and the written descriptions of it are some of the issues that I cover. Through a discussion of Silvia Milanezi's article "Beauty in Rags: On *Rhakos* in Aristophanic Theatre" (2005), I also consider problems that arise in presenting literary sources, such as Aristophanes's *Frogs*, as historical evidence for costuming practices, before my discussion then turns to the subject of dress. With respect to Lloyd Llewellyn-Jones's article "A Woman's View?: Dress, Eroticism, and the Ideal Female Body in Athenian Art" (2002) and Sue Blundell's article "Clutching at Clothes" (2002), I address issues such as the risk of anachronism in applying film theory in a historical study and the problem with categorizing evidence into reductive dualities. I conclude with a consideration of Graham Ley's article "A Material World" (2007), through which I consider the representation of properties in the extant texts versus their possible functions on the ancient stage.

In the final section on Euripides's *Bacchae*, I focus on three historiographical issues that arise in scholars' assumptions that Dionysus has a "feminine" or "effeminate" appearance. The first issue I address is the reliance on the words of a character for evidence about a performance, for critics often rely on Pentheus's words (451–59) as evidence for Dionysus's appearance, i.e., his costume. In addition, although studies of fifth-century social codes of dress are just beginning to develop, scholars often assume that Pentheus's opinion about Dionysus's costume is one that the 405 BCE audience—all of them—shared. A third and related problem is the scholarly commentary that develops around a certain interpretation to the exclusion of other interpretations, for scholarship has propagated the view of Dionysus's feminine or effeminate appearance in the play, despite other possibilities for the god's costume in the 405 BCE performance. Without a doubt, the appearance of Dionysus's costume in *Bacchae*'s performance is crucial information for an interpretation of not only the play's themes but also the significance of the god and his relationship to fifth-century Athenian theatre and its civic functions. However, because the extant text is no simple synechdochic substitute for the 405 BCE staging in the theatre, many difficulties arise in trying to determine that information.

Using the Pronomos Vase as Evidence for Costume

The recent work *The Pronomos Vase and Its Context* well illustrates the historiographical problems related to this crucial piece of evidence, which depicts Dionysus and a cast from a satyr play,[16] so I will begin this chapter with a quick overview of some critical points discussed in that important volume. One key problem concerns the origins of the vase itself. Archaeologists found the Pronomos Vase, which is said to have been discovered in 1835 and painted in Athens ca. 400 BCE, in a tomb in the non–Greek-speaking Italian town of Ruvo.[17] The vase's discovery in Ruvo has led to debate about its manufacture. Was the vase "originally intended for precisely this audience and this market—that is to say, it was painted in Athens but for a south Italian clientele"—or did it reach Italy via the secondhand market "some time after it lost its immediate, topical appeal in Athens"?[18] The answer to this question is crucial. As Mark Griffith explains:

> Obviously it makes quite a big difference to the interpretation and meaning of the vase, whether we see it, on the one hand, as an essentially Athenian product, reflective of local interests and performance activities—perhaps even of a particular victory in the City Dionysia . . . or, on the other, as a funerary monument destined from the outset to sit inside or next to an Italian tomb . . . in a context far removed from the Athenian Theatre of Dionysos and among people who might never have actually seen or heard Pronomos' pipe.[19]

The vase's artists, intended audiences, patrons, and commercial markets are all important factors for its interpretation that should not be ignored. In the case of the Pronomos Vase, historians of the ancient theatre do not overlook these issues. Their importance is clear, but the information cannot be determined with any certainty. Arguments about the vase's audience rest on possible scenarios that sometimes conflict with one another, and this uncertainty about such basic questions then extends to theories about costume. How we imagine the Pronomos Vase's audience makes "quite a big difference" not only to how we interpret the vase but also to how we interpret the costumes it represents.

Limitations in Access to Sources

The lack of access to the vase also presents problems for research. Since its discovery, the vase has inspired a vivid history of documentary images and illustrations, yet while the rise of performance studies has sparked interest in the vase, it "has been in storerooms in Naples since the disastrous earthquake of 1980."[20] Although the display of the vase at the 2010 symposium at the J. Paul Getty Museum gave many scholars an opportunity to view the vase firsthand,[21] the lack of access to the vase over the years, discussed by François Lissarrague, has led to the reliance of scholars on drawings, reproduced images, and descriptions that provide a mediated engagement with the vase. This reliance on reproduced illustrations is a problem common to all theatre historians,[22] and in many cases, unavoidable circumstances and limitations in finances affect research, and in turn influence scholarship and its quality.

For example, Lissarrague has explained the possible consequences of observing a flat representation of a voluminous vase. He states that "we need to envisage the Pronomos Vase not as a flat image on paper, in a book, or on a screen, but as a volume, round and monumental, and as a continuous frieze blending progressively Sides A [figure 1, which depicts the cast of a satyr play] and B [figure 3, a mythical scene with Dionysus and a maenad or possibly Ariadne surrounded by maenads and satyrs]."[23] Such a viewing of the vase could create a narrative that joins the two sides of the vase (figure 2) instead of creating a visual hierarchy such as that "between theatre (rite) and *thiasos* (myth)" (39). As Lissarrague's remarks make clear, the medium for viewing (two-dimensional reproduced image or three-dimensional artifact) influences interpretations. Firsthand observance is critical but unfortunately often impossible.

Preconceived Ideas

In the same volume, Rosie Wyles has argued against the idea that the Pronomos Vase can serve as evidence for a standard costume in the late fifth century.[24] She states that apart from a "methodological issue [i.e., the risk of circularity], there is also the danger that the assumption that this costume is 'standard' might stop viewers from *looking* at the vase properly" (237). Wary of this tendency to rely on preconceived ideas, Wyles has avoided extensive descriptions of costumes, for another obstacle to looking at the vase objectively is the transcription of visual images into words. She argues that "above all it is through labelling costumes with verbal tags that assumptions creep in and that costume is dismissed from further consideration since descriptions of it seem to provide 'the answer'" (253n68).

Wyles provides an example of the tendency of this verbal labeling to lead to assumptions by rebutting claims about a standardized form of tragic footwear. She argues that Heracles on the Pronomos Vase is not wearing what scholars have tagged as *kothornoi*, a standardized tragic footwear of flat-soled boots. Instead, his shoes have "upturned toes and patterned greaves on his legs" (237). She also explains that while "the word which is most commonly used by characters in tragedy to denote shoes is *arbule*," Euripides's *Orestes* (1467–70) contrasts three different characters' types of footwear: (1) the Phrygian slave's Persian slippers (*eymarides*), (2) Helen's golden sandals (*chryseosandala*), and (3) Orestes's Mycenaean boots (*arbyloi*) (240). Based on these examples, she suggests that "there is nothing to pose a semantic objection to the possible realization of a range of shoes in tragedy"

(240). However, the Pronomos Painter could have painted greaves even if Heracles wore boots on stage, and the footwear described in *Orestes* may not have been realistically portrayed. In a stylized theatre, especially, the audience may not have expected to see a literal golden sandal; instead, when they heard the word, they could have projected the image onto a uniform style of footwear that a tragic actor wore. Thus, although Wyles presents two strong points for the use of a range of shoes in tragedy and in the process explains the influence of preconceived ideas on assumptions about tragic footwear, the use of a conventional style of boot is still possible.

Because of the discrepancies between text and performance, both the literary and visual record on costuming can be misleading, and preconceived ideas can influence the interpretation of both. Looking at a vase is a most crucial step in the interpretive process. However, the lack of access to the Pronomos Vase, the reliance on written descriptions of its images, and the influence of previous scholarship can override the processes not only of seeing the image objectively but also of appreciating the distinction between the costumes depicted on the vases and the many possible types of costumes that could have potentially existed on the fifth-century stage. Nevertheless, the vase undoubtedly provides rich details about many aspects of performance, such as masks (facial characteristics, hairstyles, and whole-headed mask construction), costumes (footwear, ornate appearance, coverage of principal actors in both satyr play and tragedy[25]), properties (clubs and animal skins), and musical instruments.

Comic Metaphor or Historical Reference?: Using Dramatic Texts as Evidence

If the Pronomos Vase is arguably the most important piece of visual evidence for the study of costume, then perhaps the most important piece of textual evidence is Aristophanes's *Frogs*. In the comedian's parody[26] of the two tragic playwrights, "Aeschylus" accuses "Euripides"[27] of dressing his characters in rags: "How dare you, you son of that goddess of the vegetable-plot? *You* say that of *me*, you scraper-together of idle chatter, you creator of beggars, you stitcher of rags?" (840–42).[28] "And anyway," "Aeschylus" later states in his debate with "Euripides":

> it's only natural that the demigods should use words bigger than ours, just as they wear much more splendid clothes than we do—something in which I set a good example that you utterly perverted. . . . In the

first place by dressing men of kingly station in rags, so as to make them objects of pity. . . . Well, for a start, thanks to that, there isn't one rich man who's willing to take charge of a warship. Instead he wraps himself in rags and wails and claims to be poor. (1060–66)[29]

While several scholars, such as Eric Csapo, whose "Kallippides on the Floor-Sweepings" I discussed at length in the previous chapter, have used this passage as historical evidence for Euripides's costuming practices, Silvia Milanezi has examined the literary function of Aristophanes's references to rags. Her article "Beauty in Rags: On *Rhakos* in Aristophanic Theatre" interprets rags as a metaphor, so her consideration of the literary function of this passage raises questions about the ability of *Frogs* to serve as reliable evidence on fifth-century performance practices.[30]

Milanezi argues that *rhakos* "from epic onwards [was] the generic term for rags, tattered shabby or torn garments . . . usually associated with beggars' outfits" (75). She proposes to study "the vocabulary of rags and tatters . . . in Aristophanes, Euripides, and epigraphy: firstly to understand the relationship between women's garments and theatrical costumes and then the relationship between rags and political ideology" (75). In the process, she questions why Aristophanes would have presented Euripides as the inventor of dressing kings in rags, because extant tragedy and iconography offer little to support the gibe of "Aeschylus." She claims that the attribution is curious because Homer disguises Odysseus as a beggar and "Aeschylus brought Xerxes to the stage in rags" (76). Moreover, Milanezi suggests that "like Euripides, Aristophanes created many raggedy characters. They cannot all be explained as literary parodies, lampoons on Euripides, or a well-developed comic *topos* (*Pax* 739–40)" (83). She concludes with a political interpretation, namely that in Aristophanes:

> people are ragged because they abandon their authority. . . . Their economic situation, their beggary position is only the result of this. Aristophanes does not pity poverty or rags, because for him they are results of a perversion of the citizens' ability to make their own decisions.
> . . . By his rags, Aristophanes pledges for a new conception of political life in which blindness, selfishness and surface appearance give place to real participation. (84)

Milanezi ultimately suggests that the references to *rhakos* (rags) in *Frogs* functions not as a literal description of Euripides's costuming practices but rather as an Aristophanic metaphor for "the poverty that touches every aspect of Athenian life in the city" (83).

Whether or not scholars agree with Milanezi's argument, "Beauty in Rags" provides a perfect example of how disagreements can emerge over the use of dramatic texts as evidence, for, as also discussed in chapter 3, play-texts have a double identity. They serve the dual function of referring to both a fictional world, which Rozik calls W_1, and real-life historical events (Rozik's W_0).[31] Deciding to which world *Frogs* referred is no easy task, so the subject of study often determines a scholar's use of the sources. One scholar can read *Frogs*'s reference to rags as a literary figure; another can interpret the reference as historical evidence for costuming or other performance practices. Both arguments can be convincing, but both cannot always be correct.

Mixing Ancient and Modern Styles: Film Theory and the Risk of Anachronization

I have discussed the Pronomos Vase and *Frogs*, which are two critical fifth-century sources on costume, but no study of costume is complete without a consideration of dress. For this reason, I now turn to ancient historian Lloyd Llewellyn-Jones's article "A Woman's View?: Dress, Eroticism, and the Ideal Female Body in Athenian Art." Llewellyn-Jones "aims to evaluate how far images made in ancient Athens give an accurate or realistic picture of women's clothes, and to question how artistic representations of dress were related to the gendered conception of the female body" (171). Studying historical images with film theory[32] to aid him, his comparative approach explores the influence of social codes of gender on depictions of women's dress. He argues that both Athenian vases and Hollywood film accentuate breasts for the "male gaze."[33] The representations of women on Athenian vases share the "uplifted pointy-breasted look" (183) of female stars in the 1950s, but while women in the fifties could artificially create this look, women in Greece could not.

Although he lacks an actual garment from the ancient world on which to base his theory, his knowledge of the literal material (linen and wool) from which Athenian clothes were made serves as evidence for his argument. He claims that "although full breasts may have been sexually arousing (even underneath clothing), ancient Greek dress, unsupported by tight tailoring or corsetry and made from loose linen or opaque wool, was incapable of physically presenting the breasts as uplifted or pushed forward" (182). In other words, the artists performed an ancient style of photo-shopping in their depictions of women's breasts in order to portray them in ways that the linen and wool could not have made possible. Based on this observation, Llewellyn-Jones concludes that painters were interested in idealization more than accurate representation and that depictions of women's dress in Athenian art idealize and eroticize the female body. Furthermore, "the effect that this stylization had on the female viewers of vase-paintings is difficult to know, but women's knowledge of how to make cloth . . . coupled with their daily experiences of actually wearing clothes, must have aroused some puzzled reactions to the images of dress they encountered in the artworks" (190). Even before the days of market-driven excess, he suggests, an ideal of beauty persisted.

In contrast to Llewellyn-Jones's observations about depictions of real-life women, features of the female body do not seem to be accentuated in representations of cross-dressed actors in tragic costume (figures 10 and 11) as these features were with the padding of comic costumes (figure 14). This convention may be due to the tragic actor's need to play both male and female roles, but in any case, if Llewellyn-Jones is correct about the depictions of women's breasts in iconography, then in figure 1 the actor with a winged Eros clutching her, who sits to the right of Dionysus and Ariadne (seated in the middle of the top row of figures), may indeed be a cross-dressed actor, as some scholars have suggested. The depiction of the figure contrasts with Ariadne both because the breasts are not accentuated and the skin does not appear white, a characteristic associated with female beauty.

Despite such observations that Llewellyn-Jones's work encourages, the rewards of his study are tempered, for Llewellyn-Jones's approach of film theory inevitably risks anachronization. Because film theory has its own historicity and is embedded with the social codes and cultural systems of the interpreter's time, the theory may distort the ancient subject; for the methodology has developed in response to specific social and historical constructions of gender, which are not those of the ancient world. In addition to mismatching genres (film and iconography), the theoretical approach risks obscuring key social differences between the interpreter's world and ancient society, such as the distinction between female eroticization in a heteronormative society versus that in a culture that also eroticizes the male body. Film conceals male nudity; Athenian vases glorify it, even though the Athenian stage did not. The approach thus serves as an example of what Hayden White has described as historians' inability to "say precisely what we wish to say or mean precisely what we say. Our discourse always tends to slip away from our data towards the structures of consciousness with which we are trying to grasp them."[34] Because the gender dynamics embedded in film theory especially contribute to the inevitable slipping away from the data, scholars may question the extent to which this theory, which developed in response to trends in Euro-American culture, is applicable in a study of the fifth century BCE.[35]

Categorizing Evidence into Dualities

Another recent study of ancient dress codes from the same collection is Sue Blundell's "Clutching at Clothes." Blundell begins her article by asking why vase-painters often depicted women clutching at their clothes. She addresses that question by starting from the basic premise that clothes are associated with femininity in Greek art, "not the least because a high proportion of the men depicted in Greek art are nude" (145). Because clothing is associated with femininity, the vase-painters highlighted, "for whatever reason, the femininity of their female characters" (146).[36] To support these claims, Blundell reads images in relation to literary texts, a method similar to that of Richard Green, whose work I have discussed in chapters 4 and 6, yet Blundell also emphasizes the areas where the iconography and the literature do not correspond. Her methodology demonstrates what Peter Burke has explained as the historian's need "to read between the lines, noting the small but significant details — including significant absences — and using them as clues to information which the image-makers did not know they knew, or assumptions they were not aware of holding."[37] Applying this technique, she explores the question of why women frequently appear unshod in vase-painting, when the literary sources suggest that women and men wore shoes.[38]

Observing patterns in the depiction of shoes, she connects this information to her understanding of gender roles in ancient Athens. Her analysis suggests that shoes play an important role in demarcating public versus private space and by extension male versus female territory. One vase which she discusses is a red-figure cup by Peithinos, dated to 525–475 BCE (Antikensammlung, Staatliche Museen zu Berlin-Preussischer Kulturbesitz F2279). Interpreting the image on the vase, she constructs a narrative that incorporates her understanding of the passive role of Athenian women versus the active role of Athenian males in public life. On this vase, "the young men's sandals, coupled with their sticks, signify their ability to move around freely in outdoor, public space; and in this way their position as Athenian citizens is underlined. Their companions, by contrast, are marked out in this context as people who do not enjoy the same privileges as the youths—who as females or as under-age males are formally excluded from the public domain" (148). Examining such evidence closely, she argues that shoes are not mere accessories; they have serious social significance. They connect mobility through public and private space, which in Athens was a gender-specific process. Blundell also considers representations of skirts, belts, bags, and hairbands, and her discussion on each of these topics supports her conclusion that "in vase-painting, too, clothing is often manipulated to create a gender performance; and we as the viewers of the pot make up the audience" (163).

Combining the visual and the literary, Blundell pulls the thread of gender through each of her sources in order to examine more closely clothing's social connotations. Her methodology offers great insight into the significance of representations of women's clothing, but her focus on gender may predetermine her response to certain questions so that a preordained argument arises that uses the sources to support a previously accepted theory. For example, to support her thesis, Blundell categorizes the sources into the neat polarizations of male/female, public/private, active/passive, but imposing these preconceived categories onto the sources excludes various other possibilities for the absence of shoes. Perhaps vase-painters depicted women without shoes for aesthetic reasons,[39] or perhaps the absence of shoes relates to customs of women from distinct social classes. The reductive quality of Blundell's polar dualities, such as male/female, obscure important distinctions between classes of women, and as a result, may obscure other possible meanings and reasons for the presence or absence of shoes in visual imagery. Thus, such a study of iconography must be used with caution in making comparisons between depictions of real-life women's dress and movement and the costuming of cross-dressed actors on the stage.

Describing Props versus Reanimating Them in Performance

Before concluding my studies of costume, I want also to address the study of properties. In his article "A Material World," Graham Ley has mined the comic sources for references to *mēchanopoios* (crane maker, *Peace* 174), *skeyē* (properties), and the *skeyopoios* (*Knights* 232), which he argues (269) is the term for properties maker even though, in the context of *Knights*, the term refers to the creation of masks. In the process, he cites various examples of comic props (e.g., Heracles's lionskin in *Frogs*; Myrrhine's pillow, blanket, and perfume in *Lysistrata*; and the puppies in *Wasps*), which he then contrasts with props from tragedy (e.g., Agamemnon's boots in *Agamemnon*, Electra's lock of hair in *Libation Bearers*, and the branches decorated with woolen filaments in *Suppliants*). Observing the distinctions between tragedy's and comedy's use of properties, he explains that, in comparison to Aristophanic comedy, fifth-century tragedy represents the material world sparingly "as if comedy sensed the need or the opportunity to take the restricted material qualities of costumed and propertied tragic performance and exaggerate them exuberantly." According to Ley, "comedy rarely exploits a property for long, discarding objects quickly and absolutely. Tragedy, in contrast may cling to a property throughout its action" (275–76).

Although comedy can indeed at times provide an extended focus on a property, such as Heracles's lionskin in *Frogs*, Ley continues to emphasize a distinction between comedy's and tragedy's use of props and to explain that tragedy's practice of clinging to or emphasizing properties often occurs with staple tragic props (e.g., caskets, boxes, baskets). These items may contain something deadly, such as Medea's gifts in Euripides's *Medea*, or work in conjunction with a recognition, as does the signet ring in Sophocles's *Electra* or the birth tokens in Euripides's *Ion*. Based on this study of fifth-century tragic and comic props as well as an examination of costumes and props in satyr plays and Roman comedy, Ley concludes, "Both the selective austerity [in the use of costumes and props] of Greek tragedy and the abundance so evident in Aristophanic comedy are aesthetic exploitations of the sensual and sensory awareness of their audience, who like their Roman counterparts lived in a material world, as well as in a world of words" (283). Ley's careful listing of examples from across the fifth-century dramatic corpus illustrates patterns in the uses of props in comedy and tragedy, but he does not aim to interpret these patterns to reconstruct the meaning of properties in a multidimensional performance.

For example, Ley does not attempt to engage in a phenomenological study of props, such as that of Andrew Sofer's *The Stage Life of Props*. Challenging the semiotic dematerialization of properties into signs, Sofer argues that a prop is "*a discrete, material, inanimate object that is visibly manipulated by an actor in the course of performance* [emphasis his]" (11). Moreover props are "'triggered' by an actor in order to become a prop (objects shifted by stagehands between scenes do not qualify)" (11–12). Accordingly, a thyrsus (the fennel stalk carried by worshippers of Dionysus) resting on the stage is just a set decoration until the actors hold it. In this way, "dimensions that allow the object to mean in performance are precisely those liable to drop out of sight when the prop is treated as a textual rather than as a theatrical phenomenon" (2). Accordingly, he aims to "restore to the prop those performance dimensions that literary critics are trained not to see" (2), and he relates the emphasis on properties in a performance to "ghosting," a term coined by theatre historian Marvin Carlson.[40]

When theatre historians imagine properties phenomenologically, props reveal themselves as "not mere accessories, but time machines. As material ghosts, stage props become a concrete means for playwrights to animate stage action, interrogate theatrical practice, and revitalize dramatic form" (3). Sofer's reference to Carlson's term "ghosting" explains the ways in which props make meaning on the stage, for, according to Sofer, "props are not static symbols but precision tools whose dramaturgical role in revising outmoded theatrical contracts with the audience has long been neglected. In this sense, the function of the stage property duplicates that of theater itself: to bring dead images back to life—but with a twist" (3).

By identifying fifth-century tragedy's ways of clinging to props, such as caskets, boxes, and baskets, Ley too hints at the phenomenological meaning of ancient props. However, he does not attempt to explain the reasons for tragedy's tendency to cling to properties. Nor does he discuss the ritual and cultural significance of the items used as properties, which, according to Sofer, would contribute to their "ghosting" in the performance.

While the confines of Ley's short essay do not allow for a thorough exploration of such matters of the page versus the stage, he still presents valuable information for the study of the function of properties in performance. He opens the possibility for a discussion of the ways in which properties are activated to create theatrical and historical meaning. Indeed such an approach may be a rich subject for a future study in which the function of dramatic properties could be contextualized in relation to ancient Greek views about the agency of inanimate objects and animals which could be prosecuted and convicted for crimes according to law.[41]

What Did Dionysus Look Like?

I will now turn to my case study of Euripides's *Bacchae* in order to address historiographical issues that arise in various scholars' interpretations of Dionysus's costume in the play. Although critics rarely speculate about the costume of Dionysus when he appears *ex machina*,[42] several readings of the play hinge on Dionysus's feminine or effeminate appearance when he is disguised as the Stranger (i.e., as a priest of his cult), even though Dionysus gives no indication of what gender his mortal form entails (*morphēn d' ameipsas ek theoy brotēsian*, 4). Based on Pentheus's description of the god in lines 451–59, a fragment from Aeschylus's lost play *Edoni* quoted in Aristophanes's *Women at the Thesmophoria*,[43] a reference to Dionysus's wearing a feminine cap (*mitra*) in Sophocles's *Oedipus Tyrannus*,[44] and the predominance of images of a younger, beardless Dionysus in the last quarter of the fifth century,[45] most scholars assume that the god in *Bacchae* is feminine or effeminate.

Kirk Ormand, for example has attributed feminine characteristics to the god: "From the beginning of the play, the young king Pentheus is suspicious of the Stranger . . . and particularly suspicious of him because he has attributes of femininity. In lines 451–59, Dionysus is described as having long hair (which is specified as not suitable for wrestling, a markedly masculine activity), fair skin, and a soft body."[46] Nancy Rabinowitz has also argued that "the male playing female indicates a possible relevance of the form to Dionysos, a god associated with masks and characterized by softness, woman's curls and dress,"[47] and Helene P. Foley as well reads Dionysus and Pentheus in the dressing-up scene as "two feminine or feminized figures wearing long robes and fawnskins."[48] Much interpretation rests on these presumed effeminate or feminine characteristics of Dionysus, but the expression and reception of these characteristics in *Bacchae*'s 405 BCE performance is at best a probable if not simply a possible assumption.

As scholars tend to build a commentary around one another's ideas, Dodds's presentation of evidence in his classic study of the play may have been largely influential in these interpretations of the effeminate/feminine/feminized appearance of Dionysus. He states that "the girlishness of Dion. (*thēlumorphon* 353) is not, however, Eur.'s own invention,"[49] and he cites various parallel examples of Dionysus's effeminate appearance, including the fragment from Aeschylus's lost play *Edoni*,[50] the saffron (*krokōtos*) feminine robes that the god wears in comedy where he is mocked for his effeminacy (Ar. *Frogs* 46, cf. Cratinus fragment 38), painting and sculpture where his earlier depictions as bearded begin to be replaced with images of a beardless youth in the late fifth century, and Homeric hymn 7 to Dionysus, a work which he suggests, on the one hand, could present an ephebic depiction by referring to the god as a youth but, on the other hand, voids an effeminate characterization through a reference to strong or stout shoulders (*stibaroi ōmoi*).[51] Dodds's impressive array of references, however, still does not confirm a predominately effeminate or feminine nature of the god in *Bacchae*.[52]

Several problems arise with this evidence. For example, although *Frogs* was performed in the same year as *Bacchae*, one cannot necessarily assume that a comic rendition of the god represents the general depiction of him at the time. In addition, while images of a younger, beardless Dionysus predominate in the last quarter of the fifth century, the statistics of extant images may not reflect actual fifth-century statistics. Moreover, extant late fifth-century images of a bearded Dionysus also exist (figure 15),[53] and Thomas Carpenter has explained that "the Dionysos who appears on three of the ten surviving depictions of the death of Pentheus on Attic vases has nothing to do with the oriental stranger of the *Bacchae*."[54] In other words, because the visual depictions of Dionysus may vary, a bearded Dionysus in *Bacchae* may not have been an anomaly, but even if the god were beardless, gods are not mortals. Beardless depictions of gods do not inevitably imply effeminacy, as even Dodds acknowledges: "The change in the art type results in part from a general change in the representation of gods and heroes."[55] Although he does acknowledge that the change in representations of Dionysus may be part of a general change in art, he counters this acknowledgment with vague, circumstantial evidence, suggesting "the conception of the womanish god may have deeper roots in eastern and northern religious ideas."[56]

In addition to the inability of the external evidence to support the view of the god's effeminacy, Pentheus's description of Dionysus as having a fit body, fair skin, and flowing hair beside his cheeks (not like a wrestler's) is not indisputable evidence for the god's feminine or effeminate appearance. Concerning Pentheus's first point, it is not clear how Dionysus's form could have appeared feminine or effeminate on stage, for his costume would likely have been long and concealing his body. Regarding the second point, Dionysus's mask could have been painted white, but there is no certainty that female masks were painted white, although the mask held by the seated figure to the right of Dionysus and Ariadne on the Pronomos Vase (figure 1) suggests they may have been. On the third point, Dionysus could have had hair beside his cheeks, but as I will discuss further, there is no certain evidence that this hairstyle was an effeminate, let alone a feminine, hairstyle. Being beardless, however, could have had such connotations, but nothing in the text, including Pentheus's comments, indicates whether or not the disguised god had a beard, although a line in the text does suggest Pentheus may be just growing his.[57]

Dionysus, as the Stranger, likely looked something like Pentheus's description of him (it would indeed be odd if he did not), but scholars often assume that this dress clearly connoted femininity or effeminacy. While it could have done so to Pentheus, the audience may not have shared this view, particularly because they, unlike Pentheus, would have understood that the Priest is a god in disguise. Pentheus's words (451–59) in fact reveal little about the opinion of the historical audience and far more about the young ruler's character.[58]

The remarks especially serve to characterize him as the god's opponent in a masculine competition (*agōn*). Whereas Pentheus insulted Dionysus in the beginning of the play, the god later turns it around and aims to mock (854), punish, and defeat Pentheus by convincing him to dress as a woman-impersonating-man, who wears "woman-impersonating clothes" (*gynaikomimōi stolai*, 980; *thēlyn stolēn*, 828, 836, 852; *thēlygenē stolan*, 1156).[59] When the maddened[60] Pentheus reappears on stage, Dionysus using irony mocks Pentheus's feminine dress (*gynaikomorphos*) which is unique[61] to him in the play and consists of a *mitra*[62] (feminine headband which goes over the head and temples) (833, 929, 1115), girdle[63] (935–36), and long robes (935). Thus, if Pentheus's dressing-up serves the purpose of humiliation, then it would make no sense for the god to look feminine, like Pentheus does, for in the context of this masculine competition, how could Dionysus humiliate Pentheus by dressing him up as a woman if Dionysus too appeared feminine? While Dionysus could have perhaps looked feminine or effeminate to at least some of the audience, for others the religious connotations of the Priest's apparel may have overridden the gender connotations of them.

The various ways in which the audience may have interpreted Dionysus's costume are of course difficult to reconstruct, but a consideration of trends in fifth-century dress and hairstyles is helpful. Assuming that Pentheus describes Dionysus's costume correctly, long hair, a white mask,[64] or a long *chitōn* may not necessarily have connoted femininity or effeminacy. In the first case, although wrestlers would presumably have cut their hair short so that an opponent could not grab it, long hair[65] could be a mark of an ephebe, but also of a pampered, aristocratic lifestyle. If class did influence choice of hairstyles, then the meaning of Dionysus's presumably long hair could have evoked distinct reactions depending on the status and opinions of the individual audience members.[66] Second, in the context of the tragic stage, a long *chitōn* is also not particularly "feminine" or "effeminate," because long robes are already a convention of tragic costume. Moreover, as Françoise Frontisi-Ducroux and François Lissarrague have argued in their examination of the ambisexed figures on the so-called Anakreontic Vases (490–460 BCE): "The long khiton does not belong exclusively to women. It may refer to a particular status related to a special skill (a charioteer or a kitharode) or it may be worn by a male divinity."[67] In any case, knowing more about the conventions and connotations of men's dress at the time would be helpful in determining the audience's response, but the absence of photographs, director's notes, and reviews seriously limits any interpretation of the god's appearance and the audience's varied responses to the god's costume.

Despite these critical issues with assumptions about the god's effeminacy, scholars, in building on one another's work in the so-called "procession of history," tend to develop this one commentary to the exclusion of others. One reading of the god's "feminine" appearance that has been particularly influential is Froma Zeitlin's 1985 "Playing the Other: Theater, Theatricality, and the Feminine in Greek Drama." A closer look at this important work will help to illustrate the importance of costume to her influential argument.

While earlier scholars, such as Dodds, have commented on the effeminacy of Dionysus,[68] Zeitlin has instead emphasized the god's association with the "feminine," which functions as a metaphor that is distinct from "woman" or "female." Zeitlin contends that "there is nothing new in stressing the associations of Dionysos and the feminine for the Greek theater,"[69] but at the same time, she departs from previous readings of Dionysus as a *gynnis*, or womanish-man, expressing both male and female qualities, a reading which is based on a fragment from Aeschylus's lost play *Edoni*. She summarizes this previous reading of Dionysus as a *gynnis* (womanish-man) as follows:

> On the other hand, we might want to view the androgyny of Dionysos, already in Aiskhylos called a *gunnis* (womanish man) and *pseudanor* (counterfeit man, frag. 61 Nauck), as a true mixture of masculine and feminine. This mixture, it can be argued, is one of the emblems of his [Dionysus's] paradoxical role as disrupter of the normal social categories; in his own person he attests to the *coincidentia oppositorum* that

challenges the hierarchies and rules of the public masculine world, reintroducing into it confusions, conflicts, tensions, and ambiguities, insisting always on the more complex nature of life than masculine aspirations would allow. Such a view would stress male and female aspects alike; it would regard the god as embodying a dynamic process or as configuring in his person an alternate mode of reality. (66)

Refuting this point of view, she explains that "convincing as this view may be, it runs the risk of underrating the fact that it is precisely Dionysos' identification with the feminine that gives him and his theater their power" (66). Arguing for the god's "identification" with the feminine, she demonstrates various ways in which the god's "effeminacy is a sign of his hidden power" (64), for he uses feminine techniques such as trickery and a devious plot to punish and eventually feminize Pentheus.

Zeitlin thus suggests that the Athenian theatre's use of (1) the body, (2) space, (3) plot, and (4) *mimesis* (imitation) have a "cultural referent in the traits and aspects the society most associates with the feminine domain" (71), so "the final paradox may be that theater uses the feminine for the purpose of imagining a fuller model for the masculine self, and 'playing the other' opens that self to those often banned emotions of fear and pity" (85). Furthermore, "in a more complex view, tragedy, understood as the worship of Dionysos, expands an awareness of the world and the self through the drama of 'playing the other' whose mythic and cultic affinities with the god logically connect the god of women to the lord of the theater" (86).

Coupled with these claims, however, is a serious disclaimer. Zeitlin cautions her readers about her argument that the body, space, plot, and *mimesis* (imitation) also fall in the domain that Athenian society most associates with the feminine (71). She explains that she proposes this view at the risk of "drastic (I repeat, drastic) [her emphasis] oversimplification" (71). She also assumes what she calls "another, more dangerous risk by boldly proposing in advance that each of these traits can find not its only, to be sure, but its more radical cultural referent in the traits and aspects the society most associates with the feminine domain" (71).

In spite of these disclaimers, Zeitlin's rich and rigorous interpretation was a pioneering feminist critique that was first published in 1985, the same year as Sue-Ellen Case's renowned article "Classic Drag." These scholars' feminist perspectives influenced their interpretations, for both works present an argument that exposes the patriarchal structures of Athenian drama.

However, unlike Case's work, which focuses on the practice and meaning of cross-dressed roles, Zeitlin's argument depends, in part, on the feminine/effeminate nature of Dionysus in *Bacchae*, yet although Dionysus is associated with madness, which the society appears to have associated with the feminine domain, the god's madness comes only to those who do not worship him. Moreover, even if we agree that body, space, plot, and mimesis fall in the feminine domain, it is not clear that the god who presides over theatre "must also take on womanish traits" (65). What if Dionysus's costume was not "womanish," or what if even some members of the fifth-century audience did not interpret his costume as such? How might the religious as opposed to gender connotations of the costume challenge Zeitlin's argument? Despite these questions, Zeitlin's interpretive model has been widely accepted and influential in subsequent studies about Athenian drama.[70] Scholars tend to keep reiterating the model despite the uncertainty.

This trend thus serves as an example of scholarship's tendency to build upon certain discussions to the exclusion of others, for as Michel de Certeau has observed, "Whatever is expressed [in discourse about the past] engages a group's communication with itself through this reference to an absent, third party that constitutes its past. The dead are the objective figure of an exchange among the living."[71] Along these lines, the communal consensus about Dionysus's costume may not only reflect the persuasion of the argument but also the scholarly community's interest in feminist interpretive models.

By putting the costumes of Dionysus and Pentheus under the spotlight, I hope to have demonstrated the degree to which the god's appearance depends upon the 405 BCE performance's costumes and the audience's interpretations of them. While the image of a disguised, beardless, effeminate Dionysus may continue to be convincing to many, the limited knowledge about the social significance of clothing and costuming in the late fifth century BCE prevents a clear understanding of whether Dionysus appears to be feminine and is feminized or to whom he appears to look feminine, effeminate, or feminized. While any historical understanding of the performance's costuming may at best aim to be "no more than a tissue of mutually supporting probabilities,"[72] this particular tissue may inevitably be subject to the unavoidable wardrobe malfunctions that make the meaning of Dionysus and his theatre as ambiguous as ever.

6 { GESTURE AND MASK

Scholarship on gesture in the fifth-century theatre depends in large part upon theatrical scenes on vases[1] and upon dramatic texts. These sources provide ample examples of actions such as kneeling, weeping, kissing, embracing, sitting, lying down, running, striking, bowing the head, prostration, and the handling of objects and tokens. However, scholars must consider to what extent the movements and gestures indicated by fictive characters on static images and in texts corresponded to the actions of fifth-century actors.[2] While the codes and conventions for representing actions in iconography or a play-text may parallel in some ways the kinetic movement on the stage,[3] surely there are differences. For example, vases depict movements that are static and frozen in time, but performers in a multidimensional theatre articulate movement into that space and across a period of time. Dramatic texts signal and describe gestures but give no indication of specific characteristics such as their size, speed, intensity, or fluidity. What can be visualized, then, when, as Pickard-Cambridge has lamented, "we are simply ignorant of the degree of stylization that prevailed, even in gesture"?[4]

Oliver Taplin, Michael Halleran, Richard Green, Maria Luisa Catoni, Jan Bremmer, Herman Roodenburg, Donald Lateiner, Alan Boegehold, Glenys Davies, and Lloyd Llewellyn-Jones are some of the scholars who have addressed this difficult question.[5] The studies of representations of gesture by Bremmer and Roodenburg, Catoni, Lateiner, and Davies have helped to create a backdrop against which theatrical gestures can be compared. Green has demonstrated a method for comparing representations of everyday gesture to those of theatrical gestures, and while Taplin has focused on visual imagery as well, his well-known *The Stagecraft of Aeschylus* and *Greek Tragedy in Action* have, like Halleran's work, focused primarily on the gesture and movement represented in theatrical texts. Llewellyn-Jones, however, combines the visual and the literary in his exploration of a comparative method with Japanese Kabuki. Although their approaches are distinct, all of these scholars share the common task of deciphering the conventions of texts and iconography and translating into words the traces of gestures and movement inscribed in these artifacts.

In order to interrogate the historiographical problems that arise in the process, I limit my discussion in this chapter to a few key works on theatrical gesture and its related subject of the tragic mask of the performer. I begin with a consideration of the criticism that Oliver Taplin's *The Stagecraft of Aeschylus* (1977) has received for collapsing theatrical character and actor into a single identity. I also discuss a technique that Richard Green has applied in his "Towards a Reconstruction of Performance Style" (2002), where he compares cultural attitudes about gesture, derived from literature, to depictions of gesture in iconography. I then examine the cross-cultural approach of Lloyd Llewellyn-Jones in his "Body Language and the Female Role-Player" (2005), before turning my attention to David Wiles's *Mask and Performance* (2007) and Peter Meineck's "The Neuroscience of the Tragic Mask" (2011). The final section of the chapter addresses the information about gestures in *Bacchae*'s dressing-up scene and describes historiographical issues that arise in several scholars' arguments about the significance of those gestures. I focus in particular on two points: the problem of circular reasoning in E. R. Dodds's[6] and Richard Seaford's[7] arguments for the association of the gestures with ritual, and the search for authorial intent in Bernd Seidensticker's[8] argument for their association with comedy. I conclude the section with a discussion of the risks and rewards of David Wiles's practitioner-based approach, which contests the theory of the so-called "smiling" mask of Dionysus.[9] In this way, I attempt to illustrate both the information in the text about theatrical gesture and the mask, as well as the difficulties inherent in using that information as evidence for a reconstruction of the gestures and movements of *Bacchae*'s historical 405 BCE production.

Words versus Gesture/Character versus Actor

Oliver Taplin's *The Stagecraft of Aeschylus* speaks vividly to the historiographical questions surrounding the study of gesture. *Stagecraft*'s rigorous scholarship demonstrates with painstaking detail[10] the importance of words in the reconstruction of not only gesticulation and the handling of stage properties but also movement and the lack of it as in tableaux. Taplin argues that "extra action [in a tragic performance] would either have to take place in a dumb show or it would have to be going on while the words were being spoken. . . . Both these alternatives are . . . sufficiently objectionable to leave us still with a fair working hypothesis that there was no important action that was not also signalled in the words" (29–30). Furthermore, he maintains that "if actions are to be significant, which means they must be given concentrated attention, then time and words must be spent on them.[11] . . . [We] can hardly allow any importance to actions which are not even referred to in the words" (31). Despite this pioneering work's contribution to the study of Greek tragedy's performance, Taplin's hypothesis that "there was no important action that was not signaled in the words" has afforded him criticism from both textual critics and performance historians alike.

On the one hand, Taplin has had to defend himself against philologists who have suggested that his study dismisses words because of its focus on performance: "I am not happy that my name is cited as a 'ringleader' of those who maintain that we should concentrate on performance *rather than words*."[12] On the other hand, performance scholars have criticized Taplin's emphasis on the words, especially his so-called dumb-show theory, referred to by Douglas Cairns as "Taplin's law,"[13] which claims that "all, or at least most, stage actions of significance can be worked out from what we have [i.e., the texts]."[14] Graham Ley has contended with *Stagecraft*'s anachronistic application of terminology such as entrances and exits onto the playing space,[15] and David Wiles has presented a challenge to what he calls Taplin's Aristotelian view that argues for the closed system of Greek tragedy and an immutable authorial meaning behind the play.[16] At the same time, some scholars, such as David Bain, have supported Taplin's claims that the text can indicate gestures and movement. Bain argues that if the gestures did not follow the words, then dramatists would have had more freedom in composing: "they would be able to describe themselves as undertaking actions that were well-nigh impossible to stage or in some cases contrary to the laws of nature [presumably like Seneca]."[17] For this reason, according to Bain, "the tragedians would have composed rather differently if they were under no obligation to make their characters' actions square with their words."[18] As scholars of ancient performance continue to refine their methodologies and approaches, Taplin's pioneering study of the performance aspects of the dramatic texts will surely continue to receive both criticism and praise.

Stagecraft clearly deserves praise for its demonstration of the rich information embedded in the text about performance, but criticism still surfaces because the study cannot surmount the fundamental problem of the distinction between the character's representation on the page and the performer's enactment on the stage. Instead, character and performer collapse into a single identity. Taplin assumes that the words of characters in the text serve as a blueprint or diagram for the ways in which the performers moved, even though the historical performers of an ancient play may not have necessarily followed this plan. This basic problem of character versus actor, text versus performance, underlies all studies of ancient Greek plays, for the communication codes of the text are not the same as the semiotic codes of a performance and the phenomenological codes of the actors. Even if Taplin is correct that "there was no important action that was not signalled in the words," the performance context of a historical theatrical event would influence the delivery, the reception, and the significance of those words in ways that are especially difficult for the performance historian to determine.

Reading Literary Sources in Relation to Visual Material on Gesture

Shifting the focus away from the text alone, Taplin, together with Richard Green, has been one of the leading scholars in relating the study of dramatic texts to a study of drama-related iconography. In this section, I limit my discussion to Green's "Towards a Reconstruction of Performance Style," which I have already summarized and described in chapter 4, because I want to consider in particular one of the methods that Green employs: reading literary sources in relation to the visual material on gesture. In one section of Green's article, he examines depictions of gestures in terms of the ancient Greek concept of *sōphrosynē*, which he defines as self-restraint.[19] To illustrate this point, he provides an example from Plato's *Republic* (ca. 370 BCE), which associates reserved, restrained (*sōphrōn*) movement with the elite, upper-class members of society. Green states that "when, at the beginning of the *Republic*, Polemarchus sends his slave to catch Socrates and Glaucon whom he sees walking ahead of him back to Athens, we may suppose he does so not merely as a matter of convenience, but because a gentleman could not be seen to run or even hurry (Plato, *Rep.* 1.327b2.5-5)" (105–6). With this reference to Plato's characterization of movement, Green posits that *sōphrosynē* implied a behavioral restraint that applied to gesture: "'Proper' Greeks and the gods they created show calm and control even in the most adverse situations, whereas aliens, the outsiders of society, exhibit their emotions" (99). He thus argues that elite, upper-class gentlemen practiced or were expected to practice such calm and self-posessed (*sōphrōn*) movement.

He then applies this theory of *sōphrōn* movement in his descriptions of the gestures depicted on the early fourth-century southern Italian Tarentine[20] Chorēgos Vase (figure 9), for the vase's date (ca. 399–370 BCE) corresponds well with that of the *Republic* (ca. 370 BCE). On this vase, the name Aegisthus has been painted above the tragic actor on the left of the vase, the slave's name Pyrrhias appears over the comic character standing on an upturned basket, and the name *chorēgos* (a wealthy upper-class gentleman who financed the chorus) identifies the other two comic figures. Green studies the postures of the vase's four characters with the keenness of a socialite in training, recognizing that rounded shoulders, weighted legs, and turns of the head all have serious implications.

> Both the *chorēgoi* are respectably dressed, and although there is a contrast between the younger and the older, they are both mature figures, leaning on their staffs with slightly rounded shoulders. The older one addresses the tragic paradigm, Aegisthus (as he seems to be in this case), with a confidence which is signified by his relaxed pose, weight on one leg, whereas his counterpart on the right of the scene is given a turn of the head and a balance on his feet that might enable him to move quickly. The slave Pyrrhias standing on the up-turned basket is less confined in the way he carries himself, making a quasi-authoritative gesture with his right hand and indicating a certain force of character with his left. The improbability of his role as stand-in archon is emphasized by the elaborate detail of his slave-garment the *exōmis*. (111–12)

Describing the four figures on the vase in terms of their tragic or comic attributes, Green studies their gestures in relation to *Republic*'s description of *sōphrōn*, elite movement in order to suggest that the conventions of upper-class dress reinforced the characteristic restraint of upper-class movement. For example, the left hand bound in a *hīmation*, such as the two *chorēgoi* demonstrate, reinforced the mark of elite comportment, because, as Green explains, "the *hīmation*, which was the regular outdoor wear for mature 'free' males in the fifth century, was heavy and enveloping, and certainly did not encourage free or violent movement" (106). He further argues that even though the conventions of comedy depicted on the vase distort the *chorēgoi*'s overall appearance, the men still demonstrate their social status by wrapping up the left hand according to customs of upper-class dress. Accordingly, Green connects the gestures represented on vases to a larger, class-inflected social context of gesture, identified in Plato's work.

Although his detailed and specific descriptions help to develop a comprehensive taxonomy of gesture, several problematic issues surface in Green's method. For one, his definition of *sōphrosynē*, upon which his argument in part depends, seems narrow. As Helen North and Adrian Rademaker have demonstrated, the word carried a wide range of possible, often quite distinct meanings. Plato's use of the term is by no means representative of its meaning in all of Greek literature, or of its use in the late fifth- to early fourth-century vernacular.[21] Euripides, for example, investigates the meanings of this term in his tragedies, particularly in his *Hippolytus* and *Bacchae*. In these tragedies, the characters Hippolytus and Pentheus both think they are *sōphrōn*, but their denial of the gods Aphrodite and Dionysus respectively prevent them from possessing the quality. Euripides's cultural and class biases inevitably influenced his exploration of the term *sōphrosynē*, just as Plato's biases influenced his association of the term with certain styles of movement.[22] Despite these points, Green does not have the space in his short essay to address the implications of the nuance of *sōphrosynē* for his theory of the term's relationship to gesture.

In addition to this problem, Green's use of the visual evidence also shares some of the common problems, previously discussed in chapters 3 and 5. Questions about representation, patronage, style, and anachronism all arise. How much can still images indicate the function of movement in everyday life or within a dynamic performance? How did the interests of patrons and their social status influence the subject and style of a vase? In the task of interpretation, do certain gestures, such as the hiding of the left hand,[23] become overly significant to the critic analyzing them? Moreover, Patrice Pavis has discussed the problem of the misrepresentation and mistranslation of gesture in relation to studies of theatrical gesture in his article "Problems of a Semiology of Theatrical Gesture." He argues that "once gesture becomes the object of a descriptive discourse, it loses all specificity; reduced to the level of a text, it does not give any account of its volume, of its signifying force, of its place in the global stage message. It becomes like any other kind of text, where the gesturality has lost all of its own qualities" (65). Aware of such complications, Green arms his argument with both vivid and subtle disclaimers,[24] such as "we *should expect* [italics mine] that on stage the figures of serious drama also looked 'proper'" (99), but the gap between what we should expect and what actually comes to pass will continue to present problems for the study of ancient gesture. We should expect that theatrical practice followed the depictions represented in literature and iconography, but expectations can be wrong. We cannot definitively determine the real behind the ideal, the historical gesture behind its representation.

Cross-Cultural Analogies

While Green concentrates on ancient Greek sources alone, Llewellyn-Jones has taken a cross-cultural comparative approach to gesture.[25] He looks for parallels between the representation of gestures on Athenian vases and the practice of gesture in the theatrical tradition of Japanese Kabuki. He begins by magnifying the similarities between images of Athenian cross-dressed actors, such as the actor on the left in figure 14,[26] and representations of the cross-dressed *onnagata*. Some of these similarities include: (1) the *schēmata* (figures, patterns, poses) of Athenian drama and the *mie* ("a non-realistic, sculpturesque, dance-like pose taken by one or more actors at a climactic moment in a play, designed to make a powerful impression"[27]); (2) the Athenian *peplos* and *chitōn* and the Japanese kimono; (3) the modest expressions of the female characters including closed body poses, sloping shoulders, the lifting of fabric, etc.; and (4) the similarities in the visual depiction of poses which "offers proof that a conventionalized, and very unnatural, 'female' posture was utilized on the stage" (87). Perhaps inspired by modern productions, such as Ariane Mnouchkine's *Les Atrides* (1990–1993), which have syncretized Greek drama with Eastern theatrical practices, Llewellyn-Jones attempts to distance ancient Greek theatre from its association with the traditions of modern western theatre. However, while trying to separate the Athenian-western connection, Llewellyn-Jones also admits that the Athenian-eastern connection does not exactly match well either. While he asserts that the tone and dramatic impetus of Noh, Kabuki, and Greek theatre are similar, at the same time, he also states that "there are as many differences between *Noh, Kabuki,* and Greek theatre as there are similarities" (75). These distinctions, which Llewellyn-Jones does not explain further, are the leaks that spring while he is busy plugging other holes.

The advantage of cross-cultural approaches rests in discarding the western paradigm in order to defamiliarize Athenian theatre practices, but a comparison with the East may be a false one. For instance, the Athenian actor's S-bend stance, closed posture, and lowered head on the Heidelberg bell krater (figure 14) may seem to correspond with the Japanese *onnagata's* poses, but vases are not photographs and may not represent specific or stock theatrical poses. More significantly, Llewellyn-Jones does not have the opportunity in his short article to address the problems with using a late fourth-century vase to generalize about an unspecified period of fifth-century theatre, nor can he explain the critical distinctions between comic and tragic gestures, even though the bell krater depicts a comic actor (not a tragic one) and dates to ca. 385 BCE, about twenty years after the death of Euripides.

Some larger questions about his approach arise as well. For example, might a comparison to Kabuki gestures, which developed under social and political circumstances radically different from those of ancient Athens, obscure the unique qualities of both distinctive traditions? Is eastern theatre similar to Athenian theatre, or does the "other" simply become a tool to defamiliarize and de-westernize Athenian theatre? Graham Ley has described such comparisons as providing "a shock to our perceptions if we do not come from those cultures or are unfamiliar with the forms."[28] But is such a shock defamiliarization or exoticization? Does East-West comparative drama risk an orientalism that undermines both traditions? While the use of the conventions of Asian theatre in contemporary productions, such as Ninagawa's *Medea* (1992–1998), may inspire new perspectives on the ancient plays, does the westerner's satisfaction in viewing these revisions risk an orientalism inherent in viewing one's cultural habits played back by the foreign "other"?[29] At the same time, as Taplin has suggested, perhaps to lay "exclusive stress on the *differences* is no less of a distortion than to assume unqualified similarity."[30] Cross-cultural approaches have clear advantages, but a comparison of ancient apples to Asian oranges may run the unavoidable risk of simply replacing a western model with perhaps an equally flawed eastern one. Perhaps developing a performance vocabulary specific to fifth-century theatre may be the best means to avoid the risk of exoticization and generalization that comparative studies may risk.

Reconstructing Ancient Mask from Modern Practice

One crucial component of this Athenian performance vocabulary of theatrical gesture is the mask, which influenced the gestures of the actors and their movements. Like gesture, we have images of masks but no actual artifacts. Side A of the Pronomos Vase (figures 1 and 2) offers excellent representations of fifth-century masks, which were distinct from the later fourth-century masks with which they can be confused. Based upon such images, most scholars dismiss the once popular theory that the fifth-century masks served as a megaphone of sorts and agree that they were whole-headed with hair attached and probably made of linen, yet disagreement does exist over the mask's ritual or aesthetic function.

Two recent studies[31] that have made significant contributions to the study of theatrical mask are David Wiles's (2007) *Mask and Performance* and Peter Meineck's (2011) article "The Neuroscience of the Tragic Mask."[32] The experience of these scholars as theatre practitioners has informed both of their reconstructions of the fifth-century mask, but their methodological approaches are distinct. Wiles draws on anthropological theory and emphasizes the ritual function of the mask, and Meineck employs studies from neuroscience to examine the function of the tragic mask in performance.

Arguing that the political aims of the Athenian theatre cannot be separated from its religious aims, Wiles considers the mask not as "an *object* manipulated by humans but as an *agent* engaged in a set of transactions" (5). Informed by his practical experience and anthropological studies of the cross-cultural uses of masking, he draws examples from sources such as *Bacchae*, Plato's *Ion* and *Laws*, Aristophanes's *Women at the Thesmophoria*, and the Pronomos Vase (figures 1, 2, and 3), to argue that "theatrical masks were Dionysiac masks, and the ritual theatre divide is a modern imposition" (229). His methodology consists of interpreting vase-painting in a way that concentrates "on the function of the vase as a whole" (5), and this approach contrasts with that of viewing "representations of masks as more or less imperfect renderings of a 'real' artifact" (5). His "second methodological ploy is to draw on the evidence of twentieth-century practice" (6). Informed by his practice-based research, Wiles aims to demonstrate not "what *must* have been done in antiquity" but rather "what potentially *can* be done with a mask, and what masks *can* do to us" (7). He shows that the mask has been thought to possess twentieth-century actors in various traditions, and he aims to explain fifth-century masks in terms of these ritual functions as opposed to purely aesthetic ones (225). Contrary to previous studies on the mask, he argues that "the primary function of the tragic mask is not to seal and fix a character type, but to transform a wearer, and to take power over an audience within the context of a culture where the aesthetic domain did not separate itself off from the religious" (225). In this way, Wiles aims to explore not why the Greeks wore masks but why it is "necessary for us *not* to wear masks in *our* theatre" (2).

Whereas Wiles emphasizes the cultural and religious meaning of the mask, Meineck focuses on the operation of the mask from the perspective of spectators. He couples his practical understanding of the function of masks in performance with the methodological tool of cognitive studies. From this point of view, he proposes that the "tragic mask mediated a bi-modal ocular experience that oscillated between foveal (focused) and peripheral vision, and in the eyes of the spectators seemed to possess the ability to change emotions, and that these qualities of the mask were fundamental to the performance of tragedy and the development of narrative drama."[33] He chooses as one of his examples the Watchman's scene from the opening of Aeschylus's *Agamemnon* to demonstrate the ways in which the mask worked in conjunction with the text. Wary that his reading of the passage is "highly interpretive" (142), Meineck explains that his discussion of these lines is not for the purpose of presenting an interpretation of the Watchman's emotions. Rather he aims to illustrate, through Paul Ekman's categories of "basic emotions,"[34] the type of theatrical choices that the text presents to any director, Aeschylus included. In the process, he suggests that, in a period of thirty-nine lines, the Watchman displays "nineteen marked emotional shifts and thirteen distinct emotional states" (142). He then asks how a single mask could express so many emotions. Breaking with the scholarly consensus, Meineck proposes in response that the tragic mask was not "neutral" in its appearance. Instead, the ambiguity of the mask provoked "a highly personal response in the mind of each individual spectator" (150–51).

To support this point, he draws on research in neuroscience such as the Kuleshov experiment, an experiment recently reproduced by researchers at the University College London,[35] and he demonstrates through illustrations the ways in which "low- and high-spatial frequency neural processing" (124–25) can trick the eye to imagine the facial features of a changing mask just like the Mona Lisa smile. Based on his interpretation of this study, Meineck concludes that "a close examination of the iconographic evidence from the fifth century, the application of cognitive studies and recent neuroscientific research and the results of performance-based experiments, should lay to rest the notion that the Greek tragic mask displayed a fixed, neutral, idealized, or unchanging expression" (150). This cognitive studies approach thus raises awareness about the possible inadequacy of present terminology and aims to revise the tendency to describe the mask as neutral as opposed to multifaceted.

In this way, Wiles and Meineck draw on the texts for information but also imagine the ways in which fifth-century performance practices signify in conjunction with the words of the text and endow those words with meaning. In the process, they explain not only the mask but also its relationship to Athenian theatre and culture. Wiles interprets the theatrical mask in terms of Athenian culture and religion, and Meineck draws on neuroscience experiments to demonstrate that the audience's visual and emotional experience of ancient drama is focused on the mask. However, the very practice-based insights that distinguish these studies also present interpretive problems.

One is the issue of anachronism. Wiles asks not "what *must* have been done in antiquity" but rather "what potentially *can* be done with a mask, and what masks *can* do to us" (7). However, what can potentially be done or is done with a mask today is contingent upon culturally conditioned contemporary experiences and aesthetic tastes, a point which Wiles understands, while he still stresses that "even the most determined cultural relativist must accede to certain biological universals" (7). Because the same aesthetic and practice may not have applied to the fifth-century Greeks,[36] a cross-cultural, cross-temporal study of masks could mislead scholars about the practices of ancient masking. The kinesthetic sensibility of contemporary artists is certainly useful evidence, but historiographical questions inevitably arise in this practice.

Meineck's study too raises questions. His interdisciplinary strategy of cognitive studies is an emerging methodology in theatre, dance, and performance studies that opens up important questions about performance and the mask, yet some scholars are critical of its effectiveness. Because neuroscience is growing at a rapid rate, many debates exist, and new theories quickly become old theories. For example, current studies in neuroscience have revised previous views on the once popular theory of mirror neurons, to which many cognitive studies of theatre still refer. This point raises the question of the degree to which scholars in the humanities have the necessary access and training to stay abreast of the rapid developments in neuroscience and to interpret current debates correctly. If scientists are themselves at odds over some of the mechanisms of neural processing, then could performance studies be too quickly adopting these emerging, uncertain, and quickly changing ideas? Caution is prudent, but of course no methodology is without risk. Even if Wiles's and Meineck's strategies prove to have flaws, they nevertheless chart new territory and function successfully to expose the flaws in other methodologies and studies of the mask.

Comic and Ritual Gestures in the Dressing-up Scene

While Dionysus directs his victim in how to imitate a woman, Pentheus's head goes lop-sided (933). His curl slips out from under his *mitra* (928–29). His girdle comes loose (935–36), his pleats hang crooked, and his thyrsus simply eludes him (941–42). These textual clues about theatrical gesture are coupled with another such critical clue, the breaks in distichomythia (two line by two line dialogue) in lines 927–29 (when Dionysus comments on Pentheus's messy coiffure) and 934 (when Pentheus tells Dionysus to adjust his costume). These two breaks suggest pauses for gestural stage-play.[37] Based on them, Pentheus may gesture at this point, but is the possibility of a gesture enough? The text offers good clues, but the debate over "Taplin's law" warns that assumptions about the degree of correspondence between performance and text depend in part on conjecture.

Because the study of one text alone can be unreliable, historians of theatrical gesture can also take an intertextual approach and compare the gestures in one play to those in another. Several gestures in *Bacchae*, for example, echo those in Aristophanes's comedy *Women at the Thesmophoria*,[38] performed in 411 BCE, six years prior.[39] Pentheus's women's clothes (*gynaikomimōi stolai*, 980, also *thēlyn stolēn*, 828, 836, 852, and *thēlygenē stolan*, 1156) recall those in *Women at the Thesmophoria* (*stolēn gynaikos*, 93 and *gynaikeia stolē*, 851), and Mnesilochos, like Pentheus (925), asks how his outfit looks (261). *Women at the Thesmophoria*'s recognition scene between Euripides and Mnesilochos, which is a parody of Menelaus's rescue of Helen in Euripides's *Helen* (1032ff.), may find a perverted super-parody in Agaue and Pentheus's aborted recognition (1115ff.) just before she attacks her son, who she thinks is a lion. Like the Kinsman, who after the guard catches him for spying wants to strip off his clothes and *mitra* (feminine headgear) so as not to be mocked by the crows that will eat his body, so Pentheus also removes his *mitra* (1115–16) when he appeals to his mother for his life. This movement precedes his appeal and signifies his return to sanity. Furthermore, as Euripides refers to a Gorgon's head in his hands toward the end of the comedy, likewise Agaue holds Pentheus's head in hers, and the image of Medusa's head in the hands of Perseus visually parallels the head of Pentheus in the hands of his mother. These various intertextual references to gesture are especially significant, because as I have discussed in chapter 5, the costumes and gestures of comedy and tragedy tend to be distinct,[40] but generic overlap between the conventions of comedy and tragedy can, as here, also be exploited. This apparent exploitation of generic overlap in *Bacchae* may suggest the comic potential of Pentheus's gestures, a point that I discuss later in relation to Bernd Seidensticker's article "Comic Elements in Euripides' *Bacchae*."

The gestures of Pentheus can also be compared to those signified in other tragedies. His deluded query, about whether he could carry mountains on his shoulders or tear them up with crowbars (945–50), corresponds with maddened, grandiose ideas[41] such as those of Heracles, who desires to overturn the Cyclopian structures. Tragedy associates madness with a stinging (*oistros*) or goading (*kentron*) that has physical consequences and results in perverse postures, such as those of Heracles, who tosses his head and rolls his eyes in Euripides's *Heracles* (867ff.), or Agaue, who rolls her eyes and foams at the mouth (1122–24) in *Bacchae*. Tragic madness manifests itself as an assaulted body that in turn assaults other bodies. Thus, Pentheus's outrageous, megalomanic ambitions provide an additional clue to the style of his gestures. If he is thinking big, he could be gesturing big as well. A virtuosic actor could walk the eerie line between tragedy and comedy, playing the character at once comic and mad, but did he? Despite these intertextual comparisons, the literary sources still do not provide certain evidence for the characteristics of the actor's gestures in the 405 BCE performance.

In the search for further clues about the performance of Pentheus's gestures, Richard Green's technique of comparing the literary evidence to the visual is also useful.[42] Like Green, one may first identify certain patterns that appear in representations of theatrical gestures in fifth-century and early fourth-century iconography, such as the awkward, asymmetrical, alinear figures (*schēmata*) characteristic of comic gestures in fifth- and early fourth-century vase-painting (figures 9, 12, 13, and 14), and the proportional gestures characteristic of tragedy with their graceful lines (figures 6, 9, 10, and 11).[43] If the proportion of gesture is the key to distinguishing between comic and tragic characters on vases, then could proportion also be a clue to understanding the significance of Pentheus's gestures in the dressing-up scene? With the distinctions between comic and tragic representations in mind, Pentheus's gestures may be studied in relation to them. Did the actor playing Pentheus in the dressing-up scene stand like Aegisthus on the Chorēgos Vase, tall in his elegant costume and boots, softening his posture by standing with his feet slightly apart and one knee slightly bent, relaxing his left shoulder, which the sharp descending line of his shoulder demonstrates?[44] Or did the actor stand more like the comic characters, who appear to have both knees slightly bent with rounded shoulders that rise up or stay on an even plane with their collarbone, an effect that gives them a hunched look?

Even if Pentheus's stance did not fit clearly into either of those two categories, perhaps a relative comparison could be made. Could, for example, the representation of the gestures of the comic characters and the tragic Aegisthus on the Chorēgos Vase (figure 9) in some way parallel the relationship between the gestures of Pentheus and those of Dionysus in the 405 BCE performance of *Bacchae*? How might the stance of the actor playing Pentheus have looked in relation to the stance of Dionysus? Proportionate, or disproportionate? If disproportionate, the gestures still need not be comic, for in tragedy, disproportionate, awkward gestures could be a reference to comedy, but are frequently a characteristic of madness. To be mad is to be *aphrōn*, an imbalance of the insides that has physical manifestations. *Aphrōn* is the antithesis of *sōphrōn*. If Pentheus is mad and his gestures *aphrōn*, then they were likely performed in some way that was disproportionate. However, the individual audience member's interpretation of the either proportionate or disproportionate gestures of Pentheus is critical. Was Pentheus's disproportionate comportment comic, mad, both, or something else?

Several scholars, such as Dodds, Seaford, and Seidensticker, have debated over the significance of Pentheus's gestures. Although the textual examples of gestures and movements in the dressing-up scene may or may not have appeared in the 405 BCE performance, these scholars, like many, have assumed that these actions did in fact occur and have debated over the connotations of the gestures of Pentheus. E. R. Dodds and Richard Seaford have considered the gestures to be representative of Dionysiac ritual, while

Bernd Seidensticker has argued that the gestures have associations with the conventions of Attic comedy.[45]

Although Dodds and Seaford provide no fifth-century sources that indicate the importance of girdling and pleats in Dionysiac ceremonies, both assume from this scene as well as some references in anachronistic sources[46] that girdling and pleating have ritual connotations associated with Dionysus. Dodds has stated: "It was a ritual requirement that the linen *chitōn* of the *mystēs* should be girt in such a manner as to hang in pleats."[47] More recently, Richard Seaford has followed this argument's trajectory, noting: "Like the attention to P.'s [Pentheus's] hair, this attention to his belt and dress is curious given the vigorous movement performed by maenads. Probably it reflects the importance of girdling in the mysteries."[48] Both commentators have trouble reconciling their theories with Dionysus's instructions to Pentheus to lift his thyrsus with his right hand in time with his right foot (943–44), for they recognize that a maenad (on vase-paintings) can carry her thyrsus in either hand.[49] Despite this challenge to their assumptions, through a circular style of reasoning, the scene becomes both evidence for the gestures of ritual practice and an example of that ritual practice. While connotations of ritual are surely possible, the scene's gestural stage-play may have also had comic potential.

Because critics began to question the formerly predominant view of the scene as comic, Bernd Seidensticker used this shift as an opportunity to revisit the issue.[50] He has acknowledged the difficulty of determining the scene's tone, for "the classicist faces special problems. We have almost no stage directions ([such as] 'Harry laughs wildly') and we know too little about the techniques and conventions of staging in the fifth century in general and nothing about the production of the *Bacchae* in particular" (306). But the main problem, he notes, "is, of course, the serious limitation of comparative material (both from comedy and from tragedy)" (306n19). Sticking to the literary evidence, Seidensticker argues that "there is no need to deny the comic tone merely in order to salvage the tragic atmosphere and meaning of the two scenes" (319). To build this point, he takes a comparative approach and references examples of comedy in later drama such as *Macbeth*, which he has discussed in detail, and Ibsen's *Wild Duck*. He realizes that objective proof is often not possible, but he states that a critical interpretation can show: "a) that the comic reading which it advocates does justice to the linguistic and dramatic evidence of the scene, and b) that it makes better functional sense than other interpretations for the meaning of the entire play" (306–7).[51] Comedy makes better functional sense, he argues, for the "fundamental double nature of the god and his cult which—apart from the special functions of the comic elements in their special contexts—provides the basic reason for the importance of the tragicomic technique in the *Bacchae*" (320). At the same time as he makes these assertions, Seidensticker also carefully hedges his claims: "While it is impossible to prove that this is how Euripides intended the scene to be staged [i.e., with comic overtones], the other evidence under discussion supports the hypothesis that a comic effect is indeed what the dramatist had in mind" (313). Thus, although Seidensticker references the play's performance, his interpretation has aimed to determine not the performance itself but rather Euripides's intentions for the tone of the dressing-up scene. He states that he cannot prove that Euripides "intended the scene to be staged" with comic overtones, and this focus on the author's intention for a text's performance on a stage is not the same as a consideration of the ways in which a multidimensional historical performance functioned in theatrical space as an independent entity apart from the text.

David Wiles's *Mask and Performance in Greek Tragedy* does consider the text's position in relation to a multidimensional performance. As Wiles has argued in his *Tragedy in Athens*, his interest rests in the dimension of space not time.[52] In that work, he defines his search as a critic as one not "for an authorial meaning existing somewhere within, behind, or prior to the text, but rather for an event set in space and time, and for a process or system of communication" (8). In *Mask and Performance* as well, Wiles considers performance practices in order to contend with the traditional assumption that the mask of Dionysus in *Bacchae* is "smiling." Helene P. Foley via Dodds and Winnington-Ingram[53] based this interpretation of a smiling mask upon lines 439 and 1021 of the text. In 439, the first messenger refers to Dionysus as *gelōn* (from the verb to laugh), and in line 1021, which occurs in the fourth stasimon between the dressing-up scene and the second messenger speech, the chorus calls for Bacchus, the wild beast with the *gelōn* mask or face (*prosōpon*), to come and cast the net of death about Pentheus. Wiles argues that these instances of *gelōn* indicate laughing and should not be confused with smiling.[54] Moreover, he suggests that the idea of a smiling mask would have been impractical in terms of performance, although he does not make clear exactly why.

However, despite Wiles's assertions, Foley presumably had in mind not a comic smiling mask for Dionysus but one with the archaic (or slightly upturned) smile that frequently appears in artistic representations of Dionysus and that would not necessarily seal or fix a character type. But Wiles makes no reference to this archaic smile, even though the ancient *didaskalos* and audience would have clearly been familiar with it. Exactly why an archaic smiling mask would not work in performance, Wiles does not say, but perhaps, as per Meineck's study, Dionysus's mask did not need to be constructed with a smile at all for the mask to elicit a smile. Although Wiles's argument may not have resolved all of the questions surrounding Dionysus's enigmatic face, his approach nevertheless demonstrates that a consideration of the god's visage should take into account not only the words of the text but also the mask's operation in terms of a historic performance set in space and time.

Because the extant manuscripts of fifth-century drama are, as it were, both empty casts of an absent historical performance and tangible remnants of that performance, many types of methodological approaches are important to the historical task of interpreting fifth-century drama and its performance. Viewing the artifacts with all their inherent complications from a wide variety of perspectives allows scholarship on fifth-century theatre to inch slowly toward historical understanding as "new vistas, new angles of vision, constantly appear as the procession — and the historian with it — moves along."[55] The knowledge discovered in the process may not be absolute, but it is still worth the struggle.[56]

NOTES

Introduction

1. Euripides's *Bacchae* dramatizes the conflict between the god of wine, mask, and theatre, Dionysus, and the ruler of Thebes, Pentheus. Dionysus, disguised in mortal form as a priest of his cult, arrives in Thebes from the East with a devout band of his sincere female worshippers, maenads or bacchae. Because the city has denied Dionysus's divinity, he punishes its women with a madness that leads them to a perverse interpretation of his rites on Mt. Cithaeron until he can persuade Thebes and especially Pentheus to respect him. Nevertheless, the stubborn, young Pentheus refuses to acknowledge the stranger/foreigner as a god, so Dionysus convinces him to dress up like a maenad to spy on the women. The god then deludes Pentheus's mother, Agaue, into believing her son is a lion, and Agaue, her sisters, and the rest of the Theban maenads brutally murder him on the mountain, affixing his head to a stake. The play ends with Dionysus's pronouncement of his punishment for Agaue and Cadmus.

2. Phillip B. Zarrilli, Bruce McConachie, Gary Jay Williams, and Carol Fisher Sorgenfrei, *Theatre Histories*, 64.

3. The Fasti together with the *Didascaliae* and List of Victors provide fragmentary records of the City Dionysia or Great Dionysia and Lenaia festivals from approximately the early fifth century BCE through the mid-second century BCE. The Fasti list, for example, the names of the victorious tribes in the men's and boys' dithyrambic competitions, *chorēgos* (producer), and *didaskalos* (composer-director), who would sometimes, but not always, be the poet and an actor. For the records, see Pickard-Cambridge, *The Dramatic Festivals of Athens*, 101–25. See also Benjamin W. Millis and S. Douglas Olson, *Inscriptional Records for the Dramatic Festivals in Athens*.

4. Oliver Taplin, "Greek Theatre," 19–20.

5. As I discuss more specifically in chapter 2, classicists such as Helene P. Foley (*Female Acts in Greek Tragedy*) and Jeffrey Henderson ("Women and the Athenian Dramatic Festivals") are of the opinion that at least some women were present, whereas scholars such as Simon Goldhill ("Representing Democracy") have suggested the contrary.

6. Etymologically the word means "the writing of history." For a discussion of various aspects of historiography (descriptive, historical, and analytical or critical), see Michael Stanford, *A Companion to the Study of History*, 5–7. For further reading and references on theatre historiography, see Thomas Postlewait, *The Cambridge Introduction to Theatre Historiography*, which, on pages 1–5, discusses various possible meanings of history and historiography. See also Thomas Postlewait and Bruce A. McConachie, eds., *Interpreting the Theatrical Past*; Charlotte M. Canning and Thomas Postlewait, eds., *Representing the Past*; Bruce McConachie, "Doing Things with Image Schemas"; and Tracy C. Davis, "Between History and Event." For further reading on historiography in general, see Marc Bloch, *The Historian's Craft*; David Carr, *Time, Narrative, and History*; E. H. Carr, *What Is History?*; Michel de Certeau, *The Writing of History*; R. G. Collingwood, *The Idea of History*; Keith Jenkins, ed., *The Postmodern History Reader*; C. Behan McCullagh, *The Truth of History*; Michael Stanford, *The Nature of Historical Knowledge* and *A Companion to the Study of History*; and Hayden White, *Figural Realism* and *Tropics of Discourse*. On the history of classical scholarship, see Sir John Edwin Sandys, *A History of Classical Scholarship*; Arnaldo Momigliano, *The Classical Foundations of Modern Historiography* and *Essays in Ancient and Modern Historiography*; Rudolf Pfeiffer, *The History of Classical Scholarship* and *The History of Classical Scholarship from 1300 to 1850*; and Leighton D. Reynolds and Nigel G. Wilson, *Scribes and Scholars*.

7. The work has been revised by John Gould and D. M. Lewis.

8. While this standard reference work needs updating, *The Context of Ancient Drama* still provides a valuable summary of the available sources.

9. The comedy stages a debate (*agōn*) between "Aeschylus" and "Euripides," comic characters who are parodies of the historical tragedians. Despite this scene's use of comic exaggeration, it often serves as a historical source on tragedy's performance.

10. This vase, as discussed in chapter 5, offers more visual evidence about performance conditions than any other extant vase and is the basis for many theories about costume and mask.

11. *Bacchae*'s dramaturgy does not appear to be typical, but its atypical features are significant. They suggest that whatever scholars learn about the general modes of performance, they still must take into consideration how individual plays operated within those general modes.

12. While I aim to focus on those sources which date as closely to 405 BCE as

possible, I am not averse to any considerations of anachronistic sources, for despite the inherent historiographical issues in their application (see chapter 2), later (and earlier) sources can be useful depending on a scholar's specific approach and ability to evaluate them comprehensively within the larger context of evidence.

13. A number of sources, such as Pausanias, Diodorus Siculus, and Hermesianax place Euripides's death in Macedonia. While the popular tradition has accepted this story, some scholars doubt the validity of the testimonia, even though few doubt that Euripides visited Macedonia. Other scholars have speculated that Euripides not only composed the play for a performance in Macedonia but also staged its first performance there, for Macedonia was a region with interest in Dionysian myth and cult.

14. Despite this uncertainty, Jennifer Wise has argued in *Dionysus Writes* that the innovations of writing and literacy significantly influenced the development of drama.

15. Editions of *Bacchae*, such those of Robert Y. Tyrrell, E. R. Dodds, Jeanne Roux, and Richard Seaford, present a version of the ancient Greek text compiled from these sources as well as a line-by-line commentary, which often explains issues such as discrepancies among copies, uncertainties about the attribution of lines, and conjectures about lacunae in the text. For example, as discussed in chapter 3, *Bacchae* has a significant lacuna that occurs in Agaue's speech at line 1329.

16. Because the Loeb Classical Library also includes an English translation next to the ancient languages, I have in most cases, whenever was possible, used the most recent editions of the Loebs in referencing various other ancient texts.

17. For a discussion of the ways in which viewing modern performances of ancient plays influences scholars' views of a play's performance potential, see David Wiles, "Greek and Shakespearean Plays and Their Performance."

18. For a discussion of this term, see Sauter, *The Theatrical Event*, especially pages 2–9.

Chapter 1. Theatrical Space

1. On space in theatre, see Anne Ubersfeld's seminal semiotic work *Lire le théâtre*, the translation of which is *Reading Theatre*. (Note that David Wiles has suggested that Ubersfeld's distinction between "theatrical space" [Ubersfeld's term for the theatrical building] and "scenic space" [Ubersfeld's term for the acting area] cannot apply to the Athenian theatre, because the role of chorus prevents the separation of "scenic space" from "dramatic space" [Wiles, *Tragedy in Athens*, 16–17].) On mimetic versus diegetic space, see Michael Issacharoff, "Space and Reference in Drama." In his *Discourse as Performance* (56) Issacharoff divides space into three categories: theatre space (architectural design), stage space (stage and set design), and dramatic space (space as used by a particular dramatist, i.e., space created by discourse). Dramatic space (58) is subdivided into diegetic space (de-

scribed space that is referred to in dialogue) and mimetic space (space represented on stage and made visible). For further reading on other types of space in the theatre, see Marvin Carlson, "Space and Theatre History," and Gay McCauley, *Space in Performance*. McCauley navigates this "terminological minefield," as he calls it, by outlining various ways of thinking about and with space, from Stanton B. Garner's *Bodied Spaces* and Una Chaudhuri's *Staging Place* to Ubersfeld's *Reading Theatre*. Regarding Garner and Chaudhuri, McCauley (9) explains that they have "explored the treatment of fictional place and its thematic resonance in the work of a number of modern playwrights, and while these studies do not engage overtly with performance practice, they do reveal the importance of the category of space in theatrical meaning making." For a materialist and phenomenological theory of space in terms of social space, see Henri Lefebvre's *The Production of Space*, which I will discuss later.

2. For a discussion of the *skēnē* and other aspects of the theatre's space, see appendix C of Oliver Taplin's *The Stagecraft of Aeschylus*. For further reading on the *skēnē*, see Peter D. Arnott, *Greek Scenic Conventions*; Richard Hammond, "Cries Within and the Tragic Skene"; and Nicolaos C. Hourmouziades, *Production and Imagination in Euripides*.

3. For further reading, see Donald Mastronarde, "Actors on High"; Clifford Ashby, *Classical Greek Theatre*, especially pages 248 and 68; and Rhys Townsend, "The Fourth-Century Skene."

4. Regarding the roof, see Mastronarde, "Actors on High," and Ashby, *Classical Greek Theatre*.

5. On whether the *skēnē* was painted, see A. L. Brown, "Three and Scene-painting Sophocles,'" and Ruth Padel, "Making Space Speak," 352–53. On scene painting, see Padel, "Making Space Speak," 354ff.; Taplin, *Stagecraft*, especially 437–39; and Wiles, *Tragedy in Athens*, 161.

6. On the *ekkyklēma*, see Arnott, *Greek Scenic Conventions*, 72–90; Ashby, *Classical Greek Theatre*, 90–92; Taplin, *Stagecraft*, 442–47; and Wiles, *Tragedy in Athens*, 162.

7. On the *mēchanē*, see Arnott, *Greek Scenic Conventions*, 72–90; Ashby, *Classical Greek Theatre*, 81–87; Mastronarde, "Actors on High," 247; Taplin, *Stagecraft*, 443–47; and Wiles, *Tragedy in Athens*, 181ff.

8. Many scholars have suggested a low stage made of wood. They base their arguments on practical reasons such as making the actors more conspicuous or marking off the actors from the chorus to creating better acoustics. See Wiles, *Tragedy in Athens*, 64–66, and Taplin, *Stagecraft*, 441, for an overview of scholarship on the subject. Erika Simon also cites "a low stage" in *The Ancient Theatre*, 7. See also Mastronarde, "Actors on High," 248.

9. On the altar and tomb, see Arnott, *Greek Scenic Conventions*, 57–71; Graham Ley, *The Theatricality of Greek Tragedy*, 203n82, and "Scenic Notes on Euripides'

Helen"; Rush Rehm, "The Staging of Suppliant Plays"; and Joe Park Poe, "The Altar in the Fifth-Century Theater." Poe suggests that tombs function as the equivalents of altars in the plays since they serve similar dramatic functions. See also Ashby, *Classical Greek Theatre*, 42–61; Rehm, *The Play of Space*, 41; and Wiles, *Tragedy in Athens*, 70–73.

10. I will later provide a more detailed discussion of the *orchēstra*'s shape, with further bibliographic references.

11. On the side entrances, see Taplin, *Stagecraft*, 449–51, and on the importance of the side entrances to the east/west axis, see Wiles, *Tragedy in Athens*, chapter 6.

12. On the bleacher seats, see Taplin, *Stagecraft*, 434ff.

13. Peter Meineck has most recently cited this current consensus in his "The Embodied Space," 3. The 30,000 seat figure is based on a comment in Plato's *Symposium* (175e). The revised figure can be assessed in relation to current views on the total Athenian population, which Roselli (*Theater of the People*, 13) cites at about 300,000 — 100,000 of which may have been slaves — and 40,000 metics (resident aliens). In chapter 2 I will further discuss audience size. Note that the stone theatre of today (figure 4) is the result of rebuilding.

14. Rehm explores a variety of Athenian tragedies through spatial categories such as theatrical space, scenic space, extrascenic space, distanced space, self-referential space, and reflexive space (several of these terms derive from Ubersfeld's work *Reading Theatre*) in order to determine various spatial patterns that appear as motifs in the dramas, such as: space for return, eremitic space, space and the body, space, time and memory, and space and the other (19–20).

15. I have chosen to discuss the debate from the perspective of two theatre historians/practitioners. For some recent discussions of the *orchēstra*'s shape from the perspective of classicists, see John Scott Scullion, *Three Studies in Athenian Dramaturgy*, chapter 1, which argues for a circular shape; Marcel Lysgaard Lech, "The Shape of the Athenian *Theatron*," which discusses an overlooked passage from Aristophanes's *Knights* that supports a claim for a rectangular or trapezoidal *theatron* constructed of wooden benches (*ikria*); Martin Revermann, "The Shape of the Athenian Orchestra," which argues that Heniochus fragment 5.6–8 K.-A contributes to the circular argument and challenges the "near-orthodoxy" of a rectangular *orchēstra* in the German academic community; and Martin L. West's "Heniochus and the Shape of the Athenian Orchestra," which in a brief paragraph refutes Revermann's argument by questioning his translation of *kyklios*. See also Jessica Paga, "Mapping Politics"; Eric Csapo, "The Men Who Built the Theatres"; and Hans R. Goette, "Archaeological Appendix" to Csapo's "The Men Who Built the Theatres."

16. Richard P. Martin, *The Language of Heroes*, 7. Edith Hall has cited this same passage in her "Lawcourt Dramas" to argue that the point is "equally pertinent to Athenian forensic oratory" (58).

17. Csapo and Slater, *The Context of Ancient Drama*, 79–80.

18. See Wiles, *Tragedy in Athens*, 23–62, and Ashby, *Classical Greek Theatre*, 24–41, for a more detailed survey of studies on the Theatre of Dionysus.

19. Wiles, *Tragedy in Athens*, 44. See Wilhelm Dörpfeld and Emil Reisch, *Das griechische theater.*

20. Wiles, *Tragedy in Athens*, 45.

21. Ibid., 45. See Ernst Fiechter, *Das Dionysos-Theater in Athen.*

22. Wiles, *Tragedy in Athens*, 45.

23. Ibid., 46. See Carlo Anti, *Teatri greci arcaici da Minosse a Pericle.*

24. Elizabeth Gebhard, "The Form of the Orchestra." See also Gebhard's *The Theater at Isthmia.* For other references on this subject, see Wiles, *Tragedy in Athens*, 46n80.

25. Luigi Polacco, *Il teatro di Dioniso Eleutereo ad Atene.*

26. Mastronarde, "Actors on High," 248.

27. Wiles, *Tragedy in Athens*, 51–52.

28. Ibid., 49. Wiles aims to persuade his readers that a rectangular shape would have been too small, in part based on "a photograph taken in 1899/1900 [that] depicts Austrian classicists dancing in a circle around the edge of the *orchēstra* at Epidauros to greet the new century, and 25 people seem to occupy half the circle. It is hard to see that a circular dance involving choreographed movement could be performed by 50 in a significantly smaller space" (49). While the ingenuity of the use of this photograph as evidence is persuasive in itself, Austrian classicists of that time would likely have been considerably larger, taller and wider, than your average fifth-century Athenian male whose armor looks sized to fit a 5'3" preadolescent boy rather than an average-sized 1900 Austrian.

29. Hans R. Goette, "Archaeological Appendix" to Eric Csapo's "The Men Who Built the Theatres." For further reading on this debate in classics, see the prior note in this chapter.

30. Rehm, *The Play of Space*, 37.

31. Although Wiles appears in Ashby's bibliography, Ashby does not discuss *Tragedy in Athens* in the body of his book, perhaps because of their close dates in publication. Wiles, however, in "Seeing Is Believing," an article I will discuss later, has recently addressed Ashby's views on Thorikos. For further reading on Ashby's views of the theatre's shape, see his article, "The Case for the Rectangular/Trapezoidal Orchestra," which he has expanded upon in *Classical Greek Theatre.*

32. E. H. Carr, *What Is History?*, 36.

33. Wiles, *Tragedy in Athens*, 86. Wiles compares his critical stance to that of Nicole Loraux in her *The Children of Athena*, a work that explores Athenian ideology in relation to the Acropolis and the Kerameikos (cemetery) and which Wiles calls a "classic piece of structuralism" that is at the same time, "an exploration of fifth-century spatial practices" (22). See chapter 2 for David Roselli's critique of the influence of Loraux on what he calls Athenocentric scholarship.

34. Wiles, *Tragedy in Athens*, 19–20.

35. Lefebvre, *The Production of Space*, 26.

36. Ibid., 48.

37. Ibid., 53.

38. Wiles, *Tragedy in Athens*, 20. See Lefebvre, 33.

39. *Tragedy in Athens*, ix. As discussed further in chapter 2, the assumption of a homogeneous, all-male, Athenian audience is another aspect of the Athenocentric approach that Roselli's new study criticizes.

40. Ibid., 86.

41. Ashby, *Classical Greek Theatre*, xiii.

42. A deme was a subdivision of Attica. Demes took on greater significance after the reforms of Cleisthenes that participated in the establishment of the democracy.

43. Wiles, *Tragedy in Athens*, 36.

44. Ashby, *Classical Greek Theatre*, 39.

45. Wiles, "Seeing Is Believing," 219. Compare Ashby, *Classical Greek Theatre*, 36.

46. Wiles, "Seeing Is Believing," 219.

47. Michel de Certeau, *The Writing of History*, 30.

48. Clifford, *The Predicament of Culture*, 90.

49. Rehm, *The Play of Space*, 40, cautions against the concept of basing a theory of a circular *orchēstra* on a circular dance, an idea which he argues is based on scholars' speculation that the circle developed from the threshing floor, with the circle serving as a metaphor for the cycle of seasons.

50. Athenaeus, *The Learned Banqueters*, v.181c.

51. Pickard-Cambridge, *Dithyramb, Tragedy and Comedy*, 32–33.

52. Ley, *The Theatricality of Greek Tragedy*, xiii.

53. For further reading on dithyrambs, see Armand D'Angour, "How the Dithyramb Got Its Shape." Unlike Fearn, D'Angour does not complicate the use of the term *kyklioi choroi* and its relationship to dance. On dithyrambs, see also Naerebout, *Attractive Performances*, 13–31.

54. In his "Heniochus and the Shape of the Athenian Orchestra," Martin L. West has stated in his quick response to Martin Revermann's reliance on the term *kyklios* to argue for a circular shaped *orchēstra*, *kyklios* means not circular but "simply 'on all sides, all round', and does not (any more than the English 'round' < rotundus) imply a circular area. It can indeed be used with reference to the perimeter of a rectangular structure" (12).

55. For example, in Homer, there are dances to the double-pipe and lyre (e.g., *Odyssey* 8.256–65; *Iliad* 18.494–96, 569–72, 590–606). Claude Calame in his study of choruses in archaic poetry, *Choruses of Young Women in Ancient Greece*, discusses such examples of circular dances forming around an altar or musician.

56. Ibid., 166n12. However, in *Tragedy in Athens*, 93ff., Wiles argues for a close

connection between the tragic chorus and the dithyramb through, for example, its use of triadic form.

57. Pickard-Cambridge, *Dithyramb, Tragedy and Comedy*, 33. While the meaning of *tyrbasia* is unknown, Pickard-Cambridge explains that it could possibly mean ithyphallic but more probably implies confusion, riot, revelry.

58. Fearn, *Bacchylides*, 166.

59. Bassi, "Review," 347–48.

60. Pickard-Cambridge, *The Dramatic Festivals of Athens*, 361. One key fifth-century source which provides a reference to dithyrambs and a producer of *kyklioi choroi* is Aristophanes's *Birds* (1377–1409), which Fearn states "also uses circle metaphors, in its lampoon of Kinesias, a well-known exponent of the New Music" (167).

61. Ashby, *Classical Greek Theatre*, 25.

62. Ashby adds to his argument that vase-paintings "usually picture dancers in-line, often with hands linked" and "present-day Greek dance is serpentine, not circular" (25). However, in so doing, he suggests a direct correspondence between artistic representations and lived reality, but as I discuss further in chapter 3, the conventions of vase-paintings might distort the image of circular dancing depicted on vases.

63. Wiles, *Tragedy in Athens*, 50. Cf. Vitruvius's first-century BCE work *On Architecture*, v.iii.6.

64. A scale which Wiles may overestimate based on his suggestion of a 13,000-seat theatre, not the current estimate of 4,000 to 6,000 seats. See the prior note on demographics in this chapter and the discussion of audience size in chapter 2.

65. Wiles, *Tragedy in Athens*, 50. Wiles does not make clear whose sightlines he is referring to, presumably the male spectators', as he suggests on page ix.

66. In *Classical Greek Theatre*, Ashby refers to the later evidence, such as Pollux's *Onomasticon*, the *Suda*, and the center stones in four theatre orchestras, as "misleading; almost certainly these were benchmarks, not altar bases" (56). While such later sources can often be helpful, they were nevertheless composed centuries later and may not accurately describe the fifth-century condition, so scholars, like Ashby here, are cautious in their application.

67. Wiles, *Tragedy in Athens*, 70.

68. See also Rehm, *The Play of Space*, 41. Rehm suggests a temporary stage altar here to engage dramatic focus.

69. Wiles, *Tragedy in Athens*, 72.

70. Ibid., 67. In his *Engaging Audiences: A Cognitive Approach to Spectating in the Theatre*, theatre historian Bruce McConachie has referred to the function of the *thymelē* as the mental concept of "center-periphery," which would lead spectators to ask, "who or what is at the center of things and who or what is not?" (134).

71. Meineck, "The Embodied Space," 35.

72. Goette (116) has suggested that "future excavation in the area of the *parodoi* and the *theatron* (i.e. *koilon*) may produce a more detailed picture of the theatre of Dionysos of c. 400 BC."

73. In order to illustrate this relationship, I will focus on the spatial practices of the complete play. While in some other chapters I instead focus on those factors that appear primarily in the dressing-up scene, in a discussion of theatrical space, the specificity provided by focusing on one scene would be counterproductive.

74. See note 1 in this chapter for further discussion of the types of space and the ways in which they relate to a discussion of the Theatre of Dionysus. In his "Space and Theatre History," a discussion of the historiographical issues related to terms such as these in the study of theatrical space, Carlson has used the semiotic terms "iconic space" and "indexical space" to help describe fictive space. He calls iconic space "what actors call onstage space, where everything seen is iconic, a chair serving as a sign for a chair . . . [and] offstage space would thus be indexical, since it is not seen but is indicated or pointed to by the onstage narrative" (198). See also Carlson's "The Iconic Stage" and "Indexical Space in the Theatre."

75. I use the term physical space here to make clear that I am referring to architectural space, which Issacharoff calls the theatre space. See note 1 in this chapter for a discussion of terminology related to space.

76. Wiles does not offer a detailed interpretation of *Bacchae*'s spatial practices such as he does with the *Oresteia*.

77. Wiles's outline of the Athenian theatre's spatial practices begins with his analysis of Aeschylus's *Oresteia*. Regarding the *Oresteia*, Wiles argues: "When Troy is placed to the left/east and Athens to the right/west, the different symbolic aspects of the left/right relationship neatly coalesce.

LEFT	RIGHT
sunrise	sunset
Argos	Athens
primitive	civilized
matriarchy	male democracy
chthonic goddesses	Olympians
blood bond	citizenship

The establishment of Athenian democracy seems an evolutionary process as natural as the movement of the sun. The sense of a natural left-to-right progression must have been reinforced by the fact that the Dionysiac procession entered the sanctuary of Dionysus from the left, coming along the Street of Tripods" (Wiles, *Tragedy in Athens*, 145). He further argues that in Aeschylus's *Oresteia* "the *eisodoi* provide the means of defining a linear progression: Troy → Argos → Delphi → Athens. The journey from barbaric monarchy to progressive democracy seems to be mapped as a journeying from left to right, for there is an obvious affinity between the grand arrival of Agamemnon from the Trojan east and the rising of the sun . . . (254, 522, 767, 900, 969, etc.)" (144–45).

78. Ibid., 66–67.

79. Asia in Ancient Greek terms refers to the area of Asia Minor, such as Lydia, Phrygia, and Bactria, from where Dionysus and his maenads hail.

80. I define the term here as director instead of its more common meaning of composer-director, just to emphasize the point, as mentioned previously, that *Bacchae* was produced posthumously, probably by Euripides's son. Euripides was of course also the *didaskalos*.

81. For this scheme, see the diagram in note 77 in this chapter.

82. To clarify more specifically: Dionysus and his followers arrive from the East in their journey west (left to right). On the other hand, Agaue and Cadmus live in the town but probably exit to the east (right to left), because Cadmus and Agaue have been exiled and so likely exit in the opposite direction of the city, which is in the same direction as Cithaeron (right). Agaue asks her escorts (*pompoi* 1381ff.) to take her to where she may never set eyes on Cithaeron or a thyrsus again. (These escorts could be the men who have carried onto the stage Pentheus's limbs [*prospoloi* 1216] but in any case are not the foreign chorus. Compare Dodds, *Bacchae*, 242n1381, and Seaford, *Bacchae*, 257n1381).

83. For example, city versus wild, town versus Cithaeron, male versus female, human versus god.

84. Rehm, *The Play of Space*, 211.

85. For a discussion of the debate over the relationship between a text and its performance, see Carlson's "Theatrical Performance" and Eli Rozik's *Generating Theatre Meaning*. Whereas Carlson posits Jacques Derrida's concept of the supplement as a "new way of thinking about several of the key paradoxes which bedevil theories of performance as illustration, translation, or fulfillment" (9), Rozik argues that "a literary fallacy lies in the assumption that a play-script is a full verbal text" (93), for even though he asserts the importance of play-script analysis, he also suggests that the play-text is deficient, an observation which he states distinguishes the theatrical approach from the literary approach (94). At the risk of being simplistic here, I might suggest that literary studies of play-texts and performance studies are distinct and valid undertakings each with their own accompanying merits and historiographical problems.

Chapter 2. Audience

1. Hall, "Lawcourt Dramas," 44. See also Victor Bers's "Dikastic *Thorubos*," which argues that the noises of jurors and bystanders may have influenced the outcome of trials.

2. For example, Aristophanes, *Archarnians*, 501–8, *Peace*, 962–67, *Women at the Thesmophoria*, 390–97; Plato, *Gorgias*, 502e, *Symposium* 175e; Demosthenes, *On the False Embassy*, 337, and *Against Meidias*, 226. For further citations on the audience, see Csapo and Slater, *The Context of Ancient Drama*, 286ff.

3. In *Tragedy in Athens* (51), David Wiles has made assumptions about audience size based on Plato's 30,000 figure (Plato's *Symposium* 175e), but others have suspected exaggeration in Plato. Pickard-Cambridge states: "The size of the audience at different periods cannot be precisely determined. . . . The statement of Plato . . . cannot be accepted . . . there can never have been 30,000 spectators" (*The Dramatic Festivals of Athens*, 263). Csapo and Slater concur, stating, "Plato estimated the size of the theater audience in Athens at 30,000 (122), but modern estimates" of the capacity of the Theater of Dionysus vary between 15,000 and 20,000" (*The Context of Ancient Drama*, 286). Recent studies of audience size have been based on more precise calculations of demographics. According to Roselli, such "revised estimates for the capacity of the early Classical Theater of Dionysus range from about 3,700 to 6,000 spectators, a far cry from the traditional estimates" (*Theater of the People*, 65).

4. On judging the contest, see C. W. Marshall and Stephanie van Willigenburg, "Judging Athenian Dramatic Competitions."

5. Chris Emlyn-Jones, "The Dramatic Poet and His Audience," and Robert W. Wallace, "Poet, Public, and 'Theatrocracy.'"

6. On a model for stratified decoding by spectators (elite and nonelite) and a bottom line of expertise shared by the majority of the audience, see Revermann, "The Competence of Theatre Audiences." For a use of the visual record to study audience expectations, see Green, *Theatre in Ancient Greek Society*, xii.

7. P. E. Easterling, "Weeping, Witnessing, and the Tragic Audience"; Ismene Lada-Richards, "'Empathic Understanding'" and "Emotion and Meaning in Tragic Performance"; Charles Segal, "Catharsis, Audience, and Closure in Greek Tragedy"; William B. Stanford, *Greek Tragedy and the Emotions*; Oliver Taplin, *Greek Tragedy in Action*, 159ff. On character and audience, see David J. Schenker, "Dissolving Differences."

8. I state "response" instead of "responses" because these studies, from over a decade ago, do not engage with current scholarship that explores the heterogeneous composition and responses of the audience.

9. Hans Oranje, *Euripides' "Bacchae"*; Staurt Lawrence, "Audience Uncertainty and Euripides' *Medea*."

10. See Niall W. Slater, "Making the Aristophanic Audience." On the *parabasis* (the section of a comedy where the poet addresses the audience through the chorus), see G. M. Sifakis, *Parabasis and Animal Choruses*.

11. For example, Mark Griffith, "Brilliant Dynasts"; Simon Goldhill, "The Audi-

ence of Athenian Tragedy"; Josiah Ober, *Mass and Elite in Democratic Athens*; John J. Winkler and Froma I. Zeitlin, eds., *Nothing to Do with Dionysos?*; and P. J. Rhodes, "Nothing to Do with Democracy."

12. See Roselli, *Theater of the People*, which I will later discuss at length; David Carter, *Why Athens?*; and Christopher Pelling, *Greek Tragedy and the Historian*. Carter's work addresses the identity of the audience of the Theatre of Dionysus, and the volume's contributors lean toward a broad, heterogeneous, panhellenic model, including metics (noncitizen residents) and foreign visitors. Pelling has also cautioned against the construction of a homogeneous view of an audience with a collective attitude (Pelling, "Conclusion: Tragedy as Evidence," 219).

13. For studies of the theatre audience, see Marvin Carlson, "Theatre Audiences"; Susan Bennett, *Theatre Audiences*; Herbert Blau, *The Audience*; Jim Davis and Victor Emeljanow, *Reflecting the Audience*; Jill Dolan, *The Feminist Spectator as Critic*; Elizabeth Lee-Brown, "Performativity, Context, and Agency"; Bruce McConachie, *Engaging Audiences*; Linda M. Park-Fuller, "Audiencing the Audience"; John Tulloch, *Shakespeare and Chekhov in Production and Reception*; and Wilmar Sauter, *The Theatrical Event*.

14. For an overview of scholarship on the question of women's presence, see Roselli, *Theater of the People*, 162ff.

15. Some performance scholars, such as Park-Fuller, have been using the term "audiencing" as opposed to "viewing" or "spectating" to emphasize the audience's role in the creation of a performance's meaning.

16. Roselli, *Theater of the People*, 163.

17. Goldhill, "The Audience of Athenian Tragedy," 62.

18. See chapter 4 for further discussion on disclaimers.

19. Helene P. Foley, *Female Acts in Greek Tragedy*, 3. On women in the theatre, see also A. J. Podlecki, "Could Women Attend the Theatre in Ancient Athens?"

20. Foley, *Female Acts*, 3n1.

21. Peter Arnott, *Public and Performance*, 5.

22. Csapo and Slater, *The Context of Ancient Drama*, 286.

23. Case, "Classic Drag," 326. Especially because of its reprinting in W. B. Worthen's widely circulated *Anthology of World Drama*, "Classic Drag" has been a widely read and influential work.

24. Jeffrey Henderson, "The Training of Classicists," 94.

25. *Republic* 377c2–5ff.

26. Henderson, "Women and the Athenian Dramatic Festivals," 138.

27. See David Schaps, "The Woman Least Mentioned." For a discussion of this article in relation to the naming of women in Greek and Roman comedy, see chapters 1 and 2 of Alan Sommerstein, *Talking about Laughter and Other Studies in Greek Comedy*.

28. Goldhill, "Representing Democracy," 347.

29. David Carr, *Time, Narrative, and History*, 97

30. Michel Foucault, "What Is an Author?," 118–19.

31. Ibid., 119–20.

32. Paul Ricoeur, *Interpretation Theory*, 6–7.

33. Ibid., 13. For discussion on the limitations of a Foucaultian model of discourse, see Postlewait, *Theatre Historiography*, 99–101.

34. Ibid., 8.

35. Ibid., 8. For a discussion of the problems inherent in semiotic studies of theatre, see Eli Rozik, *Generating Theatre Meaning*, 4–8. Distinguishing between the theatre medium in the sense of *langue* and the performance-text in the sense of *parole*, Rozik considers "the traditional semiotic approach, which focuses solely on the textual function of the body on stage" to be reductive but also argues that phenomenological approaches should not focus solely on physical presence (17).

36. Michael Stanford, *The Nature of Historical Knowledge*, 37.

37. Postlewait, *Theatre Historiography*, 100. See Marshall David Sahlins, *Culture in Practice*, 287 and 295–304.

38. Goldhill, "Representing Democracy," 369.

39. Roselli, *Theater of the People*, 7.

40. Hajo Holborn, *History and the Humanities*, 79.

41. Roselli, *Theater of the People*, 4. David M. Carter's *The Politics of Greek Tragedy* (6, 16, 71) also ignores the reconstruction of individual audience responses and even cautions against them.

42. Bennett, *Theatre Audiences*, 211, qtd. in Roselli, *Theater of the People*, 3.

43. Carlson, "Theatre Audiences," 97.

44. In *Tragedy in Athens*, Wiles has argued this point, stating that unlike English renaissance drama, which was concerned with the construction of the individual as a subject, "Athenian drama was preoccupied, rather, with constructing the Athenian citizen (*politēs*) as subject" (212).

45. David Bain, *Actors and Audience*, 7. See also Bain's "Audience Address in Greek Tragedy."

46. Foley, *Ritual Irony: Poetry and Sacrifice in Euripides*, 250.

47. Ibid., 250n63. Foley references Reneé Girard's *Violence and the Sacred* for a discussion of the ritual double.

48. In addition to Girard, Foley cites for example Henri Hubert and Marcel Mauss's *Sacrifice*.

49. For example, on p. 253, she states, "For if one mask represents different identities to characters and audience, if the smile that marks the mask means both benignity and destruction, and finally, if the mask in the epiphany can be understood only as a sign that represents forces that are in fact not directly accessible to the

eye, then the audience can make sense of its theatrical *experience* [italics mine] only by becoming conscious of the god's mask as a mask in the modern rather than in the ancient tragic theatrical mode. Euripides thus achieves in the audience a sense of the mask as transcending both its previous functions as the deceptive image of the illusory god and possibly alludes to the attested use of masks of Dionysus as actual cult objects."

50. The date of this production and others cited have been checked by using the on-line database of the Archive of Performances of Greek and Roman Drama. For further information on productions, see http://www.apgrd.ox.ac.uk /research-collections/performance-database/productions.

51. For example, Seidensticker's "Comic Elements in Euripides' *Bacchae*" and Foley's *Ritual Irony*. See chapter 6 for a discussion of these works.

52. Something Cadmus is also afraid of (203).

53. Seaford, *Bacchae*, 216n854–55.

54. Orgel's *Impersonations*, a study of the practice of boys playing the roles of women in Shakespeare's England, considers the ways in which discourses can obscure historical events.

55. Ormand, "Oedipus the Queen," 2. On the conventions of cross-dressing, see Nancy Rabinowitz's "How Is It Played?" and "Embodying Tragedy." For an examination of the male body in Greek tragedy, see also Katrina Cawthorn, *Becoming Female*.

56. Dover, *Greek Homosexuality*; Winkler, *The Constraints of Desire*; Halperin, *One Hundred Years of Homosexuality*. See Ormand's note 24 for extensive bibliography. See also Laura McClure.

57. Ormand, "Oedipus the Queen," 27.

58. Jenkins, *Re-thinking History*, 16–17.

59. In chapter 5, I complicate the notion of Dionysus's presumed effeminacy in *Bacchae*.

60. See Case, "Classic Drag," for a discussion of the construction of "Woman" on the Attic stage.

61. In this 411 BCE comedy, the women at the Thesmophoria, a festival in honor of Demeter and Persephone in which only women participated, attack Euripides for his depictions of them. The comedy tells the story of how Euripides persuades the manly-man Mnesilochos to dress up as a woman in order to spy upon the women at the festival who are about to try Euripides for his negative depictions of women in his plays. Like the Theban women in *Bacchae*, the women at the Thesmophoria recognize the male intruder, but in this case, Mnesilochos and Euripides, who has come to save him, escape in a comic ending.

62. In his review of JoAnne Akalaitis's 2009 *Bacchae*, Mendelsohn suggests this point. See Melinda Powers, "Dressing-up Dramaturgy," for further discussion of

the ways in which the *Bacchae* could exploit generic overlap and gesture toward a parody of Aristophanes's work. See chapter 6 for further discussion of the ways in which the two dramas correspond.

Chapter 3. The Chorus, Music, Movement, and Dance

1. *Laws* 672e. On choral performance in initiation rituals, see Claude Calame, *Choruses of Young Women*. On mourning rituals, see Margaret Alexiou, *The Ritual Lament in the Greek Tradition*, and Gail Holst-Warhaft, *Dangerous Voices*.

2. *Poetics*, 1456a25–31. Scholars have criticized Oliver Taplin's *Greek Tragedy in Action* for following Aristotle's marginalization, but as John Gould has stated in "Tragedy and the Collective Experience": "I doubt whether Taplin would offer the same characterization now" (235n8).

3. For the records, see Pickard-Cambridge, *The Dramatic Festivals of Athens*, 101–25.

4. I will further discuss these in a later note.

5. *The Learned Banqueters* i.21.f ff.

6. *Morals, Convivial Questions* ix.732ff.

7. Aelius Aristides, *On Behalf of the Four*, 161. See Csapo and Slater, *The Context of Ancient Drama*, 361–62, and Pickard-Cambridge, *The Dramatic Festivals of Athens*, 246–257, for further discussion of these various sources on dance.

8. Pickard-Cambridge, *The Dramatic Festivals of Athens*, 249.

9. For an example of the debates over choral dancing, such as those in T. B. L. Webster, A. M. Dale, H. D. L. Kitto, Lillian Lawler, and John J. Winkler, see Wiles, *Tragedy in Athens*, 87–91.

10. See a later note in this chapter for studies on music.

11. See for example Ley, "Modern Visions of Greek Tragic Dancing" and *The Theatricality of Greek Tragedy*; Rehm, "Performing the Chorus"; Wiles, *Tragedy in Athens*, 87–132; Webster, *The Greek Chorus*; Herb Golder, "Making a Scene"; and Albert Weiner, "The Function of the Tragic Greek Chorus."

12. See R. W. B. Burton, *The Chorus in Sophocles' Tragedies*, and Helene P. Foley, "Choral Identity in Greek Tragedy."

13. See for example Helen Bacon, "The Chorus in Greek Life and Drama"; Claude Calame, *Choruses of Young Women*; Steven Lonsdale, *Dance and Ritual Play in Greek Religion*; and Peter J. Wilson, *The Athenian Institution of the Khoregia* and "Leading the Tragic *Khoros*."

14. On dance's reconstruction, see Webster, *The Greek Chorus*, xi. For a comparative analysis, see Germaine Prudhommeau, *La danse grecque antique*. On dance's social and religious functions, see Lonsdale, *Dance and Ritual Play*; H. D. L. Kitto, "The Dance in Greek Tragedy"; and Fritz G. Naerebout, *Attractive Performances*.

15. Some studies on music include: Andrew Barker, *Greek Musical Writings I* and

Greek Musical Writings II; Sheram D. Bundrick, *Music and Image in Classical Athens*; Stephen Hagel, *Ancient Greek Music: A New Technical History*; Edith Hall, "The Singing Actors of Antiquity"; John J. Landels, *Music in Ancient Greece and Rome*; Graham Ley, *The Theatricality of Greek Tragedy*, especially pp. 132ff.; Penelope Murray and Peter Wilson, eds., *Music and the Muses*; and Martin L. West, *Ancient Greek Music*. On instruments, see Warren D. Anderson, *Music and Musicians in Ancient Greece*; John J. Landels, *Music in Ancient Greece and Rome*; and Peter J. Wilson, "The *Aulos* in Athens" and "The Musicians Among the Actors."

16. Wiles, *Tragedy in Athens*, chapters 4 and 5 attempt this type of approach. See also, Graham Ley's *The Theatricality of Greek Tragedy*, which I discuss in greater detail later.

17. Gould, "Tragedy and the Collective Experience," and Goldhill, "Collectivity and Otherness."

18. As per Wiles, *Tragedy in Athens*, 89, see Lawler, *The Dance in Ancient Greece*, 82–85; Pickard-Cambridge, *The Dramatic Festivals of Athens*, 239–42; Winkler, "The Ephebes' Song."

19. Wiles, *Tragedy in Athens*, 89. I discussed Wiles's argument in chapter 1.

20. Winkler, "The Ephebes' Song," 21.

21. On the Basel Dancers (figure 6), see M. Schmidt, "Dionysien," 70ff.

22. On the five fragments, see J. D. Beazley, "Hydria-fragments in Corinth," and for the image, Oliver Taplin, "The Pictorial Record," 71. In his *Pots and Plays*, which apart from pp. 28–35 primarily addresses fourth-century images from the Greek West, Taplin has revised this statement and suggested that in addition to the Basel Dancers, the only other Attic painting depicting a scene of tragedy in performance is the Kiev Chorus, a fragment of an Attic bell krater (from Olbia), unattributed, ca. 420s, Kiev, Museum of the Academy of Sciences, unnumbered (29). See p. 30 of *Pots and Plays* for the image.

23. Taplin, "The Pictorial Record," 71.

24. Ibid., 71. While various other theatre vases represent actors in costume, Taplin is referring to the scarcity of vases that depict a play in performance. See Richard Green, *Theatre in Ancient Greek Society*, for further discussion of the visual evidence on Greek theatre from the early Athenian theatre into the Roman world.

25. For further reading on illustrations of the theatre in vase-painting, sculptures, and other monuments, see also Green and Eric W. Handley, *Images of the Greek Theatre*; Oliver Taplin, *Comic Angels*; A. D. Trendall and T. B. L. Webster, *Illustrations of Greek Drama*; and T. B. L. Webster, *Monuments Illustrating Tragedy and Satyr Play* and *Monuments Illustrating Old and Middle Comedy*.

26. Burke, *Eyewitnessing*, 14. For further reading on problems related to the use of visual sources as evidence, see Thomas Postlewait, "Eyewitnesses to History."

27. Naerebout, *Attractive Performances*, 236.

28. Mary-Kay Gamel, "Review of *The Theatricality of Greek Tragedy* by Graham Ley."

29. While no recording of fifth-century music exists, modern musicians have recorded reconstructions. For example, the modern conductor Gregorio Paniagúa has recorded his impressions of the archaeological remains of ancient Greek music, including the papyrus fragment of Euripides's *Orestes*. See his ensemble Atrium Musicae de Madrid's *Musique de la Grèce Antique*. To hear samples from the tracks, see http://store.harmoniamundi.com/ancient-greek-music.html.

30. Csapo and Slater, *The Context of Ancient Drama*, 333.

31. Martin L. West, *Ancient Greek Music*, 284. See also, Csapo and Slater, *The Context of Ancient Drama*, 341–42 and Plate 21A.

32. West, *Ancient Greek Music*, 286. Csapo and Slater, *The Context of Ancient Drama*, 342 and Plate 21B.

33. Csapo and Slater, *The Context of Ancient Drama*, 333.

34. Ibid. See 331ff., and Pickard-Cambridge, *The Dramatic Festivals of Athens*, 257–262, on theatrical music and its related sources.

35. Csapo and Slater, *The Context of Ancient Drama*, 342.

36. Ley, *The Theatricality of Greek Tragedy*, 204.

37. Iggers, *Historiography in the Twentieth Century*, 144.

38. Hayden White, *Figural Realism*, 3. On the function of narrativity in historical writing, see also White's *The Content of the Form*.

39. Ibid., 3.

40. For a discussion of history as sequence, see Michael Stanford, *A Companion to the Study of History*, 193–228.

41. The small sample of extant dramas could also leave historians with a skewed impression of the chorus's decline in the fifth century, for *Bacchae* and *Oedipus at Colonus*, Euripides's and Sophocles's last plays respectively, grant a larger role to the chorus than earlier plays did. Csapo and Slater explain: "Aeschylean tragedy averages 40–50 percent choral participation, while no extant tragedy earlier than 425 B.C. (except? *Prometheus Bound*) is less than 20 percent choral. But later tragedies are considerably less; the *Orestes* of Euripides (408 B.C.), for example, is only 10.5 percent choral. Note, however, that our two latest tragedies, *Bacchae* (405? B.C.) and *Oedipus at Colonus* (401 B.C.) with 27 percent, and 22 percent, respectively, are exceptions to a nonetheless clear trend" (*The Context of Ancient Drama*, 349). At the same time, these plays may also have been self-consciously incorporating an earlier use of choral form. On this subject, see also Pickard-Cambridge, *The Dramatic Festivals of Athens*, 233.

42. Goldhill, "Collectivity and Otherness," 244. See Jean-Pierre Vernant and Pierre Vidal-Naquet, *Myth and Tragedy in Ancient Greece*, 34.

43. Gould, "Tragedy and the Collective Experience," 218.

44. Goldhill, "Collectivity and Otherness," 249.

45. Ancient Greek has various dialects, such as Attic, Doric, Ionic, and Aeolic. The principal characters in tragedy speak in Attic dialect, while choral lyric is Doric.

46. Gould, "Tragedy and the Collective Experience," 219. Doric would sound foreign, according to Gould, because the language of tragedy's principal characters was written in Attic, a dialect which was presumably more familiar to the audience.

47. Goldhill, "Collectivity and Otherness," 251. For example, he raises the question of whether it is possible to know if the Doric dialect registered to audience members, and he presents extra-tragic examples from the fifth century (Pindar) and the fourth century (Plato and Demosthenes), as he argues that Doric registered as a competing tongue, not a marginal one.

48. Gould, "Tragedy and the Collective Experience," 218.

49. Rozik, *Generating Theatre Meaning*, 84. For further reading on the double identity of a play-text, see Postlewait, *Theatre Historiography*, 117–53.

50. On maenad dancing, see Lillian B. Lawler, *The Dance in Ancient Greece*, 76.

51. These vases, a catalogue of about seventy vases that depict scenes of Dionysiac ritual, were dubbed Lenaian by the art historian Frickenhause, who postulated their connection to the civic festival of the Lenaia. While there is no certainty about whether these scenes derive from myth or represent the actual practices of civic women, many scholars have suggested that real-life maenads, or civic women who performed rituals in honor of Dionysus, existed. Sarah Peirce, in her "Visual Language and Concepts of Cult," has explained the scholarly consensus on the Lenaia Vases as one of viewing the imagery as "a visual record of a ritual as it was observed by a vase-painter, and that this record has been embellished by the painter with mythical elements" (59–60). For a discussion of the Lenaia Vases, see also Thomas Carpenter, *Dionysian Imagery in Fifth-Century Athens*; Françoise Frontisi-Ducroux, *Le dieu-masque*; and Richard Hamilton, "Lenaia Vases in Context."

52. On this issue, see Osborne, "The Ecstasy and the Tragedy."

53. On Dionysiac rituals and Greek religion in general, see Walter Burkert, *Greek Religion*. For a feminist critique of women's rituals and their representations, see Barbara Goff, *Citizen Bacchae*, especially chapter 4.

54. I have used the second edition of this commentary, which was published in 1960. In addition to this commentary, Dodds published an article on maenadism, which was reprinted as an appendix in his *The Greeks and the Irrational*.

55. According to Nietzsche, "The effects of the Dionysiac spirit struck the Apollonian Greeks as titanic and barbaric; yet they could not disguise from themselves the fact that they were essentially akin to those deposed Titans and heroes" (34). For an opinion that reacts against Nietzsche's view of Dionysus and argues for the god's cult as a civilizing force in the *polis*, see Seaford, *Reciprocity and Ritual*.

56. On the possibility of real-life maenads, see Robin Osborne, "The Ecstasy and the Tragedy."

57. Dodds, *The Greeks and the Irrational*, 272.

58. Based on a search of the Thesaurus Linguae Graecae (http://www.tlg.uci .edu/) *sōphrosynē* and its cognates occur approximately ninety-eight times in the extant tragedians' works, with Euripides using the term most frequently. The term emphasizes the importance of balance or moderation, a critical idea in tragedy that relates to many of the genre's themes. The importance of balance also governs other aspects of ancient Greek life. For example, the Hippocratic medical texts include 154 references to *metrios* (moderation, proportion), and *isonomia* (equality of law) is an important democratic political concept. Moreover, *mēden agan* (nothing in excess) was inscribed over the Temple of Apollo at Delphi. The concept of balance is clearly an important one in tragedy, medicine, ritual, and Athenian life in general.

59. See chapter 4 regarding "general perceptions versus specific truths."

60. See Helen North, *Sophrosyne*, and Adriaan Rademaker, *Sophrosyne and the Rhetoric of Self-Restraint*.

61. North, *Sophrosyne*, and Rademaker, *Sophrosyne and the Rhetoric of Self-Restraint*. See also Henry John Franklin Jones, *On Aristotle and Greek Tragedy*, 245ff. Jones's reading of other Euripidean characters suggests Euripides's interest in associating nobility with nonelite characters. In chapters 4 and 6, I discuss Green's article "Towards a Reconstruction of Performance Style," which suggests that *sōphrosynē* is related to elite styles of comportment.

62. Foley's suggestion of Dionysus's smiling mask in her *Ritual Irony* has been recently countered by Wiles in his *Mask and Performance*. See chapter 6 for further discussion of this point.

63. See Bond, *Heracles*, 132n268. Bond notes that this scene recalls the one at the end of *Agamemnon*, when the chorus briefly confronts Aegisthus's bodyguard. See also the chorus's reaction to Creon in *Oedipus at Colonus*.

64. See Mary Whitlock Blundell, *Helping Friends and Harming Enemies*.

65. For a discussion of the ethics of revenge in Euripides's *Hecuba* with particular regard to Hecuba's blinding of Polymestor, see Judith Mossman, *Wild Justice*.

66. On the other hand, as Foley has argued, "The *eudaimonia* [or joyful fortune] promised by the chorus to the adherents of Dionysiac religion is horribly ironic when the same term is applied to Agave on her return from the mountain after the destruction of her son (1258)" (Foley, *Ritual Irony*, 249).

67. Because nothing in the text indicates the chorus went to Cithaeron and since the conventions of Greek tragedy require the chorus to stay on stage with few exceptions (e.g., they leave for Ajax's suicide in Sophocles's *Ajax*), the assumption that the chorus did not go to Cithaeron rests on very secure ground.

68. The fourth ode includes many corruptions and is especially difficult to translate for this reason.

69. See A. M. Dale, *The Lyric Metres of Greek Drama*, 257. Any relationship drawn between a type of meter and an emotion is highly suspect, for the same meter can be used in different contexts with diverse effects.

70. Foley, *Ritual Irony*, 245.

71. Except when it is at the expense of neglecting other gods as in the case of Hippolytus in Euripides's *Hippolytus*.

72. See note 69 above, on A. M. Dale, regarding the difficulty in associating meter with emotional states.

73. As mentioned in the beginning of this chapter, Plato in his *Laws* (814e–16eff.; ca. 350 BCE) states that all dances, even warlike dances (*pyrrichē*) in addition to the peaceful dances (*emmeleia*), belong to a general category of dances that are harmonious. While Plato's comment must be considered within the context of his philosophical argument, the point nevertheless suggests that dances, even violent, warlike dances or emotional ones, such as the fourth ode, consist of harmonious, organized, *sōphrōn* movement, at least by Plato's standards.

74. On the body-mind relationship in ancient Greece, see note 21 in chapter 4.

75. Foley, *Ritual Irony*, 222, 239. See also Arthur, "The Choral Odes of the *Bacchae* of Euripides," 148.

76. According to Richard Seaford, although the play bears the name of Gregory of Nazianzus (329–389 CE), the work should "perhaps more likely be attributed to a Byzantine of the eleventh or twelfth century AD" (*Bacchae*, 53). Dodds, *Bacchae*, 234n1329 and Introduction, lv–lvi.

77. Although Euripidean *amoibaia* primarily take the form of lamentations, less than half of Aeschylean *amoibaia* are lamentations, and in Sophocles only two-thirds are laments. Thus, *amoibaia* differ from *kommoi* (emotional lyrical exchanges) in that *kommoi*, according to *Poetics* 12, must be *thrēnoi* (laments, dirges) (Aristotle, *Poetics* 1452b, 23–24). Thus, not all *amoibaia* are *thrēnoi* and not all *thrēnoi* are *amoibaia*. For further discussion, see F. M. Cornford, "The So-called *Kommos*."

78. For a discussion of this performance at the University of California, Davis, see Melinda Powers, "Unveiling Euripides."

Chapter 4. Performance Style

1. E.g., Keir Elam, *The Semiotics of Theatre and Drama*.

2. Approaches to performance style in the field of theatre studies range from biographies on actors to handbooks to works on theatre semiotics to theories of representation and the body. Some representative works include: John Perry, *Encyclopedia of Acting Techniques*; Jean Benedetti, *The Art of the Actor*; Erika Fischer-Lichte, "Theatre and the Civilizing Process"; Susan Leigh Foster, ed., *Choreographing History*; Mark Franko, *Dance as Text*; David Krasner, ed., *Method Acting Reconsidered*; and Phillip B. Zarrilli, ed., *Acting (Re)Considered*.

3. For example, *Clouds* 1366ff., *Archarnians* 404ff., the fragment about Kallip-

pides in *Women Who Pitch the Tents* (a late fifth- to early fourth-century work), and especially *Frogs*, which includes a parody of the tragedians "Aeschylus" and "Euripides," who debate about each other's style in a contest.

4. *Poetics* 1461b34–35. Although *Poetics* (ca. 330 BCE) is a later source, the anecdote is said to be from a fifth-century actor.

5. For example, figures 1, 2, 6, 10, 11, 12, 13. For early fourth-century examples, see figures 9 and 14.

6. For sources on actors and acting from various periods of Greek history, see Csapo and Slater, *The Context of Ancient Drama*, 221–85.

7. I will later discuss several of the works that have attempted to address performance style. For further reading on actors, see Anne Duncan's *Performance and Identity in the Classical World*, which addresses the antitheatrical tradition in antiquity; Edith Hall's *The Theatrical Cast of Athens*, which explores the complex relationship between the fictive world of the performance and its impact on the audience; and the collection of essays which discuss various topics tangentially related to acting in Niall W. Slater and Bernhard Zimmermann's *Intertextualität in der griechisch-römischen Komödie*.

8. For further reading on this anecdote, i.e., *Poetics* 1461b34–35, see Bain, *Actors and Audience*, 7n1. Bain suggests the possibility of the anecdote's use as evidence for a movement toward realism but also comments, "What appears natural to one type of audience may often look formal to another" (7n1).

9. Sir Laurence Olivier in a statement to Dustin Hoffman succinctly encapsulated one of the major historical transitions of his trade: "Try acting, dear boy. It's much easier." This alleged gibe was aimed at Hoffman after the method actor supposedly lost sleep and looked a mess in order to get into character for a scene in the 1976 film *Marathon Man*.

10. Revised in chapter 4 of Eric Csapo, *Actors and Icons of the Ancient Theater*.

11. J. Michael Walton, "Social and Domestic Drama," 130.

12. Csapo, "Kallippides on the Floor-Sweepings," 127.

13. E. R. Dodds, *Bacchae*, 133n453–59.

14. Kostas Valakas, "The Use of the Body by Actors in Tragedy and Satyr-Play," 86.

15. Green, "Towards a Reconstruction," 111.

16. Lada-Richards, "'Estrangement' or 'Reincarnation'?," 67. In *Actors and Audience* (3–4), Bain criticizes Sifakis's use of Brecht in his *Parabasis and Animal Choruses*.

17. Taplin, *Greek Tragedy in Action*, 16.

18. Alpers, "Style Is What You Make It: The Visual Arts Once Again," 137–38.

19. Postlewait, *Theatre Historiography*, 184.

20. For further reading on problems related to the perceived antithesis of epic and method, see Duane Krause, "An Epic System."

21. The ancient Greeks had a unique sense of the mind-body relationship that might be better described as a body-mind-spirit relationship and that focused more on the outer signs of character as opposed to an inner psychology. See Beate Gundert, "Soma and Psyche in Hippocratic Medicine"; Ruth Padel, *In and Out of Mind*; Christopher Gill, *Personality in Greek Epic, Tragedy, and Philosophy*; Christopher Pelling, ed., *Characterization and Individuality in Greek Literature*; Sarah Broadie, "XIV — Soul and Body in Plato and Descartes"; Erik Ostenfeld, *Ancient Greek Psychology and the Modern Mind-Body Debate*; T. M. Robinson, *Plato's Psychology*; Bruno Snell, *The Discovery of the Mind*; Bernard A. O. Williams, *Shame and Necessity*; and John P. Wright and Paul Potter, eds., *Psyche and Soma*.

22. On the other hand, as J. Michael Walton has argued in his "Social and Domestic Drama," the mask, "far from providing a hindrance to any notion of realism, [may] actually serve to promote it by requiring from the actor strong feelings to be communicated by physical playing, through action and reaction" (132).

23. John Jory, "Review of *Actors and Icons of the Ancient Theater* by Eric Csapo."

24. I use quotation marks here to distinguish Aristophanes's comic characterization of these poets from the poets themselves.

25. Csapo, "Kallippides on the Floor-Sweepings," 127. In *Actors and Icons*, Csapo defines realism as "the choice of specific, historic or everyday life scenes that are familiar to the artists and their patrons and treated in such a way as to offer the impression of the familiarity of lived experience" (2).

26. Green, "Towards a Reconstruction," 107.

27. Csapo, "Kallippides on the Floor-Sweepings," 127.

28. Green, "Towards a Reconstruction," 93.

29. Csapo, "Kallippides on the Floor-Sweepings," 127.

30. Green, "Towards a Reconstruction," 111.

31. Stanford, *The Nature of Historical Knowledge*, 59.

32. Csapo, "Kallippides on the Floor-Sweepings," 127.

33. Peter Burke, *Eyewitnessing: The Uses of Images as Historical Evidence*, 187.

34. Green, "Towards a Reconstruction," 107.

35. For a discussion of the unparalleled use of the term "democratic" in this play, see Hall, "The Sociology of Athenian Tragedy."

36. For Csapo's references and a discussion of the scene, see "Kallippides on the Floor-Sweepings," 131–33.

37. Henderson, "The *Dēmos* and Comic Competition," 304.

38. As Lada-Richards has demonstrated in "'Estrangement' or 'Reincarnation,'" Sophocles's *Philoctetes* is another tragedy that is useful for the study of performance style in addition to the Aristophanic comedies *Women at the Thesmophoria* and *Archarnians*, but she does not reference or discuss *Bacchae* regarding performance style.

39. See chapter 2 for Richard Seaford's translation of the scene.

40. Segal, *Dionysiac Poetics*, 216. In *Ritual Irony*, Foley also discusses *Bacchae*'s metatheatre but in a quite distinct way. Unlike Foley and Seaford, Segal does not attempt to locate *Bacchae* within Athenian culture and focuses instead on the play as a work of literary art.

41. On the actor/text/character triad, see Rozik, *Generating Theatre Meaning*, 84.

42. Some other examples of disguise and deception in ancient drama include: Dionysus disguised as a mortal in *Bacchae*, Menelaus as a sailor in Euripides's *Helen*, Neoptolemus in Sophocles's *Philoctetes*, Euripides and his kinsman disguised as women in Aristophanes's *Women at the Thesmophoria*, Dionysus disguised as Heracles and Dionysus and his slave Xanthias pretending to be each other in Aristophanes's *Frogs*, and women disguised as men in Aristophanes's *Assemblywomen*.

43. His attention to detail here may be simply a by-product of his inexperience and not necessarily, as Valakas (86) has suggested, a reflection of the actor's performance style.

44. For a discussion of the dual ritual and aesthetic function of the mask, see Wiles, *Mask and Performance*. On the question of an actor's role and the lack of the term in ancient Greek, see Hall, *The Theatrical Cast of Athens*.

45. *Bacchae* was produced posthumously and likely directed by Euripides's son.

46. Euripides, whose plays, such as *Alcestis*, *Helen*, *Ion*, and *Orestes*, show an interest in experimenting with genre, must have included this scene for a reason, for while it is unclear if the scene is Euripides's invention, he clearly had the option of excluding it. Pentheus could have gone to the mountain openly or with his arms as in other versions of the story. Instead, he dresses up. Basing her argument on a comparison of the Euripides with other versions of the myth depicted on vases, Jenny March has argued that Pentheus's cross-dressing and murder by his mother is not a traditional feature of the story but a Euripidean invention.

47. Mendelsohn, "A Wild Night in the Park." For further discussion of this point, see also chapters 2 and 6.

48. For a discussion of the political and social connotations of performance style, see Joseph Roach, "Power's Body" and *The Player's Passion*.

49. In his *The Shakespeare Riots*, Nigel Cliff has framed the American actor Forrest's competition with the English Macready as a class-inflected rivalry.

50. Woodruff, *The* Bacchae *of Euripides*, xx.

51. The chorus's stated reason for opposing Pentheus is his denial of their god, not his autocratic rule.

52. Foley, *Ritual Irony*, 222 and 239; see also Marylin B. Arthur, "The Choral Odes of the *Bacchae* of Euripides," 148.

53. Foley, *Ritual Irony*, 240.

Chapter 5. Costuming and Properties

1. See Foley, "The Comic Body in Greek Art and Drama," and Revermann, *Comic Business.*

2. See chapter 3 for problems with using anachronistic sources.

3. Despite this apparent problem, Csapo has argued in *Actors and Icons* (ix) that iconography may reveal more to historians than mechanical reproductions such as photographs, because the extensive mediation further reveals the interests, preoccupations, and orientations of the artists and their patrons.

4. Although the patterned costumes depicted on vase-paintings may have been due to the style of the painter, Rosie Wyles, in her "The Tragic Costumes," which I will discuss later, has aimed to prove that the elaborate patterning of the costumes on the Pronomos Vase resembled those on actual costumes. For further discussion, see E. J. W. Barber, "The Peplos of Athena," and Peter Wilson, *The Athenian Institution of the Khoregia,* 94.

5. Women were in charge of weaving but little is known about these women's identities and how they worked. Slaves and migrants may have also contributed. For further reading, see Graham Ley's "A Material World."

6. In her recent critical study of costuming, *The Actor in Costume,* Aoife Monks proposes reasons for the limited studies on costuming from the antivisual pro-text tradition of scholarship to "the implicit assumption that costumes are frivolous and not worthy of serious analysis" (10). In her work, she argues that costuming is indistinguishable from the actor, "makes the actor's body possible, and is fundamental to the relationship between the actor and the audience" (12).

7. I will discuss Wyles's article "The Tragic Costumes" later. See also her article "Towards Theorising the Place of Costume in Performance Reception." Iris Brooke's *Costume in Greek Classic Drama* (1962) was the last full-length work on the subject.

8. For studies of comic costume, see for example Laura M. Stone's *Costume in Aristophanic Poetry*; James Robson, "New Clothes, a New You"; Gwendolyn Compton-Engle, "Control of Costume in Three Plays of Aristophanes," and her "Stolen Cloaks in Aristophanes' *Ecclesiazusae.*"

9. Apart from Wyles's *Costume in Greek Tragedy,* Linda Jones Roccos's comprehensive annotated bibliography *Ancient Greek Costume* offers an excellent overview of the history of scholarship on costume and dress. Two classic works on the subject are: Pickard-Cambridge's *The Dramatic Festivals of Athens,* which discusses issues related to costume in tragedy, comedy, and satyr play, and Iris Brooke's *Costume in Greek Classic Drama,* which includes various sketches from scenes on vases to illustrate the types and ways of wearing Athenian clothing, jewelry, armor, footwear, headdresses, and dramatic costumes.

10. See Graham Ley, "A Material World" (discussed later); Colleen Chaston, *Tragic Props and Cognitive Function*; and Oliver Taplin's chapter "Objects and Tokens" in *Greek Tragedy in Action*, 77–100. For the use of props in comedy, see Mary C. English, "The Diminishing Role of Stage Properties in Aristophanic Comedy," and Joe Park Poe, "Multiplicity, Discontinuity and Visual Meaning in Aristophanic Comedy."

11. Issues of costuming and properties are especially relevant, such as Pentheus's costume in *Bacchae*'s dressing-up scene, the bow in Sophocles's *Philoctetes*, and the infamous tapestries in Aeschylus's *Agamemnon*. For further references on the study of tragic costume in specific plays, see Wyles, *Costume in Greek Tragedy*, 2. See Ley, "A Material World," and Taplin, *Greek Tragedy in Action*, for an overview of key scenes that use properties.

12. Liza Cleland, Mary Harlow, and Lloyd Llewellyn-Jones also offer an overview of scholarship on dress in "I Wear This Therefore I Am," xii–xiii. On ancient dress, see also Liza Cleland, Glenys Davies, and Lloyd Llewellyn-Jones, *Greek and Roman Dress from A–Z*.

13. On athletic nudity, see Myles McDonell, "The Introduction of Athletic Nudity."

14. On nudity as costume, see Larissa Bonfante, "Nudity as Costume in Classical Art" and "The Naked Greek." This view has been challenged by Andrew Stewart in *Classical Greece and the Birth of Western Art*. See also Ann G. Geddes, "Rags and Riches." On clothing in initiation ritual, see Laura Gawlinksi, "'Fashioning' Initiates."

15. On the issue of the representation of the male body on the stage, see Richard Hawley, "The Male Body as Spectacle in Attic Drama."

16. Although the vase depicts the cast of a satyr play, the actors, according to sources such as Pollux, iv.118, would have worn costumes similar to those of tragedy, apart from, of course, the chorus and Silenus, who are dressed as satyrs. On satyr play, see George W. M. Harrison, ed., *Satyr Drama*; Mark Griffith, "Slaves of Dionysos"; and Edith Hall, "Ithyphallic Males Behaving Badly."

17. On the discovery of the vase and subsequent publications, see François Lissarrague, "From Flat Page to the Volume of the Pot." On the relationship of the vase to its Italian patrons, see in the same volume Mark Griffith, "Satyr Play and Tragedy, Face to Face," especially pp. 47–49.

18. Griffith, "Satyr Play and Tragedy," 48.

19. Ibid., 48. Griffith continues to argue that the vase "even if it is based on an actual celebratory *pinax*, represents not any one particular Athenian production, but an idealized synthesis of typical Dionysian moments and elements for Attic tragic-satyric performance, as conceived by or for a south Italian audience" (48).

20. Lissarrague, "From Flat Page," 33.

21. See Mary Hart, ed., *The Art of Ancient Greek Theater*, for a catalogue of this extraordinary exhibition and scholarly articles related to theatre iconography.

22. For further discussion on this point, see Postlewait, "Eyewitnesses," 580.

23. Lissarrague, "From Flat Page," 46.

24. Wyles, "The Tragic Costumes," 237.

25. As stated earlier, the assumption that the costumes of principal characters in both tragedy and satyr play are similar is based in part on a statement by Pollux, iv.18. The costumes of the two choruses would of course have differed.

26. See chapter 4 for further discussion of this parody and the issues with using it as historical evidence for performance style.

27. I here again put the tragedians' names in quotation marks to indicate the distinction between the characters in Aristophanes's comedy and the historical figures.

28. Translation by Alan H. Sommerstein.

29. Ibid.

30. See chapter 4 for further discussion on the problems with using comedy as historical evidence.

31. Rozik, *Generating Theatre Meaning*, 84. See my chapter 3 for further discussion of this point.

32. Film theory includes a number of critical frameworks that scholars have developed to analyze film in terms of social impact and influence, e.g., the way in which films construct and reflect cultural, national, and gender identities. See for example Laura Mulvey's "Visual Pleasure and Narrative Cinema," where Mulvey discusses the masculine subjectivity of film and the operation of the "male gaze" which projects its desire onto female figures. Males see, while women are to be seen. More recently, feminist works such as Judith Butler's *Bodies That Matter* have discussed views of the gaze that take into account lesbian subjectivity.

33. A term that feminist theory has adopted from the French psychoanalytic theorist Jacques Lacan to refer to the practice of presenting images from the perspective of heteronormative culture, a practice which results in an unequal power dynamic of gender.

34. Hayden White, *Tropics of Discourse*, 1.

35. For a discussion of the perception of vision in the ancient world from Plato to Seneca, see Shadi Bartsch, *The Mirror of the Self*.

36. For further discussion on the concept of gender in fifth-century Athens, see my discussion of Kirk Ormand's article "Oedipus the Queen" in chapter 2.

37. Burke, *Eyewitnessing*, 188. See also Thomas Postlewait, "Eyewitnesses to History," for further discussion on the techniques for reading images and the related problems.

38. Examples of the literary sources she studies include: Aristophanes's *Women at the Thesmophoria* (253–68), *Assemblywomen* (74–75, 269–71, 319, 345, 508), and *Clouds*

(102–3); Aeschylus's *Prometheus Bound* (135) and *Agamemnon* (944–45); Homer's *Odyssey* 1.96; Plato's *Symposium* 174A and 203D; and Xenophon's *Oeconomicus* 9.19.2.

39. On the erotics of feet, see Daniel Levine, "ERATON BAMA ('Her Lovely FootStep')."

40. On "ghosting" or "theater as a vast recycling project," see Marvin Carlson's *The Haunted Stage*.

41. On the prosecution of inanimate objects in Greek law, see Walter Woodburn Hyde's "The Prosecution of Lifeless Things and Animals in Greek Law: Part I" and "The Prosecution of Lifeless Things and Animals in Greek Law: Part II."

42. David Wiles in his *Mask and Performance* argues that the god's human and divine forms would not have differed (228).

43. Discussed later in relation to Froma Zeitlin's article.

44. Because only Pentheus in the play wears a *mitra*, Sophocles's reference to a "golden-mitraed Dionysus," in the ca. 429 BCE *Oedipus Tyrannus*, cannot be easily assumed into the context of *Bacchae* any more than the mid-fifth-century representations of a full-bearded, armed, muscular version of Dionysus can. Moreover, Dionysus most often appears in vase-painting with an ivy wreath, so the *mitra*'s pronounced association with women specifically may override any remote Dionysiac associations with the headgear.

45. A later note will discuss examples of bearded images of Dionysus which also existed at the time.

46. Ormand, "Oedipus the Queen," 10–11.

47. Rabinowitz, "How Is It Played?"

48. Foley, *Ritual Irony*, 250.

49. Dodds, *Bacchae*, 133n453–59.

50. Discussed later in relation to Froma Zeitlin's article.

51. Dodds, *Bacchae*, 133–34n453–59.

52. For a discussion of the suggestion of Dionysus's passivity, see Csapo, "Riding the Phallus," which argues that Dionysus's ambiguous nature would make him capable of playing both an active and a passive role.

53. See for example the image of the bearded Dionysus on the Attic, red-figure, terracotta pelike (ca. 420–410 BCE), attributed to the Somzée Painter, Metropolitan Museum of Art 75.2.7 (figure 15), the reverse of which depicts three youths. In addition, the on-line Beazley archive presents at least six examples of a bearded Dionysus on Athenian red-figure pottery from the period 425–375 BCE including Beazley 9024294, Odessa Archeological Museum: 76449; Beazley 217518, Ruvo, Museo Jatta: 36933; Beazley 217480, Gotha, Schlossmuseum: 75; Beazley 217553, Paris, Musée du Louvre: G433; Beazley 217595, Agrigento, Museo Archeologico Regionale: XXXX217595; Beazley 217593, Munich, Antikensammlungen: S68. http://www.beazley.ox.ac.uk/archive/default.htm.

54. Carpenter, *Dionysian Imagery*, 106. However, while the god does not appear

to be depicted as a foreigner in these images, Carpenter explains that he does appear as a beardless youth in at least two of the images from the late fifth century BCE (107).

55. Dodds, *Bacchae*, 134n453–59.

56. Ibid.

57. A point often assumed from Agaue's comment that the "lion's" (i.e., Pentheus's) head is just sprouting hair (1185–87). However, Agaue's comment is difficult to take as certain evidence for the length of Pentheus's beard and thus his age. She is after all still deluded into believing that her son's head is a lion's.

58. For comparison, see my discussion in chapter 2 of Ormand's "Oedipus the Queen," which uses the fictive world of the play to make an argument about social codes of gender. See also chapter 4 on the distinction between character and actor.

59. *Thēly-* and *gynaiko-* refer to different words for woman.

60. Pentheus dresses up because Dionysus sends him into a "light madness" (*elaphran lyssan* 850–51). He does not go into a "light-minded madness" from dressing up in his new costume, as Aoife Monks has suggested in her introduction, or from wearing a *mitra*, as per Dodds's argument (*Bacchae*, 181n854–55). For one, Dionysus states that he must first delude Pentheus, because the sane king would never have considered dressing up (851–53) and donning a *mitra* otherwise. Second, Pentheus's lingering sanity is marked by his uncertainty about whether or not to dress up when he exits the stage (845–46). Third, Pentheus's *mitra* does not *accidentally* fall off and as a result make him sane. Pentheus removes the *mitra*, so he must have first come to his senses to realize that he should take off the headgear, which serves to disguise him (1115–18). Thus, wearing the headgear alone could not have made him mad.

61. Pentheus's costume (*skeyēn*) resembles those of neither Cadmus nor Teiresias, who do not wear *mitras*, nor the feminine (*thēlyn*) costume of the uninitiated Theban women, nor the (*skeyēn*, 180) of the god, which includes a thyrsus, fawnskin, and an ivy wreath (176–77).

62. Maenads on vase-painting do not consistently wear *mitras*. Although the chorus and Agaue could theoretically wear them, there is no reference to their doing so.

63. The only references to women who girdle themselves, as Pentheus does, are to the Theban women who girdle their fawnskins with snakes that lick their cheeks (*katezdōsanto*, 698). However, maenads (good and bad) on vase-paintings often wear girdles (figures 7 and 8). See Blundell's "Clutching at Clothes" on the significance of girdles or belts (156–58), which often signify preparation for a wedding—in Pentheus's case, perhaps a marriage to death.

64. Presumably upper-class women would have stayed indoors and therefore avoided the sun. Slaves and lower-class women, however, would have presumably

had tanned skin. Vase-painting may not reliably indicate the convention of the use of white in masking, and because various painters may use distinct stylistic conventions, the use of pigment may be contingent upon the preferences and styles of the individual painters. Therefore, in *Women at the Thesmophoria*, it is uncertain whether Agathon's mask (*leykos*, 147–49) actually was white, but even if it were, the color could have been difficult for all to see in a large outdoor theatre in the sunlight. From my observations of the vase at the 2010 J. Paul Getty exhibit "The Art of Ancient Greek Theater," the barefoot figure who is presumed to be a cross-dressed actor on the Pronomos Vase appears to have larger and darker feet than those of Ariadne, who has white skin, which is a characteristic associated with feminine beauty. On whiteness and femininity in ancient Greece, see Bridget M. Thomas, "Constraints and Contradictions: Whiteness and Femininity in Ancient Greece," in *Women's Dress in the Ancient Greek World*.

65. Seaford cites two fifth-century sources as evidence to suggest that long hair "was worn by Greek men generally (so far as we can tell) until the second half of the 6th c. BC, and thereafter by some gods (especially D. [Dionysus]). In Athens of Eur.'s time, it [long hair] was a mark of aristocratic young men, and so caused resentment (Lysias 16.18, Ar. *Knights* 580)" (*Bacchae* 187n455–56). Seaford also suggests (187n455–56) that despite the manliness of short hair, "P. [Pentheus] himself may have long hair, but held up in a band," because line 831 suggests that Pentheus either wore a wig or had long hair.

66. If Dionysus's hair did flow long beside his cheeks (150, 240, 455) and proves him "no wrestler," determining the social significance of hair is still difficult. Representations on vase-paintings from the period suggest that women bound their hair and did not wear it long in public. Maenads often tie their hair up but sometimes wear it long. On the Pronomos Vase, ca. 400 BCE (figures 1, 2, and 3), which on one side depicts a cast from a satyr play, the unidentified woman in figure 1, who could also be a cross-dressed actor with his hair tied up (fourth figure from viewer's right), wears her hair up perhaps to fit it better under the mask. The actor playing Heracles (third figure from viewer's right), on the other hand, who is an athletic hero and often appears with short hair, and about four of the chorus members have shorter-cropped hair. However, the majority of men depicted (bearded and unbearded), including the beardless Dionysus, have curls that "flow beside their cheeks."

67. Frontisi-Ducroux and Lissarrague, "From Ambiguity to Ambivalence," 217–18.

68. See for example Dodds, *Bacchae*, 133–34n453–59.

69. Zeitlin, "Playing the Other," 65.

70. For example, Karen Bassi's *Acting Like Men*, 141, a study which suggests that Athenian cross-dressing is appropriative and aims to master the other.

71. de Certeau, *The Writing of History*, 46.

72. Michael Stanford, *The Nature of Historical Knowledge*, 59.

Chapter 6. Gesture and Mask

1. For examples of relevant fifth- and early fourth-century theatrical images, see figures 1, 2, 6, 9, 10, 11, 12, 13, and 14. For further discussion of these images, see chapters 3 and 5.

2. For a discussion of performance style, see chapter 4.

3. Semioticians have developed a vocabulary for reading and describing gestural language on the stage. See for example Patrice Pavis's "Problems of a Semiology of Theatrical Gesture" and *Languages of the Stage*; Keir Elam's *The Semiotics of Theatre and Drama*; and also Elaine Aston and George Savona's *Theatre as Sign-System*. For studies on reading the body and its cultural, historical, and gender-specific movement, see Susan Foster, Mark Franko, and Marcel Mauss.

4. Pickard-Cambridge, *The Dramatic Festivals of Athens*, 176.

5. Taplin, *The Stagecraft of Aeschylus*; Green, "Towards a Reconstruction"; Michael Halleran, *Stagecraft in Euripides*; Maria Luisa Catoni, *Schemata*; Jan Bremmer and Herman Roodenburg, *A Cultural History of Gesture*; Donald Lateiner, *Nonverbal Behavior in Homeric Epic*; Alan Boegehold, *When a Gesture Was Expected*; Glenys Davies, "The Language of Gesture in Greek Art" and "The Significance of the Handshake Motif in Classical Funerary Art"; Lloyd Llewellyn-Jones, "Body Language and the Female Role-Player." For a full survey on studies of nonverbal communication in the ancient world, see Douglas L. Cairns's introduction to *Body Language in the Greek and Roman Worlds*. Much recent work in classics on nonverbal communication has focused on Roman oratory, perhaps because the source material offers such a rich commentary on gestural practices.

6. Dodds, *Bacchae*.

7. Seaford, *Bacchae*.

8. Seidensticker, "Comic Elements in Euripides' *Bacchae*."

9. David Wiles, *Mask and Performance in Greek Tragedy*.

10. An example of Taplin's use of evidence is as follows. Regarding line 231 of *Eumenides*, Taplin discusses the departure of the chorus in mid-play: "It is not usual, of course, for the chorus to leave the scene in the course of a tragedy. . . . There are four other instances in surviving fifth-century tragedy: each is in various ways different from the others, and is similar to and different from *Eum*. I catalogue them here, and as I come to each point of dramatic technique, I shall note the variations: (i) S. *Aj* 814–66, (ii) E. *Alc* 746–861, (iii) E. *Hel* 385–515, (iv) *Rh* 564–674. Other examples have been posited among the lost plays, but only two deserve serious consideration. One is the Aeschylean play (presumably *Aitnaiai*) which is the subject of the hypothesis in *POxy* 2257 fr. 1, where *Eum* is given as a parallel for

repeated changes of scene. This seems to imply that the chorus repeatedly left the scene and returned to it: but see pp. 416f. Since we know nothing concrete about the way this was done, there is no more to be said in this context. Secondly it has been supposed that the chorus went off and re-entered in E. *Phaethon* (226–70). But there is no sign in the chorus's own words that it has been away; and so it is best to suppose that it simply retreated into the background during 226–70" (Taplin, *The Stagecraft of Aeschylus*, 375–76).

11. For example, demonstrative pronouns and deictics in particular suggest gesture.

12. Taplin, *Greek Tragedy in Action*, ix.

13. Cairns, "Introduction," xiv.

14. Taplin, *Stagecraft*, 2.

15. Ley, *The Theatricality of Greek Tragedy*, 3.

16. Wiles, *Tragedy in Athens*, 7–8.

17. Bain, *Actors and Audience*, 8.

18. Ibid.

19. In my discussion of *Bacchae* in chapter 3, I define this term as "balance" or "moderation" in order to capture better the nuance of the word's meaning in that play.

20. One problem with using this vase as evidence for fifth-century drama is its Tarentine, not Attic origin, even though some scholars assume that vases from the Greek West were produced according to Athenian tastes and for the Athenian market. Another issue is that the vase is an early fourth-century work, not a late fifth-, and was produced approximately twenty years after *Bacchae*'s 405 BCE production.

21. On the wide-ranging use of this term, see Helen North, *Sophrosyne*, and Adriaan Rademaker, *Sophrosyne and the Rhetoric of Self-Restraint*.

22. See chapter 3 for further discussion on the bias in the philosophic works of Plato.

23. On this gesture in depictions of messengers, see Green's "Messengers from the Tragic Stage."

24. See my chapter 4 for Green's other disclaimers.

25. For a comparative study of Athenian and Noh theatre, see Mae Smethurst, *The Artistry of Aeschylus and Zeami*, and Martha Johnson, "Reflections of Inner Life."

26. For cross-dressed actors, see also figures 10, 11, and possibly 1 (the "woman" in the top row seated to the right of Dionysus and Ariadne).

27. Llewellyn-Jones, "Body Language and the Female Role-Player," 79. See especially his note 37 on *mie*.

28. Ley, *Theatricality of Greek Tragedy*, 206. Ley cautions against such studies

because the so-called traditional theatres to which scholars often compare the Athenian theatre (e.g., Peking Opera, Noh, Kathakali, Kutiyattam, Balinese, etc.) are "not necessarily or even probably what they have always been" (206).

29. On mimicry and alterity, see for example Homi Bhabha's *The Location of Culture* and Michael Taussig's *Mimesis and Alterity*.

30. Taplin, *Greek Tragedy in Action*, 7.

31. I will limit my discussion in this section to some key historiographical issues that arise in Wiles's and Meineck's recent works, but for further reading on the history of scholarship on the mask, see: Henry John Franklin Jones, *On Aristotle and Greek Tragedy*; Stephen Halliwell, "The Function and Aesthetics of the Greek Tragic Mask"; C. W. Marshall, "Some Fifth-Century Masking Conventions"; David Napier, *Masks, Transformation, and Paradox*; Thomas A. Carpenter and Christopher A. Faraone, eds., *Masks of Dionysus*; Martha Johnson, "Reflections of Inner Life"; Claude Calame, "Vision, Blindness, and Mask"; Frontisi-Ducroux, *Le dieu-masque* and *Du masque au visage*; and Jean-Pierre Vernant, *Myth and Society in Ancient Greece*.

32. Meineck notes (152) that the article is part of a forthcoming wider study of the visual aspects of ancient drama.

33. Meineck, "The Neuroscience of the Tragic Mask," 114.

34. Meineck (156n44) notes the categories are not without controversy.

35. Meineck (148) explains that the study offered a neurobiological basis for contextual framing effects on social attributions, and in so doing provides a glimpse into how the human brain operates when watching a mask in a drama.

36. See chapter 1 for a discussion of the historian's ability to see outside of culturally conditioned modes of seeing.

37. Dodds, *Bacchae*, 194n927–29.

38. See chapter 2 for a summary of this play and for further discussion of its potential connection to *Bacchae*.

39. For further discussion of *Bacchae*'s possible allusion to *Women at the Thesmophoria*, see Mendelsohn's review of JoAnne Akalaitis's *Bacchae* and Powers, "Dressing-up Dramaturgy in Charles L. Mee's *Bacchae* 2.1."

40. The principal characters of tragedy are thought to wear the same costumes as those in satyr plays, which is of course why the costumes depicted on the Pronomos Vase are so significant.

41. Dodds notes: "With him [Pentheus] this consciousness takes the form of megalomaniac delusions, like those of the mad Heracles (*Her.* 943ff.) and those which are in fact experienced by the insane" (*Bacchae*, 195n945–46).

42. Discussed earlier in this chapter.

43. The Chorēgos Vase (figure 9) especially demonstrates the distinction in proportion between comic and tragic bodies. Proportion is a key difference in the

appearance of the three comic characters versus the tragic character Aegisthus. Aegisthus's staff is straight and erect. He holds his staff firmly. He grips it elegantly with his index finger slightly separate from his fist. His other hand rests on his head and also keeps three fingers together with the index finger held apart. On the other hand, the slave character whose name, Pyrrhias, is inscribed on the vase and who gestures with his right hand, separates all of the fingers on his left hand, which rests on his hip. His fingers are slightly crooked, giving the impression that they are bent, and the *chorēgos* to the far right also has bent fingers and holds all of them together, without separating the index finger. The characters seem to attempt the same mannerisms as Aegisthus, but their comic context distorts their comportment. Aegisthus's body is proportionate, the comic actors' are not.

44. Another example relevant to this discussion is the chous from Anavyssos (figure 12), ca. 420 BCE. In this scene, a naked, comic actor stands on a stage before a seated, bearded gentleman and a boy, and raises his right arm and leg in unison (perhaps in a gesture like Pentheus's at 943–44). This Attic image juxtaposes an elite character from everyday life with a comic actor performing on stage.

45. On comedy in *Bacchae*, see also Foley, *Ritual Irony*, 217–19, 225–34, 237, 244–45, 250–51, and 257.

46. Dodds (194n935–36) and Seaford (224–25n935–38) primarily use the second-century CE author Pollux (7.54) to make their claims about the importance of pleats in rituals. On the importance of girdling, Seaford notes a second-century CE inscription from Torre Nova. He also notes the Scholia Parisina on Apollonius Rhodius 1.918, which refers to "Samothracian initiands girdled with red bands."

47. Dodds, *Bacchae*, 194n935–36.

48. Seaford, *Bacchae*, 224–25n935–38.

49. Ibid., 225n941–43, and Dodds, *Bacchae*, 195n943–44.

50. Seidensticker, "Comic Elements," 304–5.

51. See also Seidensticker's note 21 on the importance of tone in a scene.

52. Wiles, *Tragedy in Athens*, 4.

53. On the Greek word *gelōn* (from the verb to laugh), Dodds, *Bacchae*, 131n439 comments: "The actor who played the Stranger no doubt wore a smiling mask throughout." R. P. Winnington-Ingram also suggests a smiling Dionysus (8, 9, and 19), as does Foley, *Ritual Irony*, 246ff.

54. Wiles, *Mask and Performance*, 221.

55. E. H. Carr, *What Is History?*, 36.

56. I here concur with Appleby, Hunt, and Jacob, who state: "Truths about the past are possible, even if they are not absolute, and hence are worth struggling for" (7).

WORKS CITED

Alexiou, Margaret. *The Ritual Lament in Greek Tradition*, 2nd ed. Rev. by
Dimitrios Yatromanolakis and Panagiotis Roilos. Lanham, MD: Rowman
& Littlefield Publishers, 2002.

Alpers, Svetlana. "Style Is What You Make It: The Visual Arts Once Again."
In *The Concept of Style*, edited by Berel Lang, 137–62. Ithaca, NY: Cornell
University Press, 1987.

Anderson, Warren D. *Music and Musicians in Ancient Greece*. Ithaca, NY: Cornell
University Press, 1994.

Anti, Carlo. *Teatri greci arcaici da Minosse a Pericle*. Padua, Italy: Le Tre Venezie,
1947.

Appleby, Joyce, Lynn Hunt, and Margaret Jacob. *Telling the Truth about History*.
New York: W. W. Norton & Co., 1994.

Arnott, Peter D. *Greek Scenic Conventions in the Fifth Century B.C.* Oxford, UK:
Clarendon Press, 1962.

———. *Public and Performance in the Greek Theatre*. New York: Routledge, 1989.

Arthur, Marylin B. "The Choral Odes of the *Bacchae* of Euripides." *Yale Classical
Studies* 22 (1972): 145–79.

Ashby, Clifford. "The Case for the Rectangular/Trapezoidal Orchestra." *Theatre
Research International* 13 (1988): 1–20.

———. *Classical Greek Theatre: New Views of an Old Subject*. Iowa City: University of Iowa Press, 1999.

Aston, Elaine and George Savona. *Theatre as Sign-System: A Semiotics of Text and
Performance*. New York: Routledge, 1991.

Bacon, Helen H. "The Chorus in Greek Life and Drama." *Arion* 3.1 (Fall
1994–Winter 1995): 6–24.

Bain, David. *Actors and Audience: A Study of Asides and Related Conventions in Greek Drama.* 1977. Reprint. Oxford, UK: Clarendon Press, 1987.

———. "Audience Address in Greek Tragedy." *Classical Quarterly* 25.1 (1975): 13–25.

Barber, E. J. W. "The Peplos of Athena." In *Goddess and Polis: The Panathenaic Festival in Ancient Athens,* edited by Jenifer Neils, 103–18. Princeton, NJ: Princeton University Press, 1992.

Barker, Andrew. *Greek Musical Writings I: The Musician and His Art.* Cambridge, UK: Cambridge University Press, 1984.

———. *Greek Musical Writings II: Harmonic and Acoustic Theory.* Cambridge, UK: Cambridge University Press, 1989.

Bartsch, Shadi. *The Mirror of the Self: Sexuality, Self-Knowledge, and the Gaze in the Early Roman Empire.* Chicago: University of Chicago Press, 2006.

Bassi, Karen. *Acting Like Men: Gender, Drama and Nostalgia in Ancient Greece.* Ann Arbor: University of Michigan Press, 1998.

———. "*Tragedy in Athens: Performance Space and Theatrical Meaning,* Review." *Theatre Journal* 53.2 (2001): 347–48.

Beazley, J. D. "Hydria-fragments in Corinth." *Hesperia* 24.4 (1955): 305–19.

Benedetti, Jean. *The Art of the Actor: The Essential History of Acting from Classical Times to the Present Day.* London: Methuen, 2005.

Bennett, Susan. *Theatre Audiences: A Theory of Production and Reception,* 2nd ed. New York: Routledge, 1997.

Bers, Victor. "Dikastic *Thorubos.*" In *Crux: Essays in Greek History Presented to G. E. M. de Ste. Croix,* edited by Paul A. Cartledge and F. D. Harvey, 1–15. London: Duckworth, 1985.

Bhabha, Homi. *The Location of Culture.* New York: Routledge, 1994.

Blau, Herbert. *The Audience.* Baltimore: Johns Hopkins University Press, 1990.

Bloch, Marc. *The Historian's Craft.* Translated by Peter Putnam. New York: Alfred A. Knopf, 1953.

Blundell, Mary Whitlock. *Helping Friends and Harming Enemies: A Study in Sophocles and Greek Ethics.* Cambridge, UK: Cambridge University Press, 1989.

Blundell, Sue. "Clutching at Clothes." In *Women's Dress in the Ancient Greek World,* edited by Lloyd Llewellyn-Jones, 143–70. Swansea, Wales, and London: Classical Press of Wales/Duckworth, 2002.

Boegehold, Alan L. *When a Gesture Was Expected: A Selection of Examples from Archaic and Classical Greek Literature.* Princeton, NJ: Princeton University Press, 1999.

Bond, Godfrey W., ed. *Heracles.* 1981. Reprinted with corrections. Oxford, UK: Clarendon Press, 1990.

Bonfante, Larissa. "The Naked Greek: How Ancient Art and Literature Reflect the Custom of Civic Nudity." *Archaeology* 43.5 (1990): 28–35.

————. "Nudity as a Costume in Classical Art." *American Journal of Archaeology* 93.4 (1989): 543–70.

Böttinger, Karl August. "Waren die Frauen in Athen Zuschauerinnen bei den dramatischen Vorstellungen?" In *Kleine schriften: archäologischen und antiquarischen*, vol. 1, edited by Julius Sillig, 297–307. Dresden and Leipzig: Arnoldische Buchhandlung, (1796) 1837.

Bremmer, Jan and Herman Roodenburg. *A Cultural History of Gesture: From Antiquity to the Present Day.* Ithaca, NY: Cornell University Press, 1992.

Broadie, Sarah. "XIV — Soul and Body in Plato and Descartes." *Proceedings of the Aristotelian Society* 101.1 (2001): 295–308.

Brockett, Oscar G. *History of the Theatre*, 3rd ed. Boston: Allyn and Bacon, 1977.

Brockett, Oscar G. and Franklin J. Hildy. *History of the Theatre*, 10th ed. New York: Pearson, 2008.

Brooke, Iris. *Costume in Greek Classic Drama.* London: Methuen, 1962.

Brown, A. L. "Three and Scene-painting Sophocles." *Proceedings of the Cambridge Philological Society* 210 (1984): 1–17.

Bundrick, Sheram D. *Music and Image in Classical Athens.* Cambridge, UK: Cambridge University Press, 2005.

Burke, Peter. *Eyewitnessing: The Uses of Images as Historical Evidence.* Ithaca, NY: Cornell University Press, 2001.

Burkert, Walter. *Greek Religion.* Cambridge, MA: Harvard University Press, 1985.

Burton, R. W. B. *The Chorus in Sophocles' Tragedies.* Oxford, UK: Clarendon Press, 1980.

Butler, Judith. *Bodies that Matter: On the Discursive Limits of Sex.* New York: Routledge, 1993.

Cairns, Douglas. "Introduction." In *Body Language in the Greek and Roman Worlds*, edited by Douglas L. Cairns, ix–xxii. Swansea, Wales: Classical Press of Wales, 2005.

Calame, Claude. *Choruses of Young Women in Ancient Greece: Their Morphology, Religious Role, and Social Functions*, rev. ed. Translated by Derek Collins and Janice Orion. New York: Rowman & Littlefield Publishers, 2001.

————. "Vision, Blindness, and Mask: The Radicalization of the Emotions in Sophocles' *Oedipus Rex.*" In *Tragedy and the Tragic: Greek Theatre and Beyond*, edited by Michael S. Silk, 17–37. Oxford, UK: Clarendon Press, 1996.

Canning, Charlotte M. and Thomas Postlewait, eds. *Representing the Past: Essays in Performance Historiography.* Iowa City: University of Iowa Press, 2010.

Carlson, Marvin. *The Haunted Stage: The Theatre as Memory Machine.* Ann Arbor: University of Michigan Press, 2001.

————. "The Iconic Stage." *Journal of Dramatic Theory and Criticism* 3.2 (Spring 1989): 3–18.

———. "Indexical Space in the Theatre." *Assaph* 10 (1994): 1–10.

———. "Space and Theatre History." In *Representing the Past: Essays in Performance Historiography*, edited by Charlotte M. Canning and Thomas Postlewait, 195–214. Iowa City: University of Iowa Press, 2010.

———. "Theatre Audiences and the Reading of Performance." In *Interpreting the Theatrical Past: Essays in the Historiography of Performance*, edited by Thomas Postlewait and Bruce A. McConachie, 82–98. Iowa City: University of Iowa Press, 1989.

———. "Theatrical Performance: Illustration, Translation, Fulfillment, or Supplement?" *Theatre Journal* 37.1 (1985): 5–11.

Carpenter, Thomas H. *Dionysian Imagery in Fifth-Century Athens.* Oxford, UK: Clarendon Press, 1997.

Carpenter, Thomas H. and Christopher A. Faraone, eds. *Masks of Dionysus.* Ithaca, NY: Cornell University Press, 1993.

Carr, David. *Time, Narrative, and History.* Bloomington: Indiana University Press, 1988.

Carr, E. H. *What Is History?* New York: Random House, 1961.

Carter, David M. *The Politics of Greek Tragedy.* Exeter, UK: Bristol Phoenix Press, 2007.

Carter, David M., ed. *Why Athens?: A Reappraisal of Tragic Politics.* Oxford, UK: Oxford University Press, 2011.

Casaubon, Isaac. *Theophrasti "Characteres ethici," sive descriptions morum.* Lyon, France: Franciscum le Preux, 1592.

Case, Sue-Ellen. "Classic Drag: The Greek Creation of Female Parts." *Theatre Journal* 37.3 (1985): 317–27.

Catoni, Maria Luisa. *Schemata: Comunicazione non verbale nella Grecia antica.* Pisa, Italy: Edizioni della Normale, 2005.

Cawthorn, Katrina. *Becoming Female: The Male Body in Greek Tragedy.* London: Duckworth, 2008.

Chaston, Colleen. *Tragic Props and Cognitive Function: Aspects of the Function of Images in Thinking* (*Mnemosyne* Suppl. 317). Boston and Leiden, Netherlands: Brill, 2010.

Chaudhuri, Una. *Staging Place: The Geography of Modern Drama.* Ann Arbor: University of Michigan Press, 1995.

Cleland, Liza, Glenys Davies, and Lloyd Llewellyn-Jones. *Greek and Roman Dress from A–Z.* New York: Routledge, 2007.

Cleland, Liza, Mary Harlow, and Lloyd Llewellyn-Jones. "'I Wear This Therefore I Am': The Clothed Body in the Ancient World [Introduction]." In *The Clothed Body in the Ancient World*, edited by Liza Cleland, Mary Harlow, and Lloyd J. Llewellyn-Jones, xi–xv. Oxford, UK: Oxbow Books, 2005.

Cliff, Nigel. *The Shakespeare Riots: Revenge, Drama and Death in Nineteenth-Century America.* New York: Random House, 2007.

Clifford, James. *The Predicament of Culture: Twentieth-Century Ethnography, Literature, and Art.* Cambridge, MA: Harvard University Press, 1988.

Collingwood, R. G. *The Idea of History,* rev. ed. Edited by Jan Van Der Dussen. Oxford, UK: Clarendon Press, 1993.

Compton-Engle, Gwendolyn. "Control of Costume in Three Plays of Aristophanes." *American Journal of Philology* 124.4 (2003): 507–35.

———. "Stolen Cloaks in Aristophanes' *Ecclesiazusae.*" *Transactions of the American Philological Association* 135.1 (2005): 163–76.

Cornford, F. M. "The So-called *Kommos* in Greek Tragedy." *Classical Review* 27 (1913): 41–45.

Csapo, Eric. *Actors and Icons of the Ancient Theater.* Malden, MA: Wiley-Blackwell, 2010.

———. "Kallippides on the Floor-Sweepings: The Limits of Realism in Classical Acting and Performance Styles." In *Greek and Roman Actors: Aspects of an Ancient Profession,* edited by Pat Easterling and Edith Hall, 127–47. Cambridge, UK: Cambridge University Press, 2002.

———. "The Men Who Built the Theatres: *Theatropolai, Theatronai,* and *Arkhitektones.*" In *The Greek Theatre and Festivals: Documentary Studies,* edited by Peter Wilson, 87–115. Oxford, UK: Oxford University Press, 2007.

———. "Riding the Phallus for Dionysus: Iconology, Ritual, and Gender-Role De/Construction." *Phoenix* 51.3/4 (1997): 253–95.

Csapo, Eric and William J. Slater. *The Context of Ancient Drama.* Ann Arbor: University of Michigan Press, 1995.

D'Angour, Armand. "How the Dithyramb Got Its Shape." *Classical Quarterly* 47.2 (1997): 331–51.

Dale, A. M. *The Lyric Metres of Greek Drama,* 2nd ed. Cambridge, UK: Cambridge University Press, 1968.

Davies, Glenys. "The Language of Gesture in Greek Art: Gender and Status on Grave Stelai." *Apollo* CXL.389 (1994): 6–11.

———. "The Significance of the Handshake Motif in Classical Funerary Art." *American Journal of Archaeology* 89.4 (1985): 627–40.

Davis, Jim and Victor Emeljanow. *Reflecting the Audience: London Theatregoing, 1840–1880.* Iowa City: University of Iowa Press, 2001.

Davis, Tracy C. "Between History and Event: Rehearsing Nuclear War Survival." *Drama Review* 46.4 (2002): 11–45.

de Certeau, Michel. *The Writing of History.* Translated by Tom Conley. New York: Columbia University Press, 1988.

Dionysus in 69. Directed by Brian de Palma. 1970. New York: International Film Forum, 2011. DVD.

Dodds, E. R. *The Greeks and the Irrational* (Sather Classical Lectures 25). Berkeley: University of California Press, 1951.

Dodds, E. R., ed. *Bacchae,* 2nd ed. Oxford, UK: Clarendon Press, 1960.

Dolan, Jill. *The Feminist Spectator as Critic.* Ann Arbor: University of Michigan Press, 1988.

Dörpfeld, Wilhelm and Emil Reisch. *Das griechische theater: Beiträge zur geschichte des Dionysos-theaters in Athen und anderer griechischer theater.* Athens: Barth & von Hirst, 1896.

Dover, Sir Kenneth. *Greek Homosexuality.* Cambridge, MA: Harvard University Press, 1978.

Duncan, Anne. *Performance and Identity in the Classical World.* Cambridge, UK: Cambridge University Press, 2006.

Easterling, P. E. "Weeping, Witnessing, and the Tragic Audience: Response to Segal." In *Tragedy and the Tragic: Greek Theatre and Beyond,* edited by Michael Silk, 173–82. Oxford, UK: Clarendon Press, 1996.

Easterling, Pat and Edith Hall, eds. *Greek and Roman Actors: Aspects of an Ancient Profession.* Cambridge, UK: Cambridge University Press, 2002.

Edmunds, Lowell. *Theatrical Space and Historical Place in Sophocles' Oedipus at Colonus.* New York: Rowman & Littlefield Publishers, 1996.

Ekman, Paul. "Basic Emotions." In *Handbook of Cognition and Emotion,* edited by Mick J. Power and Tim Dalgleish, 45–60. New York: John Wiley & Sons, 1999.

Elam, Keir. *The Semiotics of Theatre and Drama,* 2nd ed. London: Methuen, 2002.

Emlyn-Jones, Chris. "The Dramatic Poet and His Audience: Agathon and Socrates in Plato's *Symposium.*" *Hermes* 132.4 (2004): 389–405.

English, Mary C. "The Diminishing Role of Stage Properties in Aristophanic Comedy." *Helios* 27.2 (2000): 149–62.

Fearn, David. *Bacchylides: Politics, Performance, Poetic Tradition.* Oxford, UK: Oxford University Press, 2007.

Fiechter, Ernst. *Das Dionysos-Theater in Athen.* 4 vols. Stuttgart: W. Kohlhammer, 1935–1950.

Fischer-Lichte, Erika. "Theatre and the Civilizing Process: An Approach to the History of Acting." In *Interpreting the Theatrical Past: Essays in the Historiography of Performance,* edited by Thomas Postlewait and Bruce A. McConachie, 19–36. Iowa City: University of Iowa Press, 1989.

Foley, Helene P. "Choral Identity in Greek Tragedy." *Classical Philology* 98.1 (2003): 1–30.

———. "The Comic Body in Greek Art and Drama." In *Not the Classical Ideal:*

Athens and the Construction of the Other in Greek Art, edited by Beth Cohen, 275–314. Boston and Leiden, Netherlands: Brill, 2002.

———. *Female Acts in Greek Tragedy*. Princeton, NJ: Princeton University Press, 2001.

———. *Ritual Irony: Poetry and Sacrifice in Euripides*. Ithaca, NY: Cornell University Press, 1985.

Foster, Susan Leigh. "Choreographies of Gender." *Signs* 24.1 (1998): 1–33.

Foster, Susan Leigh, ed. *Choreographing History*. Bloomington: Indiana University Press, 1995.

Foucault, Michel. "What Is an Author?" Translated by Josuè V. Harari. In *The Foucault Reader*, edited by Paul Rabinow, 101–20. New York: Pantheon, 1984.

Franko, Mark. *Dance as Text: Ideologies of the Baroque Body*. Cambridge, UK: Cambridge University Press, 1993.

Frontisi-Ducroux, Françoise. *Du masque au visage. Aspects de l'identité en Grèce ancienne*. Paris: Flammarion, 1995.

———. *Le dieu-masque: Une figure du Dionysos d'Athènes*. Paris-Rome: La Découverte-École Française de Rome, 1991.

Frontisi-Ducroux, Françoise and François Lissarrague. "From Ambiguity to Ambivalence: A Dionysiac Excursion through the 'Anakreontic' Vases." In *Before Sexuality: The Construction of Erotic Experience in the Ancient Greek World*, edited by David M. Halperin, John J. Winkler, and Froma I. Zeitlin, 211–57. Princeton, NJ: Princeton University Press, 1990.

Gamel, Mary-Kay. Review of *The Theatricality of Greek Tragedy: Playing Space and Chorus*, by Graham Ley. *Bryn Mawr Classical Review*, October 11, 2008. http://www.bmcr.brynmawr.edu/2008/2008-10-11.html.

Garner, Stanton B. *Bodied Spaces: Phenomenology and Performance in Contemporary Drama*. Ithaca, NY: Cornell University Press, 1994.

Gawlinski, Laura. " 'Fashioning' Initiates: Dress at the Mysteries." In *Reading a Dynamic Canvas: Adornment in the Ancient Mediterranean World*, edited by Maura Heyn and Cynthia Colburn. Newcastle, UK: Cambridge Scholars, 2008.

Gebhard, Elizabeth R. "The Form of the Orchestra in the Early Greek Theatre." *Hesperia* 43.4 (1974): 428–40.

———. *The Theater at Isthmia*. Chicago: University of Chicago Press, 1973.

Geddes, Ann G. "Rags and Riches: The Costume of Athenian Men in the Fifth Century." *Classical Quarterly* 37.2 (1987): 307–31.

Gibson, James J. *The Ecological Approach to Visual Perception*. Boston: Houghton Mifflin, 1979.

Gill, Christopher. *Personality in Greek Epic, Tragedy, and Philosophy: The Self in Dialogue*. Oxford, UK: Clarendon Press, 1996.

Girard, Reneé. *Violence and the Sacred.* Translated by Patrick Gregory. Baltimore: Johns Hopkins University Press, 1979.

Goette, Hans R. "Archaeological Appendix" to Eric Csapo's "The Men Who Built the Theatres: *Theatropolai, Theatronai,* and *Arkhitektones.*" In *The Greek Theatre and Festivals: Documentary Studies,* edited by Peter J. Wilson, 87–121. Oxford, UK: Oxford University Press, 2007.

Goff, Barbara. *Citizen Bacchae: Women's Ritual Practice in Ancient Greece.* Berkeley: University of California Press, 2004.

Golder, Herb. "Making a Scene: Gesture, Tableau, and the Tragic Chorus." *Arion* 4.1 (Spring 1996): 1–19.

Goldhill, Simon. "The Audience of Athenian Tragedy." In *The Cambridge Companion to Greek Tragedy,* edited by P. E. Easterling, 54–68. Cambridge, UK: Cambridge University Press, 1997.

———. "Collectivity and Otherness—The Authority of the Tragic Chorus: Response to Gould." In *Tragedy and the Tragic: Greek Theatre and Beyond,* edited by Michael S. Silk, 244–56. Oxford, UK: Clarendon Press, 1996.

———. "Representing Democracy: Women at the Great Dionysia." In *Ritual, Finance, Politics: Athenian Democratic Accounts Presented to David Lewis,* edited by Robin Osborne and Simon Hornblower, 347–69. Oxford, UK: Clarendon Press, 1994.

Gould, John. "Tragedy and Collective Experience." In *Tragedy and the Tragic: Greek Theatre and Beyond,* edited by Michael S. Silk, 217–43. Oxford, UK: Clarendon Press, 1996.

Green, J. Richard. "Messengers from the Tragic Stage: The A. D. Trendall Memorial Lecture." *British Institute of Classical Studies* 41.1 (1996): 17–30.

———. *Theatre in Ancient Greek Society.* New York: Routledge, 1994.

———. "Towards a Reconstruction of Performance Style." In *Greek and Roman Actors: Aspects of an Ancient Profession,* edited by Pat Easterling and Edith Hall, 93–126. Cambridge, UK: Cambridge University Press, 2002.

Green, J. Richard and Eric W. Handley. *Images of the Greek Theatre.* Austin: University of Texas Press, 1995.

Griffith, Mark. "Brilliant Dynasts: Power and Politics in the *Oresteia.*" *Classical Antiquity* 14.1 (1995): 62–129.

———. "Satyr Play and Tragedy, Face to Face." In *The Pronomos Vase and Its Context,* edited by Oliver Taplin and Rosie Wyles, 47–64. Oxford, UK: Oxford University Press, 2010.

———. "Slaves of Dionysos: Satyrs, Audience, and the End of the *Oresteia.*" *Classical Antiquity* 21.2 (2002): 195–258.

Gundert, Beate. "Soma and Psyche in Hippocratic Medicine." In *Psyche and Soma: Physicians and Metaphysicians on the Mind-Body Problem from Antiquity to Enlightenment*, edited by John P. Wright and Paul Potter, 13–36. Oxford, UK: Clarendon Press, 2000.

Hagel, Stephen. *Ancient Greek Music: A New Technical History*. Cambridge, UK: Cambridge University Press, 2009.

Hall, Edith. "Ithyphallic Males Behaving Badly, or, Satyr Drama as Gendered Tragic Ending." In *Parchments of Gender: Deciphering the Bodies of Antiquity*, edited by Maria Wyke, 13–37. Oxford, UK: Clarendon Press, 1998.

———. "Lawcourt Dramas: The Power of Performance in Greek Forensic Oratory." *British Institute of Classical Studies* 40.1 (1995): 39–58.

———. "The Singing Actors of Antiquity." In *Greek and Roman Actors: Aspects of an Ancient Profession*, edited by Pat Easterling and Edith Hall, 3–38. Cambridge, UK: Cambridge University Press, 2002.

———. "The Sociology of Athenian Tragedy." In *The Cambridge Companion to Greek Tragedy*, edited by P. E. Easterling, 93–126. Cambridge, UK: Cambridge University Press, 1997.

———. *The Theatrical Cast of Athens: Interactions between Ancient Greek Drama and Society*. Oxford, UK: Oxford University Press, 2006.

Halleran, Michael R. *Stagecraft in Euripides*. London: Croom Helm, 1985.

Halliwell, Stephen. "The Function and Aesthetics of the Greek Tragic Mask." In *Intertextualität in der griechisch-römischen Komödie (Drama-Beiträge zum antiken Drama und seiner Rezeption 2)*, edited by Niall W. Slater and Bernhard Zimmerman, 195–211. Stuttgart, Germany: Metzlerschen & Poeschel, 1993.

Halperin, David M. *One Hundred Years of Homosexuality and Other Essays on Greek Love*. New York: Routledge, 1990.

Hamilton, Richard. "Lenaia Vases in Context." In *Poetry, Theory, Praxis. The Social Life of Myth, Word, and Image in Ancient Greece. Essays in Honor of William J. Slater*, edited by Eric Csapo and Margaret Miller, 48–68. Oxford, UK: Oxbow Books, 2003.

Hammond, Richard. "Cries Within and the Tragic Skene." *American Journal of Philology* 108 (1987): 585–99.

Harrison, George W. M., ed. *Satyr Drama: Tragedy at Play*. Swansea, Wales: Classical Press of Wales, 2005.

Hart, Mary Louise, ed. *The Art of Ancient Greek Theater*. Los Angeles: J. Paul Getty Museum, 2010.

Hawley, Richard. "The Male Body as Spectacle in Attic Drama." In *Thinking Men: Masculinity and Its Self-Representation in the Classical Tradition*, edited by Lin Foxhall and John Salmon, 83–99. New York: Routledge, 1998.

Henderson, Jeffrey. "The *Dēmos* and the Comic Competition." In *Nothing to Do with Dionysos?*, edited by John J. Winkler and Froma I. Zeitlin, 271–313. Princeton, NJ: Princeton University Press, 1990.

————. "The Training of Classicists." In *Classics: A Discipline and Profession in Crisis*, edited by Phyllis Culham and Lowell Edmunds, 89–98. Lanham, MD: University Press of America, 1989.

————. "Women and the Athenian Dramatic Festivals." *Transactions of the American Philological Association* 121 (1991): 133–47.

Holborn, Hajo. *History and the Humanities*. New York: Doubleday, 1972.

Holst-Warhaft, Gail. *Dangerous Voices: Women's Laments and Greek Literature*. New York: Routledge, 1992.

Hourmouziades, Nicolaos C. *Production and Imagination in Euripides: Form and Function of the Scenic Space*. Athens: Greek Society for Humanistic Studies, 1965.

Hubert, Henri and Marcel Mauss. *Sacrifice: Its Nature and Functions*. Translated by W. D. Halls. 1964. Reprint. Chicago: University of Chicago Press, 1981.

Hyde, Walter Woodburn. "The Prosecution of Lifeless Things and Animals in Greek Law: Part I." *American Journal of Philology* 38.2 (1917): 152–75.

————. "The Prosecution of Lifeless Things and Animals in Greek Law: Part II." *American Journal of Philology* 38.3 (1917): 285–303.

Iggers, Georg G. *Historiography in the Twentieth Century: From Scientific Objectivity to the Postmodern Challenge*. Middletown, CT: Wesleyan University Press, 1997.

Issacharoff, Michael. *Discourse as Performance*. Palo Alto, CA: Stanford University Press, 1989.

————. "Space and Reference in Drama." *Poetics Today* 2.3 (1981): 211–24.

Jenkins, Keith. *Re-thinking History*. New York: Routledge, 1991.

Jenkins, Keith, ed. *The Postmodern History Reader*. New York: Routledge, 1997.

Johnson, Martha. "Reflections of Inner Life: Masks and Masked Acting in Ancient Greek Tragedy and Japanese Noh Drama." *Modern Drama* 35 (1992): 20–34.

Jones, Henry John Franklin. *On Aristotle and Greek Tragedy*. New York: Oxford University Press, 1962.

Jory, John. Review of *Actors and Icons of the Ancient Theater*, by Eric Csapo. *Bryn Mawr Classical Review*, April 11, 2011. http://www.bmcr.brynmawr.edu /2011/2011–04–11.html.

Kitto, H. D. L. "The Dance in Greek Tragedy." *Journal of Hellenic Studies* 75 (1955): 36–41.

Krasner, David, ed. *Method Acting Reconsidered: Theory, Practice, Future*. New York: Palgrave Macmillan, 2000.

Krause, Duane. "An Epic System." In *Acting (Re)considered: Theories and Practices*, edited by Phillip Zarrilli, 262–74. New York: Routledge, 1995.

Lada-Richards, Ismene. "'Empathic Understanding': Emotion and Cognition in

Classical Dramatic Audience-Response." *Proceedings of the Cambridge Philological Society* 39 (1993): 94–140.

———. "Emotion and Meaning in Tragic Performance." In *Tragedy and the Tragic: Greek Theatre and Beyond*, edited by Michael S. Silk, 397–413. Oxford, UK: Clarendon Press, 1996.

———. "'Estrangement' or 'Reincarnation'?: Performers and Performance on the Classical Athenian Stage." *Arion* 5.2 (Fall 1997): 66–107.

Landels, John G. *Music in Ancient Greece and Rome*. New York: Routledge, 1999.

Lateiner, Donald. *Nonverbal Behavior in Homeric Epic*. Ann Arbor: University of Michigan Press, 1995.

Lawler, Lillian B. *The Dance in Ancient Greece*. Middletown, CT: Wesleyan University Press, 1964.

Lawrence, Stuart. "Audience Uncertainty and Euripides' *Medea*." *Hermes* 125.1 (1997): 49–55.

Lech, Marcel Lysgaard. "The Shape of the Athenian *Theatron* in the Fifth Century: Overlooked Evidence." *Greek, Roman, and Byzantine Studies* 49.2 (2009): 223–26.

Lee-Brown, Elizabeth. "Performativity, Context, and Agency: The Process of Audience Response and Its Implication for Performance." *Text and Performance Quarterly* 22.2 (2002): 138–48.

Lefebvre, Henri. *The Production of Space*. Translated by Donald Nicholson-Smith. Oxford, UK: Blackwell, 1991.

Levine, Daniel. "ERATON BAMA ('Her Lovely FootStep'): The Erotics of Feet in Ancient Greece." In *Body Language in the Greek and Roman Worlds*, edited by Douglas Cairns, 55–72. Swansea, Wales: Classical Press of Wales, 2005.

Ley, Graham. "A Material World: Costume, Properties, and Scenic Effects." In *The Cambridge Companion to Greek and Roman Theatre*, edited by Marianne McDonald and J. Michael Walton, 268–85. Cambridge, UK: Cambridge University Press, 2007.

———. "Modern Visions of Greek Tragic Dancing." *Theatre Journal* 55.3 (2003): 467–80.

———. "Scenic Notes on Euripides' *Helen*." *Eranos* 89 (1991): 25–34.

———. *The Theatricality of Greek Tragedy: Playing Space and Chorus*. Chicago: University of Chicago Press, 2007.

Lissarrague, François. "From Flat Page to the Volume of the Pot." In *The Pronomos Vase and Its Context*, edited by Oliver Taplin and Rosie Wyles, 33–46. Oxford, UK: Oxford University Press, 2010.

Llewellyn-Jones, Lloyd. "Body Language and the Female Role-Player in Greek Tragedy and Japanese Kabuki Theatre." In *Body Language in the Greek and*

Roman Worlds, edited by Douglas L. Cairns, 73–105. Swansea, Wales: Classical Press of Wales, 2005.

———. "A Woman's View?: Dress, Eroticism, and the Ideal Female Body in Athenian Art." In *Women's Dress in the Ancient Greek World*, edited by Lloyd Llewellyn-Jones, 171–202. Swansea, Wales and London: Classical Press of Wales/Duckworth, 2002.

Lonsdale, Steven. *Dance and Ritual Play in Greek Religion*. Baltimore: Johns Hopkins University Press, 1993.

Loraux, Nicole. *The Children of Athena: Athenian Ideas about Citizenship and the Division between the Sexes*. Translated by Caroline Levine. Princeton, NJ: Princeton University Press, 1993.

March, Jenny. "Euripides' *Bakchai*: A Reconsideration in the Light of the Vase-Paintings." *British Institute of Classical Studies* 36.1 (1989): 33–65.

Marshall, C. W. "Some Fifth-Century Masking Conventions." *Greece and Rome* 46.2 (1999): 188–202.

Marshall, C. W. and Stephanie van Willigenburg. "Judging Athenian Dramatic Competitions." *Journal of Hellenic Studies* 124 (2004): 90–107.

Martin, Richard P. *The Language of Heroes: Speech and Performance in the* Iliad. Ithaca, NY: Cornell University Press, 1989.

Mastronarde, Donald. "Actors on High: The Skene Roof, the Crane, and the Gods in Attic Drama." *Classical Antiquity* 9.2 (1990): 247–94.

Mauss, Marcel. "Techniques of the Body." *Economy and Society* 2.1 (1973): 70–88.

McCauley, Gay. *Space in Performance: Making Meaning in the Theatre*. Ann Arbor: University of Michigan Press, 2000.

McClure, Laura K., ed. *Sexuality and Gender in the Classical World: Readings and Sources*. Oxford, UK: Blackwell, 2002.

McConachie, Bruce. *Engaging Audiences: A Cognitive Approach to Spectating in the Theatre*. New York: Palgrave Macmillan, 2008.

———. "Doing Things with Image Schemas: The Cognitive Turn in Theatre Studies and the Problem of Experience for Historians." *Theatre Journal* 53.4 (2001): 569–94.

McCullagh, C. Behan. *The Truth of History*. New York: Routledge, 1998.

McDonell, Myles. "The Introduction of Athletic Nudity: Thucydides, Plato, and the Vases." *Journal of Hellenic Studies* 111 (1991): 182–93.

Meineck, Peter. "The Embodied Space: Performance and Visual Cognition at the Fifth Century Athenian Theatre." *New England Classical Journal* 39.1 (2012): 3–46.

———. "The Neuroscience of the Tragic Mask." *Arion* 19.1 (Spring/Summer 2011): 113–58.

Mendelsohn, Daniel. "A Wild Night in the Park." (Rev. of *The Bacchae*, dir. by

JoAnne Akalaitis, presented by the Public Theater at the Delacorte Theater, New York City, August 11–30, 2009.) http://www.nybooks.com/articles /archives/2009/oct/22/a-wild-night-in-the-park/?pagination=false.

Milanezi, Silvia. "Beauty in Rags: On *Rhakos* in Aristophanic Theatre." In *The Clothed Body in the Ancient World*, edited by Liza Cleland, Mary Harlow, and Lloyd J. Llewellyn-Jones, 75–86. Oxford: Oxbow Books, 2005.

Miller, Walter. "The Theatre of Thorikos, Preliminary Report." In *Papers of the American School of Classical Studies at Athens*, vol. 4 (1885–1886), 1–10. Boston: Damrell and Upham, 1888.

Millis, Benjamin W. and S. Douglas Olson, eds. *Inscriptional Records for the Dramatic Festivals in Athens: IG II² 2318–2325 and Related Texts*. Boston and Leiden, Netherlands: Brill, 2012.

Momigliano, Arnaldo D. *The Classical Foundations of Modern Historiography* (Sather Classical Lectures). Berkeley: University of California Press, 1990.

———. *Essays in Ancient and Modern Historiography*. Oxford, UK: Basil Blackwell, 1977.

Monks, Aoife. *The Actor in Costume*. New York: Palgrave Macmillan, 2010.

Mossman, Judith. *Wild Justice: A Study of Euripides' Hecuba*. Oxford, UK: Clarendon Press, 1995.

Mulvey, Laura. "Visual Pleasure and Narrative Cinema." *Screen* 16.3 (Autumn 1975): 6–18.

Murray, Penelope and Peter Wilson, eds. *Music and the Muses: The Culture of Mousike in the Classical Athenian City*. Oxford, UK: Oxford University Press, 2004.

Naerebout, Fritz G. *Attractive Performances: Ancient Greek Dance: Three Preliminary Studies*. Amsterdam: J. C. Gieben, 1997.

Napier, David. *Masks, Transformation, and Paradox*. Berkeley: University of California Press, 1986.

Nietzsche, Friedrich. *The Birth of Tragedy and the Genealogy of Morals*. Translated by Francis Golffing. Garden City, NY: Doubleday Anchor, 1956.

North, Helen. *Sophrosyne: Self-knowledge and Self-restraint in Greek Literature*. Ithaca, NY: Cornell University Press, 1966.

Ober, Josiah. *Mass and Elite in Democratic Athens: Rhetoric, Ideology, and the Power of the People*. Princeton, NJ: Princeton University Press, 1989.

Oranje, Hans. *Euripides' Bacchae: The Play and Its Audience*. Boston and Leiden, Netherlands: Brill, 1984.

Orgel, Stephen. *Impersonations: The Performance of Gender in Shakespeare's England*. Cambridge, UK: Cambridge University Press, 1996.

Ormand, Kirk. "Oedipus the Queen: Cross-Gendering without Drag." *Theatre Journal* 55.1 (2003): 1–28.

Osborne, Robin. "The Ecstasy and the Tragedy: Varieties of Religious Experience in Art, Drama and Society." In *Greek Tragedy and the Historian*, edited by Christopher Pelling, 187–212. Oxford, UK: Clarendon Press, 1997.

Ostenfeld, Erik. *Ancient Greek Psychology and the Modern Mind-Body Debate.* Aarhus, Denmark: Aarhus University Press, 1986.

Padel, Ruth. *In and Out of Mind: Greek Images of the Tragic Self.* Princeton, NJ: Princeton University Press, 1992.

———. "Making Space Speak." In *Nothing to Do with Dionysos?*, edited by John J. Winkler and Froma I. Zeitlin, 336–65. Princeton, NJ: Princeton University Press, 1990.

Paga, Jessica. "Mapping Politics: An Investigation of Deme Theatres in the Fifth and Fourth Centuries B.C.E." *Hesperia* 79 (2010): 351–84.

Paniagúa, Gregorio. Atrium Musicae de Madrid's *Musique de la Grèce Antique.* © 2000, 1978 by Harmonia Mundi. HMA1951015. Compact disc.

Park-Fuller, Linda M. "Audiencing the Audience: Playback Theatre, Performative Writing, and Social Activism." *Text and Performance Quarterly* 23.3 (2003): 288–310.

Pavis, Patrice. *Languages of the Stage: Essays in the Semiology of the Theatre.* New York: Performing Arts Journal, 1982.

———. "Problems of a Semiology of Theatrical Gesture." Translated by Elena Biller-Lappin. *Poetics Today* 2.3 (1981): 65–93.

Peirce, Sarah. "Visual Language and Concepts of Cult on the 'Lenaia Vases.'" *Classical Antiquity* 17.1 (1998): 59–95.

Pelling, Christopher. "Conclusion: Tragedy as Evidence." In *Greek Tragedy and the Historian*, edited by Christopher Pelling, 213–33. Oxford, UK: Clarendon Press, 1997.

Pelling, Christopher, ed. *Characterization and Individuality in Greek Literature.* Oxford, UK: Clarendon Press, 1990.

———. *Greek Tragedy and the Historian.* Oxford, UK: Clarendon Press, 1997.

Perry, John. *Encyclopedia of Acting Techniques.* Cincinnati: Betterway Books, 1997.

Pfeiffer, Rudolf. *The History of Classical Scholarship: From the Beginnings to the Ends of the Hellenistic Age.* Oxford, UK: Clarendon Press, 1968.

———. *The History of Classical Scholarship from 1300 to 1850.* Oxford, UK: Clarendon Press, 1976.

Pickard-Cambridge, Sir Arthur. *Dithyramb, Tragedy and Comedy*, 2nd ed. Oxford, UK: Clarendon Press, 1962.

———. *The Dramatic Festivals of Athens*, 2nd ed. Rev. by John Gould and D. M. Lewis. Oxford, UK: Clarendon Press, 1968. Revised with a new supplement and corrections, 1988.

Podlecki, A. J. "Could Women Attend the Theatre in Ancient Athens? A Collection of Testimonia." *Ancient World* 21 (1990): 27–43.

Poe, Joe Park. "The Altar in the Fifth-Century Theater." *Classical Antiquity* 8.1 (1989): 116–39.

———. "Multiplicity, Discontinuity and Visual Meaning in Aristophanic Comedy." *Rheinisches Museum* 14.3 (2000): 256–95.

Polacco, Luigi. *Il teatro di Dioniso Eleutereo ad Atene.* Rome: "L'Erma" di Bretschneider, 1990.

Poole, William. "Male Homosexuality in Euripides." In *Euripides, Women, and Sexuality,* edited by Anton Powell, 108–50. New York: Routledge, 1990.

Postlewait, Thomas. *The Cambridge Introduction to Theatre Historiography.* Cambridge, UK: Cambridge University Press, 2009.

———. "Eyewitnesses to History: Visual Evidence for Theatre in Early Modern England." In *The Oxford Handbook of Early Modern Theatre,* edited by Richard Dutton, 575–606. Oxford, UK: Oxford University Press, 2009.

Postlewait, Thomas and Bruce A. McConachie, eds. *Interpreting the Theatrical Past: Essays in the Historiography of Performance.* Iowa City: University of Iowa Press, 1989.

Powers, Melinda. "Dressing-up Dramaturgy in Charles L. Mee's *Bacchae 2.1.*" *Text and Presentation* (2007): 182–93.

———. "Unveiling Euripides." *Journal of Dramatic Theory and Criticism* 23.2 (Spring 2009): 5–19.

Prudhommeau, Germaine. *La danse grecque antique.* 2 vols. Paris: Éditions du Centre national de la recherche scientifique, 1965.

Rabinowitz, Nancy. "Embodying Tragedy: The Sex of the Actor." *Intertexts* 2.1 (1998): 3–25.

———. "How Is It Played? The Male Actor of Greek Tragedy: Evidence of Misogyny or Gender Bending." *Didaskalia: Ancient Theatre Today* 1.6 (1995). http://www.didaskalia.net/issues/supplement1/rabinowitz.html.

Rademaker, Adriaan. *Sophrosyne and the Rhetoric of Self-Restraint: Polysemy and Persuasive Use of an Ancient Greek Value Term* (*Mnemosyne* Suppl. 259). Boston and Leiden, Netherlands: Brill, 2005.

Rehm, Rush. "Performing the Chorus: Choral Action, Interaction, and Absence in Euripides." *Arion* 4.1 (Spring 1996): 45–60.

———. *The Play of Space: Spatial Transformation in Greek Tragedy.* Princeton, NJ: Princeton University Press, 2002.

———. "The Staging of Suppliant Plays." *Greek, Roman and Byzantine Studies* 29.3 (1988): 263–307.

Revermann, Martin. *Comic Business: Theatricality, Dramatic Technique, and Performance Context of Aristophanic Comedy.* Oxford, UK: Oxford University Press, 2006.

———. "The Competence of Theatre Audiences in Fifth- and Fourth-Century Athens." *Journal of Hellenic Studies* 126 (2006): 99–124.

———. "The Shape of the Athenian Orchestra in the Fifth Century: Forgotten Evidence." *Zeitschrift für Papyrologie und Epigraphik* 128 (1999): 25–28.

Reynolds, Leighton D. and Nigel G. Wilson. *Scribes and Scholars: A Guide to the Transmission of Greek and Latin Literature*, 3rd ed. Oxford, UK: Clarendon Press, 1991.

Rhodes, P. J. "Nothing to Do with Democracy: Athenian Drama and the *Polis*." *Journal of Hellenic Studies* 123 (2003): 104–19.

Ricoeur, Paul. *Interpretation Theory: Discourse and the Surplus of Meaning*. Fort Worth: Texas Christian University Press, 1976.

Roach, Joseph. *The Player's Passion: Studies in the Science of Acting*. Ann Arbor: University of Michigan Press, 1985.

———. "Power's Body: The Inscription of Morality as Style." In *Interpreting the Theatrical Past*, edited by Thomas Postlewait and Bruce A. McConachie, 99–118. Iowa City: University of Iowa Press, 1989.

Robinson, T. M. *Plato's Psychology*, 2nd ed. Toronto: University of Toronto Press, 1995.

Robson, James. "New Clothes, a New You: Clothing and Character in Aristophanes." In *The Clothed Body in the Ancient World*, edited by Liza Cleland, Mary Harlow, and Lloyd J. Llewellyn-Jones, 65–74. Oxford, UK: Oxbow Books, 2005.

Roccos, Linda Jones. *Ancient Greek Costume: An Annotated Bibliography: 1784–2005*. Jefferson, NC: McFarland & Co., 2006.

Roselli, David Kawalko. *Theater of the People: Spectators and Society in Ancient Athens*. Austin: University of Texas Press, 2011.

Roux, Jeanne, ed. *Les Bacchantes*. 2 vols. Paris: Les Belles Lettres, 1970 and 1972.

Rozik, Eli. *Generating Theatre Meaning: A Theory and Methodology of Performance Analysis*. Toronto: Sussex Academic Press, 2008.

Sahlins, Marshall David. *Culture in Practice: Selected Essays*. New York: Zone Books, 2000.

Sandys, Sir John Edwin. *A History of Classical Scholarship*, 3rd ed. 3 vols. New York: Hafner Publishing Co., 1958.

Sauter, Wilmar. *The Theatrical Event: Dynamics of Performance and Perception*. Iowa City: University of Iowa Press, 2000.

Schaps, David. "The Woman Least Mentioned: Etiquette and Women's Names." *Classical Quarterly* 27.2 (1977): 323–30.

Schenker, David J. "Dissolving Differences: Character Overlap and Audience Response." *Mnemosyne* Fourth Series 52.6 (1999): 641–57.

Schmidt, M. "Dionysien." *Antike Kunst* 10 (1967): 70–81.

Scullion, John Scott. *Three Studies in Athenian Dramaturgy*. Stuttgart, Germany: Teubner, 1994.

Seaford, Richard. *Reciprocity and Ritual: Homer and Tragedy in the Developing City-State*. Oxford, UK: Clarendon Press, 1994.

Seaford, Richard, ed. and trans. *Bacchae*. Warminster, UK: Aris & Phillips, 1997.

Segal, Charles. "Catharsis, Audience, and Closure in Greek Tragedy." In *Tragedy and the Tragic: Greek Theatre and Beyond*, edited by Michael S. Silk, 149–72. Oxford, UK: Clarendon Press, 1996.

———. *Dionysiac Poetics and Euripides' Bacchae*. Princeton, NJ: Princeton University Press, 1982. Preface to Expanded Edition and Afterword, 1997.

Seidensticker, Bernd. "Comic Elements in Euripides' *Bacchae*." *American Journal of Philology* 99.3 (1978): 303–20.

Sifakis, G. M. *Parabasis and Animal Choruses: A Contribution to the History of Attic Comedy*. London: Athlone Press, 1971.

Simon, Erika. *The Ancient Theatre*. Translated by C. E. Vafopoulou-Richardson. New York: Methuen, 1982.

Slater, Niall W. "Making the Aristophanic Audience." *American Journal of Philology* 120.3 (Autumn 1999): 351–68.

Slater, Niall W., and Bernhard Zimmermann, eds. *Intertextualität in der griechisch-römischen Komödie (Drama-Beiträge zum antiken Drama und seiner Rezeption 2)*. Stuttgart, Germany: Metzlerschen & Poeschel, 1993.

Smethurst, Mae. *The Artistry of Aeschylus and Zeami: A Comparative Study of Greek Tragedy and Nō*. Princeton, NJ: Princeton University Press, 1989.

Snell, Bruno. *The Discovery of the Mind: In Greek Philosophy and Literature*. New York: Dover, 1982.

Sofer, Andrew. *The Stage Life of Props*. Ann Arbor: University of Michigan Press, 2003.

Sommerstein, Alan H. *Talking about Laughter and Other Studies in Greek Comedy*. Oxford, UK: Oxford University Press, 2009.

———, ed. and trans. *Frogs*. Oxford, UK: Oxbow, 1996.

Stanford, Michael. *A Companion to the Study of History*. Oxford, UK: Blackwell, 1994.

———. *The Nature of Historical Knowledge*. Oxford, UK: Blackwell, 1986.

Stanford, William B. *Greek Tragedy and the Emotions: An Introductory Study*. London and Boston: Routledge/Kegan Paul, 1983.

Stewart, Andrew. *Classical Greece and the Birth of Western Art*. Cambridge: Cambridge University Press, 2008.

Stone, Laura M. *Costume in Aristophanic Poetry*. New York: Arno, 1981.

Taplin, Oliver. *Comic Angels and Other Approaches to Greek Drama through Vase-Painting*. Oxford, UK: Clarendon Press, 1993.

———. "Greek Theatre." In *The Oxford Illustrated History of Theatre*, edited by

John Russell Brown, 13–48. 1995. Reissued. Oxford, UK: Oxford University Press, 2001.

———. *Greek Tragedy in Action.* 1978. Reprinted with revisions. New York: Routledge, 1985.

———. "The Pictorial Record." In *The Cambridge Companion to Greek Tragedy,* edited by P. E. Easterling, 69–92. Cambridge, UK: Cambridge University Press, 1997.

———. *Pots and Plays: Interactions between Tragedy and Greek Vase-Painting of the Fourth Century B.C.* Los Angeles: J. Paul Getty Museum, 2007.

———. *The Stagecraft of Aeschylus: The Dramatic Use of Exits and Entrances in Greek Tragedy.* Oxford, UK: Clarendon Press, 1977.

———. "Women in the Tragedies: Women in the Theatres?" Presentation at the Celebrating Suzanne Said Conference, Columbia University, New York, NY, October 15, 2011.

Taussig, Michael. *Mimesis and Alterity: A Particular History of the Senses.* New York: Routledge, 1993.

Teevan, Colin, trans. *Bacchai.* Introd. by Edith Hall. London: Oberon Books, 2002.

Thomas, Bridget M. "Constraints and Contradictions: Whiteness and Femininity in Ancient Greece." In *Women's Dress in the Ancient Greek World*, edited by Lloyd Llewellyn-Jones, 1–16. Swansea, Wales and London: Classical Press of Wales/Duckworth, 2002.

Townsend, Rhys. "The Fourth-Century Skene of the Theater of Dionysos at Athens." *Hesperia* 55.4 (1986): 421–38.

Trendall, A. D. and T. B. L. Webster. *Illustrations of Greek Drama.* London: Phaidon, 1971.

Tulloch, John. *Shakespeare and Chekhov in Production and Reception: Theatrical Events and Their Audiences.* Iowa City: University of Iowa Press, 2005.

Tyrrell, Robert Y., ed. *Bakchai,* 2nd ed. New York: Macmillan & Co., 1951.

Ubersfeld, Anne. *Reading Theatre.* Translated by Frank Collins. Edited by Paul Perron and Patrick Debbèche. Toronto: University of Toronto Press, 1999.

Valakas, Kostas. "The Use of the Body by Actors in Tragedy and Satyr-Play." In *Greek and Roman Actors,* edited by P. E. Easterling and Edith Hall, 69–92. Cambridge, UK: Cambridge University Press, 2002.

Vernant, Jean-Pierre. *Myth and Society in Ancient Greece.* Translated by Janet Lloyd. New York: Zone Books, 1990.

Vernant, Jean-Pierre and Pierre Vidal-Naquet. *Myth and Tragedy in Ancient Greece.* Translated by Janet Lloyd. New York: Zone Books, 1988.

Wallace, Robert W. "Poet, Public, and 'Theatrocracy': Audience Performance in Classical Athens." In *Poet, Public, and Performance in Ancient Greece*, edited by Lowell Edmunds and Robert W. Wallace, 97–111. Baltimore: Johns Hopkins University Press, 1997.

Walton, J. Michael. "Social and Domestic Drama." In *The Art of Ancient Greek Theater*, edited by Mary Louise Hart, 128–35. Los Angeles: J. Paul Getty Museum, 2010.

Webster, T. B. L. *The Greek Chorus*. London: Methuen, 1970.

———. *Monuments Illustrating Old and Middle Comedy*, 3rd ed. Rev. by J. Richard Green. London: Institute of Classical Studies, 1978.

———. *Monuments Illustrating Tragedy and Satyr Play*, 2nd ed. London: Institute of Classical Studies, 1967.

Weiner, Albert. "The Function of the Tragic Greek Chorus." *Theatre Journal* 32.2 (1980): 205–12.

West, Martin L. *Ancient Greek Music*. Oxford, UK: Clarendon Press, 1992.

———. "Heniochus and the Shape of the Athenian Orchestra." *Zeitschrift für Papyrologie und Epigraphik* 130 (2000): 12.

White, Hayden. *The Content of the Form: Narrative Discourse and Historical Representation*. Baltimore: Johns Hopkins University Press, 1987.

———. *Figural Realism: Studies in the Mimesis Effect*. Baltimore: Johns Hopkins University Press, 1999.

———. *Tropics of Discourse: Essays in Cultural Criticism*. Baltimore: Johns Hopkins University Press, 1978.

Wiles, David. "Greek and Shakespearean Plays and Their Performance." In *Theorising Performance: Greek Drama, Cultural History, and Critical Practice*, edited by Edith Hall and Stephe Harrop, 43–55. London: Duckworth, 2010.

———. *Mask and Performance in Greek Tragedy: From Ancient Festival to Modern Experimentation*. Cambridge, UK: Cambridge University Press, 2007.

———. "Seeing Is Believing: The Historian's Use of Images." In *Representing the Past: Essays in Performance Historiography*, edited by Charlotte M. Canning and Thomas Postlewait, 215–39. Iowa City: University of Iowa Press, 2010.

———. *Tragedy in Athens: Performance Space and Theatrical Meaning*. Cambridge, UK: Cambridge University Press, 1997.

Williams, Bernard A. O. *Shame and Necessity*. Berkeley: University of California Press, 1993.

Wilson, Peter J. *The Athenian Institution of the Khoregia: The Chorus, the City and the Stage*. Cambridge, UK: Cambridge University Press, 2000.

———. "The *Aulos* in Athens." In *Performance Culture and Athenian Democracy*, edited by Simon Goldhill and Robin Osborne, 58–95. Cambridge, UK: Cambridge University Press, 1999.

————. "Leading the Tragic *Khoros*: Tragic Prestige in the Democratic City." In *Greek Tragedy and the Historian*, edited by Christopher Pelling, 81–108. Oxford, UK: Clarendon Press, 1997.

————. "The Musicians among the Actors." In *Greek and Roman Actors*, edited by P. E. Easterling and Edith Hall, 39–68. Cambridge, UK: Cambridge University Press, 2002.

Wilson, Peter J., ed. *The Greek Theatre and Festivals: Documentary Studies*. Oxford, UK: Oxford University Press, 2007.

Winkler, John J. *The Constraints of Desire: The Anthropology of Sex and Gender in Ancient Greece*. New York: Routledge, 1990.

————. "The Ephebes' Song: *Tragōidia* and *Polis*." In *Nothing to Do with Dionysos?: Athenian Drama in Its Social Context*, edited by John J. Winkler and Froma I. Zeitlin, 20–62. Princeton, NJ: Princeton University Press, 1990.

Winkler, John J. and Froma I. Zeitlin, eds. *Nothing to Do with Dionysos?: Athenian Drama in Its Social Context*. Princeton, NJ: Princeton University Press, 1990.

Winnington-Ingram, R. P. *Euripides and Dionysus: An Interpretation of the* Bacchae. Cambridge, UK: Cambridge University Press, 1948.

Wise, Jennifer. *Dionysus Writes: The Invention of Theatre in Ancient Greece*. Ithaca, NY: Cornell University Press, 1998.

Woodruff, Paul, trans. and notes. *The* Bacchae *of Euripides*. New York: Hackett, 1998.

Wright, John P. and Paul Potter, eds. *Psyche and Soma: Physicians and Metaphysicians on the Mind-Body Problem from Antiquity to Enlightenment*. Oxford, UK: Clarendon Press, 2000.

Wyles, Rosie. *Costume in Greek Tragedy*. London: Bristol Classical Press, 2011.

————. "Towards Theorising the Place of Costume in Performance Reception." In *Theorising Performance: Greek Drama, Cultural History, and Critical Practice*, edited by Edith Hall and Stephe Harrop, 171–80. London: Duckworth, 2010.

————. "The Tragic Costumes." In *The Pronomos Vase and Its Context*, edited by Oliver Taplin and Rosie Wyles, 231–54. Oxford, UK: Oxford University Press, 2010.

Zarrilli, Phillip B., ed. *Acting (Re)Considered: Theories and Practices*, 2nd ed. New York: Routledge, 2002.

Zarrilli, Phillip B., Bruce McConachie, Gary Jay Williams, and Carol Fisher Sorgenfrei. *Theatre Histories: An Introduction*, 2nd ed., edited by Gary Jay Williams. New York: Routledge, 2010.

Zeitlin, Froma. *Playing the Other: Gender and Society in Classical Greek Literature.* Chicago: University of Chicago Press, 1996.

———. "Playing the Other: Theater, Theatricality, and the Feminine in Greek Drama." In *Nothing to Do with Dionysos?*, edited by John J. Winkler and Froma I. Zeitlin, 63–96. Princeton, NJ: Princeton University Press, 1990. First published in *Representations* 11 (1985): 63–94.

in the dressing-up scene, 113; and terminology for/views of theatrical space, 17–18, 101; and views of dance, 21, 49; and views of gender, 43. *See also* sources: anachronistic; vision

Anakreontic Vases, 95

anthropological studies, 40, 53, 107

Anti, Carlo, 14

Archive of Performances of Greek and Roman Drama, 130n50

arguments based on possibility or probability, 8, 20, 28, 70, 71, 92. *See also* disclaimers

arguments by analogy, 12, 18–21, 34

arguments *ex silentio*, 4, 30, 31–33

aristocrats. *See* class

Aristophanes, 29, 32, 33, 36, 69, 76, 85; works of: *Archarnians*, 73, 127n2, 136n3, 138n38, 139n42; *Assembly-women*, 139n42, 142n38; *Birds*, 124n60; *Clouds*, 73, 136n3, 142n38; *Frogs*, 6, 20, 40, 52, 72, 73, 79, 80, 84–86, 90, 92, 93, 137n3, 139n42; *Knights*, 89, 121n15, 145n65; *Lysistrata*, 90; *Peace*, 85, 89, 127n2; *Wasps*, 90; *Women at the Thesmophoria*, 44, 76, 92, 107, 110–11, 127n2, 130n61, 130–31n62, 138n38, 139n42, 144–45n64; *Women Who Pitch the Tents*, 137n3. See also *agōn*: *Frogs*; democracy: *Frogs*

Aristotle's *Poetics*: and anecdote about acting style, 65, 69, 70–71, 72; and *kommoi*, 136n77; and role of chorus in tragedy, 47, 131n2; as source on performance, 6; and spectacle, 8; and women in audience, 31

Arnott, Peter, 31

Arthur, Marylin B., 61

Ashby, Clifford, 12, 15, 16–23

assumption: of the ideal case, 12, 21; influence of cultural and individual perspectives on, 12

Astor Place Riots, 76

Athenaeus: *The Learned Banqueters*, 19, 20, 36, 47

Athenocentric approaches. *See* David Roselli

audience, 29–45; in Aristophanes, 29; and "audiencing," 128n15; emotions of 29, 127n7; ideal or homogenized, 9, 29, 30, 38, 41–44; individual spectator vs. target audience groups, 30, 37–38; perspective on mask, 108–9; and physical size of spectator, 122n28; position of in Theatre of Dionysus, 24; response vs. responses of, 29, 37–38, 42; size of, 11, 29, 121n13, 124n64, 127n3. *See also Bacchae*: audience's perspective on; theatrical event

audience identity: boys, 2, 3; foreigners, 29, 36; men, 2, 3, 16, 30, 36; metics, 31, 36, 121n13, 128n12; slaves, 2, 3, 31, 36, 121n13, 128n12; women, 2, 3, 9, 29–38, 44–45

aulos. *See* musical instruments

author intention, 100, 101, 114

Bacchae: audience's perspective on, 28, 38–45, 76–77, 92, 94–95, 97, 112; composition of, 7; costume in, 81, 91–97; dramaturgy of, 6, 28, 118n11; earthquake scene in, 60; gesture in, 58; lacuna in, 62; manuscripts of (P and L), 7; messenger speeches in, 26, 58, 59, 60, 61, 114; papyri fragments of, 7; political commentary in, 9, 62, 66, 76–77; reconstruction of choral performance in, 48, 56–63;

Cithaeron. *See* Mt. Cithaeron

City Dionysia: characterization of, 55; and dithyramb, 19, 29; records of, 117n3; and women, 30, 31–36

class: *dēmos*, 69, 76; elites, 69, 94, 145n65; and tension between elites and non-elites, 69. *See also* bias: in sources; clothing: of elites; Euripides: and associating nobility with non-elites; gesture: class; women: class

classicists, 3, 4, 5–6, 14, 101, 113

Clifford, James, 18

clothing, 80; of elites, 103–4; *chitōn*, 79, 92, 94, 95, 105, 113; construction /material of, 80, 86; *exōmis* (slave garment), 103; girdles, 94, 110, 113, 144n63, 149n46; of gods, 93, 94; *himation*, 104; *peplos*, 105; scholarship on, 80, 141n12; shoes, 88–89. *See also* costume; women: and clothing

cognitive studies, 107, 108–10

context (historical), 6–9, 15–16, 44, 55–56, 72, 91, 102. *See also* ahistoricism; periodization

costume (*skeyēn*), 79–97; and comedy, 79, 80, 87, 103–4; and comedy vs. tragedy, 148–49n43, 149n44; makers of, 80, 140n4; footwear/bare feet, 83–84; *mitra*, 40, 92, 94, 110, 111, 143n44, 144n60, 144n61, 144n62; patterning on, 140n4; sources on, 79, 81–86; standard style of in tragedy, 79, 80, 83, 84, 87; in tragedy vs. satyr play, 141n16, 148n40. *See also* actors: costume/body of; *Bacchae*: costume in; clothing; cross-dressing; Dionysus: costume; disguise; fawnskins; nudity; Pentheus: costume of; mask

cross-cultural approaches, 105–7, 107–8, 109

cross-dressing: and gender, 42–43; representations of, 87, 105–6, 145n64, 145n66. *See also* actors; dressing-up scene

cross talk (generational). *See* generational cross talk

Csapo, Eric, 31, 52, 66, 67, 68–73, 76, 77, 85

cultural blinders, 16–18

cultural history, 56

cultural studies, 6, 35

dance: as discourse, 51; dithyramb, 14, 19–20, 23, 117n3; *emmeleia*, 47, 136n73; *geranos*, 19; *kordax*, 47; *pyrrichē*, 47, 136n73; reconstruction of, 4, 50; and shape of space, 18–21; *sikinnis*, 47; and social and religious functions of, 48; and transcription into words, 51; *tyrbasia*, 19, 124n57. *See also* *Bacchae*: reconstruction of choral performance in; chorus; maenads; music

Davies, Glenys, 99

de Certeau, Michel, 18, 97

deictics, 74, 147n11

delivery, 41, 47, 51, 52, 102

deme, 32, 123n42

deme theatres, 16, 17. *See also* Theatre at Thorikos

democracy: and *Bacchae*, 76–77; and *Frogs*, 73, 138n35; and "radical democracy," 69

dēmos. *See* class: *dēmos*

Demosthenes, 6, 29, 36, 127n2, 134n37

deus ex machina. *See* Dionysus: as *deus ex machina*

dialect, 54–55, 134n35, 134n46, 134n47

Didascaliae, 117n3

didaskalos: choices of, 24, 26, 28, 42, 75, 77; and the Fasti, 117n3

Aulis, 6, 51; *Medea*, 90, 106; *Orestes*, 51, 83, 84, 133n29, 133n41, 139n46; *Phaethon*, 147n10; *Suppliants*, 51. *See also Bacchae*

event (historical): and context, 72; fictional vs. historical, 54–56, 76, 81, 86. *See also* theatrical event

evidence (historical): influence of distinct types on an argument's conclusion, 48, 53–56; use of comedy as, 66, 73–74, 80, 84. *See also* play-text; sources; visual sources

Fasti, 2, 47, 117n3
fawnskins, 40, 41, 56, 57, 92
Fearn, David, 19
feminism, 6, 31, 96–97, 142n32
Fiechter, Ernst, 14
film theory, 81, 86–88, 142n33
Foley, Helene P.: *Female Acts*, 31; *Ritual Irony*, 30, 38, 40–41, 43, 61–62, 76–77, 92, 114
folk dancing, 21
Forrest, Edwin. *See* actors: Forrest and Macready
Foucault, Michel, 34
Frontisi-Ducroux, François, 95

Gamel, Mary-Kay, 51
Gebhard, Elizabeth, 14
gender roles: in Athens, 42–43; and depictions of women's dress, 86–89; and theatre, 95–97
general perceptions vs specific truths, 66, 71–74
generational cross talk, 15–16
genre: 111, 113–14, 130n62, 139n46
geranos. *See* dance: *geranos*
gesture, 99–115; and class, 102–4; comic vs. tragic, 106, 110–12; cross-cultural

approaches to, 105–7; misrepresentation/mistranslation of, 104–5; sources on, 99. *See also Bacchae*: gestures in; dressing-up scene: gesture/movement in; mask; movement; performance style; *schēma*; *sōphrosynē*

ghosting, 91
Gibson, James J., 12
girdles. *See* clothing: girdles
Goette, Hans R., 14
Goldhill, Simon, 5; "Collectivity and Otherness," 48, 53–56; "Representing Democracy," 30, 31, 32, 33–35, 36
Gould, John, 48, 53–56
Great Dionysia. *See* City Dionysia
Green, J. Richard: "Messengers from the Tragic Stage," 72; "Towards a Reconstruction," 66, 67, 68–73, 88, 99, 100, 102–5, 111
Griffith, Mark, 82
gynnis, 95

hairstyles, 84; of elites, 94, 145n65; length of, 92, 93, 94, 145n65, 145n66; of maenads, 145n66. *See also* Dionysus: beard/beardless; Pentheus: beard
Hall, Edith, 121n16, 137n7, 139n44
Halleran, Michael, 99–100
Halperin, David, 42
Heidelburg bell krater, 106. *See also* visual sources
"helping friends and harming enemies," 60
Henderson, Jeffrey: "The *Dēmos* and the Comic Competition," 73; "The Training of Classicists," 32; "Women and the Athenian Dramatic Festivals," 30, 31–33, 36

Heniochus, 121n15, 123n54
hēsychia, 58, 62
Hildy, Franklin J., 2
historical event. *See* event; theatrical event
historical narratives. *See* narratives (historical)
historical record. *See* sources; visual sources
historical time: as diachronic, 35; as synchronic, 4, 30, 33–35
historiography, 3, 5, 8, 10, 33, 53, 118n6. *See also* history; theatre/performance historians
history, 6, 8, 9, 33, 35, 51, 53, 68, 95; theatre history, 8, 15. *See also* historiography; theatre/performance historians
Hoffman, Dustin. *See* actors: Hoffman and Olivier
Holborn, Hajo, 37
Homer, 19, 20, 85; Homeric hymn to Dionysus, 92; *Iliad*, 123n55; *Odyssey*, 123n55, 142–43n38
hybris, 28, 59
Hysiai, 26
hysteria, 57, 61, 63

iconography. *See* vases; visual sources
ideology, 43, 52, 55, 68, 85, 122n33
Iggers, Georg G., 52
individuality (in Athens), 37, 129n44
instincts and opinions. *See* disclaimers
interpretive patterns, 4, 69, 72, 90, 111
intertextuality, 110–11
Issacharoff, Michael, 12, 119n1

J. Paul Getty Museum, 82, 145n64
Jenkins, Keith, 44
Jory, John, 68

judging (of theatre competition), 29, 73, 74

Kabuki theatre, 100, 105–6
Kallippides. *See* actors
kommoi, 136n77. *See also amoibaion*
kothornoi. *See* costume: footwear/bare feet
krokōtos, 40, 92
kyklioi khoroi (circular dance), 19–20, 124n60. *See also* dance: dithyramb; Heniochus

lacuna. See *Bacchae*: lacuna in
Lada-Richards, Ismene, 67
langue, 34, 129n35. *See also* discourse
Lateiner, Donald, 99
law courts, 29, 33, 91
Lawler, Lillian B., 49
Lefebvre, Henri, 12, 16
Lenaia festival, 73
Lenaia Vases, 56, 134n51. *See also* visual sources
Ley, Graham: "A Material World," 81, 89–91; *The Theatricality of Greek Tragedy*, 19, 49, 50–51, 52, 101, 106
Lissarrague, François, 82, 83, 95
List of Victors, 117n3
Llewellyn-Jones, Lloyd: 5; "Body Language and the Female Role Player," 99, 100, 105–6; "A Woman's View," 80–81, 86–87
Loraux, Nicole, 36, 122n33
lyre. *See* musical instruments

Macready, William Charles. *See* actors: Forrest and Macready
madness, 59, 97, 111, 112, 144n60
maenad, 24–27, 41, 56–63, 74, 75, 77; in iconography, 56, 57, 59, 113, 146n66;

in real-life, 56. See also *Bacchae*; chorus; dance

"male gaze," 86, 88, 142n33

mannerism, 67, 68

Martin, Richard P., 13

mask, 23, 100, 107–9, 114–15; makers of, 89; and Pentheus 59, 75; in performance, 107–10; whiteness of, 93, 94, 144–45n64; and whole-headed structure, 79, 107. *See also* Dionysus: smiling mask of

Mastronarde, Donald, 14

McConachie, Bruce, 2, 5, 117n2, 124n70

mēchanē, 11, 68

mēden agan, 61, 135n58

Meineck, Peter: "The Embodied Space," 21–22, 23; "The Neuroscience of the Tragic Mask," 100, 107–10, 115

Menander, 67

Mendelsohn, Daniel, 44, 76

messenger scenes, 72. *See also Bacchae*: messenger speeches in

metatheatre, 74, 75

meter, 48, 51, 61

method acting, 68, 75

methodology: distinct types or eras of, 15–16, 53–56, 107–10; limitations in, 37, 38, 43, 45, 49, 66, 83; and scholars, 6, 8. *See also* historiographical topics; methodologies

metics. *See* audience: identity of (metics)

Milanezi, Silvia, 80, 85–86

Miller, Walter, 17

mimesis (imitation), 96, 97. *See also* representation

mimicry (and alterity), 148n29

mimicry (vocal), 71

mind-body relationship, 61, 68, 138n21

modern misnomers. *See* anachronism: and performance style terminology

mitra. *See* costume: *mitra*

modern performances of Greek tragedy: and influence on scholarship, 8, 119n17

modern productions of Greek tragedy: JoAnne Akalaitis' *Bacchae*, 130n62; Sir Peter Hall's *Bacchae*, 41, 62; Bill T. Jones' *Bacchae*, 62; Charles L. Mee's *Bacchae 2.1*, 148n39; Ariane Mnouchkine's *Les Atrides*, 105; Ninagawa's *Medea*, 106; Richard Schechner's *Dionysus in 69*, 62–63; Tadashi Suzuki's *Bacchae*, 41; John Tiffany's *Bacchae*, 41

molpē, 48

morphē, 57, 92

moysikē, 48

movement: and costume, 80, 89; and gesture, 101–5; and performance style, 65–66; and (problem with) reconstruction of, 49, 50–51; and song (*molpē*), 48. *See also Bacchae*: reconstruction of choral performance in; *Bacchae*: reconstruction of spatial operations; chorus; dance; gesture; performance style; spatial patterning (blocking)

Mt. Cithaeron: and chorus, 60, 135n67; and theatrical space, 24, 25, 26, 27, 28, 126n82; and Theban women, 60, 74

music: harmonics and acoustic theory, 48; New Music, 51–53; notation of on papyri, 48, 51; reconstruction of, 48, 133n29; social function of, 48. *See also* chorus; musical instruments

musical instruments: aulos, 48, 123n55;

Seidensticker, Bernd, 100, 111, 112–14
semantics, 35
Semele, 59
semiotics: semiotic codes, 28, 35, 37, 102; theatre semiotics, 65, 90, 125n74, 129n35, 146n3
Shakespeare, 76, 113, 130n54
sight lines, 21
skēnē, 5, 11, 51
skin, 87, 92, 93, 144–45n64. *See also* mask
Slater, William, 31, 52
slaves. *See* audience: identity of (slaves); chorus: identity of in play; costume: makers of; skin
sociolect in Athenian drama, 69, 76
Socrates, 73, 103
Sofer, Andrew, 90–91
Sophocles, 136n77; works: *Ajax*, 135n67; *Andromeda*, 72, 73; *Antigone*, 27; *Electra*, 90; *Oedipus at Colonus*, 6, 12, 51, 60, 133n41; *Oedipus Tyrranus*, 92, 143n44; *Philoctetes*, 138n38, 139n42, 141n11
sōphrosynē, sōphrōn: and elite comportment, 102–5; in Greek literature, 104; in Greek tragedy, 135n58; and madness, 112; as theme in *Bacchae*, 48, 57–63, 74, 104. See also women: and *sōphrosynē*
Sorgenfrei, Carol, 2, 117n2
sources: anachronistic, 7, 118–19n12; fifth-century vs. fourth, 6, 118n12; limited, 2, 3, 4, 7, 28, 29, 48, 49, 51, 62, 65–66, 69, 70–71, 72, 79, 97, 99, 111; mixing and matching of, 4, 87, 106; overreading significance of, 48, 49–50, 104–5; and reading the literary against the visual, 4, 7, 56, 88, 100, 102–5, 111; types of, 2, 6, 15, 70;

two-dimensional for study of multi-dimensional subject, 48, 50–51, 104. *See also* arguments *ex silentio*; bias; evidence; visual sources
space, 16. *See also* spatial practices; theatrical space
spatial patterning (blocking), 11, 23, 24, 50, 51. See also *Bacchae*: reconstruction of spatial operations in; movement
spatial practices, 12, 16, 22, 24, 27, 28, 125n77
spectators. *See* audience
stage, 11, 120n8
stage directions, 7, 113
Stanford, Michael, 13, 35, 71
Stanislavski, Konstantin, 67
stichomythia. *See* distichomythia
structuralism, 12, 15, 26, 27, 28, 34, 122n33
structure and event, 35
styles, 67, 68. *See also* performance style
symbolism, 68
synchronic approaches. *See* historical time

tableaux, 101
Taplin, Oliver: *Greek Tragedy in Action*, 67, 100, 106; "The Pictorial Record," 49; *Oxford Illustrated History of the Theatre*, 3; *Pots and Plays*, 132n22; and *Stagecraft of Aeschylus*, 55, 99, 100, 101, 102, 110, 146n10; "Women in the Tragedies: Women in the Theatres?" 33
Teevan, Colin, 62
Teiresias, 58, 59, 61, 75, 144n61
text. *See* play-text
theatre audience. *See* audience

Theatre at Epidauros, 18, 22, 122n28

Theatre at Thorikos, 16–18

Theatre of Dionysus at Athens, 12, 26; excavation of, 13, 14; future excavation of, 125n72; geographical coordinates of, 23, 24, 25; material remains of, 13, 14; *orchēstra*, 11–25, 49; rebuilding of, 13; size of, 11. See also *eisodos*

theatre/performance historians, 5, 12, 15, 56, 67, 71, 82, 91, 101, 102

theatricality, 51, 74

theatrical event, 9, 30, 38, 43, 44, 45, 56, 102

theatrical space, 11–28; terminology/ types of, 11, 12, 13, 119n1, 121n14, 125n74. See also altar; *Bacchae*: reconstruction of spatial operations in; bleacher seats; *eisodos*; *ekkyklēma*; *mēchanē*; *skēnē*; spatial patterning (blocking); Theater of Dionysus; *theatron*; tomb

theatron, 3, 14, 17, 21, 37, 121n15

thrēnos, 62, 136n77

thymelē, 22, 124n70

thyrsus, 56, 75, 90, 110, 113

time. See historical time

tomb, 11, 50, 51

tyrbasia. See dance

Ubersfeld, Anne, 12, 119–20n1

Valakas, Kostas, 67

vase painting. See visual sources

vases. See Anakreontic Vases; Basel Dancers Vase; Chorēgos Vase; *chous* from Anavyssos; Heidelburg bell krater; Lenaia Vases, Pronomos Vase

Vernant, John-Pierre, 53, 54

vision (historical conditions of seeing), 16, 17–18, 142n35. *See also* cognitive studies

visual sources: drama-related, 49; as evidence for performance, 49, 105–6; and flat representation vs. voluminous object, 83; and idealization vs. representation, 79–80, 87, 105; and methods of interpretation, 69–70, 88; and separating painters' interpretations from the theatrical subject of vases, 70–73, 104; transcription of into words, 80, 83, 99, 100, 104; and vase-painting vs. photographs, 106, 107; and women's clothing, 86–89. *See also* anachronism; Anakreontic Vases; Basel Dancers Vase; Chorēgos Vase; *chous* from Anavyssos; Heidelburg bell krater; Lenaia Vases; preconceived ideas, Pronomos Vase; sources.

Vitruvius, 21, 124n63

Walton, J. Michael, 66

White, Hayden, 52, 53, 87

Wiles, David: *Mask and Performance*, 100, 107–10, 114–15; "Seeing Is Believing," 17; *Tragedy in Athens*, 11–12, 13, 14, 15, 16–23, 24, 27, 49, 101, 114. *See also* spatial practices

Williams, Gary, 2, 117n2

Wilson, Peter, 20, 55

Winkler, John J., 42, 49

Winnington-Ingram, R. P., 43, 114

women: and choral dance, 50, 55; and class, 32, 36–37, 89; and clothing, 85–89, 110; and hairstyles, 145n66; and identity of chorus in play, 54, 73; and *mitra*, 143n44; naming of in public, 33; as real-life maenads,

134n51; and ritual, 31, 36, 44, 56; and skin, 144n64; and *sōphrosynē*, 58; and weaving, 140n5. *See also* audience: identity of (women); Euripides: and women

Woodruff, Paul, 76–77

Wyles, Rosie, 80, 83–84

Xenophon, 36, 142–43n38

Zarrilli, Phillip, B., 2, 117n2

Zeitlin, Froma, 95–97